Port Hudson,
Confederate Bastion
on the Mississippi

LAWRENCE LEE HEWITT

Port Hudson, Confederate Bastion on the Mississippi

Louisiana State University Press
Baton Rouge and London

Designer: Laura Roubique Gleason
Typeface: Trump
Typesetter: CSA Press
Printer: Thomson-Shore, Inc.
Binder: John H. Dekker, Inc.

The author gratefully acknowledges Maurice Garb for granting permission to quote from the diary of Private James Very Waters, and Russell Surles, Jr., for granting permission to quote from the diary of Richard W. Ford.

10 9 8 7 6 5 4 3 2 1

Library of Congress Cataloging-in-Publication Data

Hewitt, Lawrence L.
    Port Hudson, Confederate bastion on the Mississippi.

    Bibliography: p.
    Includes index.
    1. Port Hudson (La.)—History—Siege, 1863.
I. Title.
E475.42.H49   1987   973.7'33   87-3198
ISBN 0-8071-1351-4

For
J. Larry Crain,
who determined the subject,
Carol J. Greenfield,
who restored my determination to finish,
and my beloved wife,
Jean

Contents

Illustrations

Figures
Following p. 109
Brigadier General William Nelson Rector Beall
Confederate Barracks
Commander William David "Dirty Bill" Porter
USS *Essex*
Major General Nathaniel Prentiss Banks
Major General Franklin Gardner
Rear Admiral David Glasgow Farragut
Lieutenant George Dewey
USS *Mississippi*
Colonel Isaiah George Washington Steedman
Fort Desperate
Colonel William R. Miles
Scene of Negro charge on May 27, 1863
Recruiting poster sponsored by black abolitionists in Philadelphia
Black infantry at Port Hudson

Maps

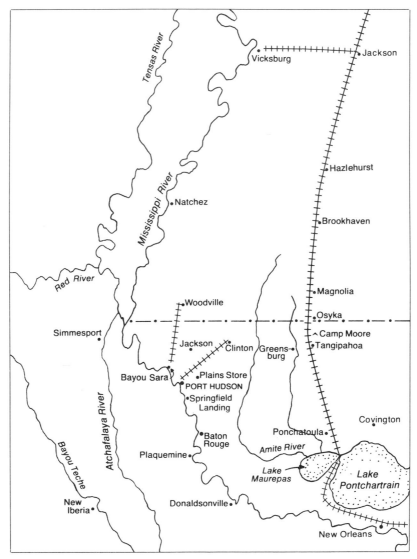

The Environs of Port Hudson

Preface

Although nearly vanished and nearly forgotten, Port Hudson, Louisiana, holds a distinct place in our nation's past. Located seventeen miles by road north of Baton Rouge, the village was the last Confederate stronghold on the Mississippi River and the site of the longest genuine siege in American military history. It was here, too, that black soldiers in the regular United States Army first participated in a major assault.

Control of the Mississippi River was a key objective of Union strategy at the beginning of the Civil War. By the second year of the war only Vicksburg, Mississippi, remained in Confederate hands. The southerners capitalized on their successful defense of that city to expand their control over the river. In August, 1862, they occupied Port Hudson and constructed a bastion stronger than that at Vicksburg. Together these fortresses denied the Federals safe use of the Mississippi.

At the same time, the twin bastions safeguarded the vital Red River connection with western Louisiana and Texas. That waterway facilitated the east-west flow of manpower, munitions, and foodstuffs between the heart of the Confederacy and the trans-Mississippi. This supply line was vital to the Confederates; control of the Mississippi River was therefore a primary goal of the Confederate government. The garrisons at Port Hudson and Vicksburg achieved these objectives for almost a year.

This study examines the Confederate occupation of Port Hudson and the Union efforts to capture the stronghold. Although it recounts the garrison life of the soldiers, its emphasis is the strategic importance the village held for the opposing governments and the enormous effect the struggle for Port Hudson—especially the Union assault of May 27, 1863—had on the course of the Civil War.

Within this framework I recount the events that brought about the Confederate occupation and fortification of Port Hudson and its relationship to Vicksburg. The strength of the bastion influenced Union Admiral David G. Farragut and Major General Nathaniel P. Banks to attempt to circumvent Port Hudson by controlling the mouth of the Red River. Their failure to starve out the Confederates eventually led Banks to launch a direct assault on the bastion. The unsuccessful attack was followed by an equally disastrous siege; Port Hudson capitulated only after Vicksburg had fallen. The Confederates' surprisingly successful defense of Port Hudson when finally assaulted wrought significant consequences for the war.

Why has history overlooked Port Hudson? The standard explanation is that its downfall followed so closely Robert E. Lee's repulse at Gettysburg and Ulysses S. Grant's capture of Vicksburg. I believe also that the siege has been overlooked because neither Lee, Grant, nor any other Civil War luminary fought at Port Hudson. An additional possibility is the absence of a local constituency. As the river continued to shift its course farther from the village, the residents gradually moved away and the town vanished. Moreover, the site never became a national park with the concurrent publicity and visitors that popularized similar places.

Numerous unit histories and individual memoirs describing the struggle for Port Hudson began appearing within a few months of the garrison's surrender, but the first scholarly work devoted to the Confederate occupation of Port Hudson was not published until 1963. Edward Cunningham's *The Port Hudson Campaign, 1862–1863* attempted to elevate Port Hudson from obscurity, but the effort proved unsuccessful. In 1983–1984 a massive two-volume compendium of details was published by David C. Edmonds. Regrettably, *The Guns of Port Hudson* does not place Port Hudson in the context of the war.[1]

I have attempted to cover the entire Confederate occupation with an emphasis on the strategy employed by both sides. I have not, however, gone beyond the assault of May 27, 1863, in detail. The additional material required to recount the siege would only prove anticlimactic and detract from the strategic importance of

1. Edward Cunningham, *The Port Hudson Campaign, 1862–1863* (Baton Rouge, 1963); David C. Edmonds, *The Guns of Port Hudson* (2 vols.; Lafayette, La., 1983–84).

Port Hudson. I made this exclusion in an effort to bring Port Hudson into the forefront of Civil War history—a position I believe it justly deserves. Gettysburg and Vicksburg are regarded as turning points of the war. Yet Gettysburg assured neither Lee's final defeat nor Vicksburg Grant's eventual triumph. Although a small engagement in comparison, the struggle for Port Hudson on May 27, 1863, had a momentous impact on the war. The attack was an excellent example of Civil War assault tactics, and it influenced Union leadership and the role of black troops, both with tremendous consequences.

In the foreword to Cunningham's book, T. Harry Williams wrote: "The Confederates at Port Hudson, by their dogged resistance, stalled the Union victory schedule and thereby prolonged the conflict." I believe the reverse was true. When the fighting ended on May 27 with the opponents deadlocked, Banks had no alternative but to besiege the garrison. Consequently, he could not join Grant at Vicksburg. Despite a recent claim to the contrary, Union General in Chief Henry W. Halleck desperately wanted the armies of Grant and Banks combined, with the latter in command.[2] Had Banks reached Vicksburg in early June of 1863—following his dispersement of Confederates in western Louisiana and a quick, glorious victory at Port Hudson—he would have been hailed as the conquering hero. As senior major general, Banks would have assumed overall command of the combined armies and received the credit for capturing Vicksburg. Until Banks met with disaster on some battlefield, he would have blocked Grant's rise to general in chief. Such a turn of events would have prolonged the war longer than the Confederates' "dogged resistance" for forty-three days following the May 27 assault.

The Confederates hastened the ultimate defeat of their cause in a more tangible way. The failure of the initial Union attack brought black soldiers into the assault. The newspaper coverage of the charge by black troops at Port Hudson proved pivotal in convincing northern whites to accept the enlistment of nearly 180,000 black soldiers in the Federal army. Though generally stationed in rear

2. T. Harry Williams, Foreword to Cunningham, *Port Hudson Campaign*, vi; Herman Hattaway and Archer Jones, *How the North Won: A Military History of the Civil War* (Urbana, 1983), 345; U.S. War Department, *The War of the Rebellion: A Compilation of the Official Records of the Union and Confederate Armies* (128 vols.; Washington, D.C., 1880–1901), ser. I, XV, 302. Hereinafter cited as *OR*.

areas, the black troops freed whites for combat duty. By the spring of 1865, the number of blacks in the Union army nearly equaled the number of Confederate infantrymen present for duty.[3] Moreover, this fresh source of manpower appeared just as the war-weary North had grown tired of the seemingly endless list of casualties.

Regardless of the consequences of the May 27 assault, for almost a year the Confederate garrison at Port Hudson influenced the course of the Civil War. While that bastion secured the Mississippi River south of Vicksburg, the twin fortresses dominated Federal strategy in the western theater, the trans-Mississippi, and along the Gulf coast. Port Hudson was important—a major Civil War event—and should be understood as such.

3. "Notes on the Union and Confederate Armies," in Robert Underwood Johnson and Clarence Clough Buel (eds.), *Battles and Leaders of the Civil War* (4 vols.; 1887–88; rpr. New York, 1956), IV, 767–68.

Acknowledgments

During the course of my research I incurred numerous obligations. I here record my gratitude to the staffs of Hill Memorial Library, Louisiana State University, Baton Rouge; State of Louisiana Office of State Parks, Department of Culture, Recreation and Tourism, Baton Rouge; Special Collections Division, Howard-Tilton Memorial Library, Tulane University, New Orleans; Special Collections Division, Chicago Public Library; Illinois State Historical Library, Springfield, Illinois; Arkansas History Commission Library, Little Rock; and the U.S. Army Military History Institute, Carlisle Barracks, Pennsylvania, for rendering exceptional assistance beyond the norm. Financial support for this work has come from a grant by Pelican Arms Collectors Association, Inc., Baton Rouge.

I wish to express my thanks to everyone associated with the Louisiana State University Press who worked to produce this volume; the outside readers who made invaluable suggestions; Trudie Calvert, who edited the manuscript for Louisiana State University Press; and Diane B. Didier, who drew the maps.

Nothing gives me greater pleasure than having this opportunity to acknowledge those individuals who have assisted me in countless ways, from opening their homes to a virtual stranger to voicing an amiable quip about my testudinate pace. Many new friendships resulted from this endeavor. My special thanks to Maurice Garb, Gary A. Crump, John L. Loos, Charles W. Royster, James J. Bolner, Pierre E. Conner, Jr., Kenneth R. McDaniel, Joan E. Vogel, Edward J. Gonzales III, Ronald L. McCallum, David R. Perdue, Estelle Williams, Roman J. Heleniak, Dr. Edward M. Boagni III, John R. Bangs, John D. Winters, Russell Surles, Jr., William Gladstone, Charles N. Elliott, Daniel J. Stari, Roy E. Crittenden, Benton O.

Bickham III, Frederick W. Graul, Danny M. Sessums, Thomas E. Schott, E. Russ Williams, Bertram H. Groene, William A. Spedale, Sidney J. Frugia, Philip B. Eckert, John E. Dutton, Fred G. Benton, Jr., Ray W. Burgess, Charles E. Hinton, John L. Heflin, Jr., Thomas MacDonald, Edgar Chesnutt, Jerry Fertitta, Charles Vincent, and William C. Davis.

I also wish to acknowledge the significant influence the late T. Harry Williams, the late Holman Hamilton, Charles P. Roland, and Charles K. Messmer had on my academic career. Above all, however, I am grateful for the unfaltering support and encouragement provided by my family and my former wife, Shirley. Their devotion, love, and understanding enabled me to pursue my goal.

In addition to those individuals to whom the book is dedicated, there are six others without whom the significance of Port Hudson might yet remain a mystery. William J. Cooper, Jr., of Louisiana State University, influenced my decision to write about Port Hudson, in part by his prophecy that the Yankees who attacked Fort Desperate lacked the will to succeed. His sage advice, constant good cheer, and unceasing encouragement while he directed my research prevented me from following in their footsteps. An unyielding taskmaster adept in balancing choice and exclusion, Bill deserves credit for making the original manuscript publishable.

Arthur W. Bergeron, Jr., formerly of the Louisiana State Archives and Records Management Center and the Louisiana Office of State Parks, provided much needed encouragement throughout the project. A boon companion on several research trips, Art read the entire manuscript and more than once provided that elusive grain of sand for which I had searched.

Carolyn E. Lochhead, formerly of the St. Francisville (Louisiana) *Democrat* and now of the Washington *Post*, out of friendship and love diligently labored over every page. Her ability to tighten the text proved indispensable.

William D. Moore, Jr., Sidney L. "Cotton" McCallum, and Evelyn W. McDaniel assisted me in numerous ways, particularly by convincing me to make the career change that enabled me to complete the manuscript. My thanks to each of you.

Port Hudson,
Confederate Bastion
on the Mississippi

I

Occupation: August, 1862

I want Baton Rouge and Port Hudson.
> —Major General Earl Van Dorn,
> District of the Mississippi

On a topographical map, the great river system that flows through the American heartland resembles nothing less than a huge arterial network, a lifeline that before the Civil War provided the farmers of the Midwest with access to world markets through New Orleans, the most important port on the Gulf of Mexico.

Following the secession of the slave states and the onset of the Civil War, the newly established Confederate States of America applied a tourniquet to the lower Mississippi and threatened the economic well-being of the farmers in the states between the Ohio River and the Great Lakes. Perhaps no place else in the United States did President Abraham Lincoln's warning about a house divided have more urgent meaning.

Conversely, the Mississippi River provided northern military planners the greatest opportunity to divide the Confederacy. Union control of the entire length of the Mississippi River would isolate Confederate states west of the river from the rest of the secessionist states.

At the outset of the war in 1861, Winfield Scott, the Union's first general in chief, recognized the importance of securing the Mississippi—and New Orleans—for the North. President Abraham Lincoln agreed. Not only would northern control of the river divide the newly united Confederacy, it would clear the way for shipment of produce by disgruntled midwestern farmers. Yet neither Scott nor his successor, George B. McClellan, made much headway toward claiming the waterway during the first year of the war.

Federal efforts to secure the Mississippi made the river critically important to the Confederate leaders. At the beginning of the war the Confederate government's primary concern was to repel Union invasions until the aggressors exhausted themselves. A secondary objective was to retain territory, for a nation that cannot secure its own borders confesses its inability to protect its citizens.

Strategically, the defense of New Orleans was essential. Located near the mouth of the river, New Orleans was by far the most populous city in the Confederacy and its leading financial and commercial center. When the war began, the Confederacy moved swifty to secure the city. Thousands of volunteers poured into New Orleans, and the authorities in Richmond shipped in scores of cannon. Everyone in the South believed that a force advancing from the Gulf of Mexico could not take New Orleans because brick fortifications guarded every approach. Consequently, they assumed the threat to the city lay upriver.

The northernmost Confederate garrison on the Mississippi occupied Columbus, Kentucky, almost a thousand miles upstream. But the loss of Forts Henry and Donelson in February, 1862, forced the Confederates to abandon this position. Foreseeing the possible evacuation of Columbus, the South had garrisoned New Madrid, Missouri, Island No. 10, Fort Pillow, Tennessee, and Vicksburg, Mississippi—all for the purpose of defending New Orleans. In March, General Pierre G. T. Beauregard, commander of the Army of the Mississippi, recommended to Major General Mansfield Lovell, commander of the defenses along the lower Mississippi, "the fortification of Port Hudson as a measure of precaution against the fall of our defenses north of Memphis."[1] Acting on Beauregard's suggestion, Lovell constructed the earthworks for a battery at Port Hudson in early April.

But before cannon and troops could arrive, disaster struck. On April 24, 1862, the Union navy succeeded in passing Forts Jackson and St. Philip on the river below New Orleans. The city fell within a week. Land forces followed, and the United States Army soon occupied much of southern Louisiana. By mid-June only Vicksburg remained under Confederate control.

1. *OR*, XV, 811.

Under naval attack from north and south, this bastion too seemed certain to fall, allowing the Union to achieve its first objective. Responsibility for defending Vicksburg fell upon Beauregard's successor, General Braxton Bragg. In late June, Major General Earl Van Dorn took charge of Vicksburg's defense and Bragg provided him with the necessary reinforcements. Van Dorn thwarted all Union efforts to drive him from the city, and by mid-July the strategic situation in the area had changed drastically. The Union forces had adopted a defensive posture.

Wanting to strengthen his hold on Vicksburg, Van Dorn sought to fortify Port Hudson. The Federal navy had hardly left Vicksburg when Van Dorn issued orders for an offensive into southeastern Louisiana. He wrote President Jefferson Davis, "I want Baton Rouge and Port Hudson." If the Confederates could capture the Federal garrison at Baton Rouge, they would secure navigation of the Red River (a vital east-west supply line), allow for the fortification of Port Hudson, and simplify the reoccupation of New Orleans. Brigadier General Daniel Ruggles, the district commander headquartered at Tangipahoa, Louisiana, had earlier requested reinforcements for such an expedition. On July 26 Van Dorn dispatched Major General John C. Breckinridge with just under four thousand troops to gain control of southeastern Louisiana.[2]

On July 28 Breckinridge joined Ruggles just north of Tangipahoa at Camp Moore, and their combined forces advanced on Baton Rouge. Because illness kept a large number of Confederates at Camp Moore and many more dropped out along the march, Breckinridge reached the outskirts of Baton Rouge with only twenty-eight hundred men. Federal naval vessels anchored before the city bolstered a Yankee land force that nearly equaled that of the southerners, but Breckinridge counted on the C.S.S. *Arkansas* to eliminate this additional hazard. The Confederates attacked at dawn on August 5, crushed the Union left wing, and pushed on toward the river. But the devastating fire of the Union fleet brought their advance to a halt, and Breckinridge listened in vain for the guns of the *Arkansas* to engage the enemy vessels. The Confederate ship had developed engine trouble four miles above the city, and the crew set the vessel afire to prevent her capture. When

2. *Ibid.*, Vol. LII, Pt. 2, p. 334, XV, 76, 747, 771, 1235; Archer Jones, *Confederate Strategy from Shiloh to Vicksburg* (Baton Rouge, 1961), 74; Robert G. Hartje, *Van Dorn: The Life and Times of a Confederate General* (Nashville, 1967), 205.

Breckinridge learned the fate of the *Arkansas*, he abandoned any hope of resuming the attack and withdrew from the field.[3]

Although repulsed, Breckinridge did not allow the campaign to end in failure. A few days later, fulfilling Van Dorn's wishes, Breckinridge ordered Ruggles to occupy Port Hudson. With heavy guns mounted along the precipitous eighty-foot bluff, the Confederates would have a southern anchor on the Mississippi below the mouth of the Red River. If they could hold Port Hudson and Vicksburg, east-west communications via the Red River would remain open. The trans-Mississippi states provided thousands of recruits for depleted regiments serving east of the river. Texas grain and beef cattle, Louisiana salt, sugar, and molasses, and European products shipped via Mexico all flowed down the Red River. Small arms, cannon, ammunition, and currency moved westward on the waterway.[4] The Confederate government could not afford to lose so important a lifeline. The Red River was an avenue between east and west, guarded on either side by two strongholds, Vicksburg and Port Hudson, that flanked and protected each other.

Port Hudson was located on the east bank twenty-five miles up the river from Baton Rouge where the Mississippi made a 150-degree turn. The town had grown with the swelling flow of cotton from the surrounding area. The state legislature authorized its incorporation in 1832, and the following year construction started on a railroad link with Clinton, nineteen miles to the northeast. Approximately thirty thousand bales of cotton and two thousand hogsheads of sugar passed through the port annually. Some twelve or fifteen business establishments sprang up along the bluff, but the town never became a social center. Remaining a paltry village of about two hundred inhabitants, it contained, besides the stores, only four or five houses and a Methodist church. The Mississippi steadily shifted its course southward and away from the town before the war. By 1862 the principal steamboat landing had been moved half a mile to the south. The railroad relocated its Port

3. William C. Davis, *Breckinridge: Statesman, Soldier, Symbol* (Baton Rouge, 1974), 319; *OR*, XV, 76–77; John D. Winters, *The Civil War in Louisiana* (1963; rpr. Baton Rouge, 1979), 120–21.

4. *OR*, XV, 808, Vol. XVII, Pt. 2, p. 752; Richard Taylor, *Destruction and Reconstruction: Personal Experiences of the Late War*, ed. Richard B. Harwell (1879; rpr. New York, 1955), 137; Baton Rouge *Weekly Gazette and Comet*, December 3, 1862.

Hudson terminus and depot at the new landing. A hotel sprang up nearby, and a ferry service operated to the west bank. Roads ran north to Bayou Sara and Jackson, east to Clinton, and south to Ross and Springfield landings and Baton Rouge.

The terrain immediately around Port Hudson varied immensely. Across the Mississippi a broad alluvial plain bordered the river. A plateau east of the village contained extensive fields of sugarcane and cotton. A mile and a half below Port Hudson a ravine, about three hundred yards wide and eighty feet deep, ran northeast from the river and bounded the plateau on the south. Just north and northeast of the village the gently rolling fields became almost impassable. Canyonlike ravines—many forty to sixty feet deep— and dense woods stretched for a few hundred yards to Little Sandy Creek. Above the bend in the river a marsh, bordered on the north by Big Sandy Creek and on the west by Thompson's Creek, covered much of the old riverbed. Thus fortified by nature, Port Hudson presented a formidable stronghold.[5]

5. Virginia Lobdell Jennings, *The Plains and the People: A History of Upper East Baton Rouge Parish* (New Orleans, 1962), 43, 146; Calvin D. Cowles (comp.), *Atlas to Accompany the Official Records of the Union and Confederate Armies* (1891-95; rpr. New York, 1958), plate XXXVIII, 3; Daniel P. Smith, *Company K, First Alabama Regiment, or Three Years in the Confederate Service* (Prattville, Ala., 1885), 40; Mobile *Advertiser and Register*, March 18, 1863; Wickham Hoffman, *Camp, Court and Siege: A Narrative of Personal Adventure and Observation During Two Wars, 1861-1865, 1870-1871* (New York, 1877), 66; John S. Kendall, "Recollections of a Confederate Officer," *Louisiana Historical Quarterly*, XXIX (October, 1946), 1092, 1107; Sarah Morgan Dawson, *A Confederate Girl's Diary*, ed. James I. Robertson, Jr. (1913; rpr. Bloomington, 1960), 173, 458; "Fortification and Siege of Port Hudson—Compiled by the Association of Defenders of Port Hudson; M. J. Smith, President; James Freret, Secretary," *Southern Historical Society Papers*, XIV (1886), 305; Milledge L. Bonham, Jr., *Man and Nature at Port Hudson: 1863, 1917* (Baton Rouge, 1965), [1–4].

II

Fortification: August–November, 1862

Everything is fair, they say, in love and war.
—Lieutenant Howard C. Wright,
30th Louisiana Infantry

On the morning of August 15, 1862, the 4th Louisiana Infantry marched north along the road between Baton Rouge and Bayou Sara. Casually resting their rifles on their shoulders, the men moved at an easy pace. Battle-hardened veterans of Shiloh, Vicksburg, and Baton Rouge, they carried little baggage besides their indispensable blankets, which each carried slung over one shoulder. When they passed a house, the residents lined the roadside for their first glimpse of soldiers on active duty in their neighborhood. The citizens cheered the troops heartily for their recent exploits but at the same time must have felt some foreboding, for this sight meant an end to their life of relative peace and tranquillity away from the bloody conflict.[1]

The column turned westward toward Port Hudson. Two miles before it reached that village a field of corn stretched far off to the south. An officer inquired of a resident standing nearby the name of the plantation owner and was answered, "It is Slaughter's field." "It will be the field of Slaughter yet, or I am much mistaken,"

---

1. [Howard C. Wright], *Port Hudson: Its History from an Interior Point of View as Sketched from the Diary of an Officer* (St. Francisville, La., 1937), 5; John S. Kendall, "The Diary of Surgeon Craig, Fourth Louisiana Regiment, C.S.A., 1864–65," *Louisiana Historical Quarterly*, VIII (1925), 54; F. Jay Taylor (ed.), *Reluctant Rebel: The Secret Diary of Robert Patrick, 1861–1865* (Baton Rouge, 1959), 45; Kendall, "Recollections," 1091. Unless otherwise indicated, all units mentioned in the text are infantry.

responded the officer.[2] He could not have imagined the truth in his ironic prophecy.

Experienced soldiers know that they can forage better in advance than in the wake of an army. Some six or eight members of the 4th Louisiana entered Port Hudson early and learned from a citizen that the enemy was nearby. Sailors from the ironclad U.S.S. *Essex* had come ashore at the landing to destroy the flatboats used in ferrying supplies from the west bank; the destruction of the C.S.S. *Arkansas* enabled Federal vessels to navigate the Mississippi below Vicksburg in relative safety.

Seeing an opportunity to earn the thanks of their commander and gain promotion, the Louisianians decided to ambush the Federal sailors. His comrades in position, Private John R. Nesbit approached the enemy officer, Fourth Master Spencer Kellogg, and demanded that he cease destroying the flatboats. Kellogg, angered by the impudent Confederate, threatened to capture him, and moved toward Nesbit, followed by three sailors. Nesbit led them past his hidden companions, who jumped out with their rifles pointed at the Federals; the latter, armed only with pistols, gave up without firing a shot.

Proud of their achievement, the Louisianians marched their prisoners to headquarters. But instead of congratulating them, Brigadier General Daniel Ruggles seethed with anger. He threatened to have them shot for alerting the Yankee warship to their presence. An armed guard took the Louisianians to a cabin on the edge of the bluff and held them captive, guarded by a sentinel. Realizing that they were in serious trouble, the men resolved to tunnel their way out. They succeeded, slipped past the guard, and slid down the bluff. Reaching bottom, the fugitives made a wide circuit of the town and returned to camp, where their comrades supposed they had fallen behind during the march from the Comite River three days before. Ruggles had neglected to get their names and, keeping the escapade to themselves, all escaped punishment.[3]

2. [Wright], *Port Hudson*, 5.

3. Kendall, "Recollections," 1091–92; U.S. Navy Department, *The War of the Rebellion: Official Records of the Union and Confederate Navies* (30 vols.; Washington, D.C., 1894–1922), ser. I, XIX, 186. Hereinafter cited as *ORN*. Unless otherwise indicated, all citations are to Series I; Andrew B. Booth, *Records of Louisiana Confederate Soldiers and Louisiana Confederate Commands* (4 books in 3 vols.; New Orleans, 1920), Vol. III, Bk. 1, p. 1267.

The incident did not end there. Commodore William D. Porter, commander of the *Essex*, wrote Major General Benjamin F. Butler, Union commander of the Department of the Gulf, about the ambush. Porter believed that local guerrillas had captured his men. He stated further that "the next day they [sailors] were hanged. . . . I would ask you, under the circumstances, that retribution be carried out, and would respectfully suggest that for each seaman of mine hanged one guerrilla be shot, and for my officer ten."[4] No one was hanged but Butler mentioned the matter in a letter to Major General Richard Taylor, commander of Confederate forces in western Louisiana: "I do not believe the report made by Commodore Porter. If true, it only adds another example of the infelicity of employing such partisan forces; if false, it shows the damage of reprisals and retaliation upon any report whatever."[5] The Confederates had not heard the last of Porter's fantasies.

The 4th Louisiana camped between William Slaughter's residence and Port Hudson on August 15 and 16. The regiment entered the village on the seventeenth. At noon the men stacked their arms and pitched their tents in the common, just east of the church in the center of town. The only infantry present, the Louisianians performed guard duty. They kept away from the river to avoid drawing fire from Federal naval vessels. A detachment of the 30th Louisiana shortly joined them.[6]

The arriving troops were under the command of General Ruggles. A native of Massachusetts, Ruggles graduated from West Point in 1833, fought in the Seminole War of 1839–40, and distinguished himself during the Mexican War. He remained in the U.S. Army until May 7, 1861, when he cast his lot with the Confederacy; his Virginia in-laws were the deciding factor. Commissioned a brigadier general on August 9, 1861, he served in Virginia and at New Orleans, and he led a division at the Battle of Shiloh. There he amassed the largest concentration of field artillery ever assembled in the Western Hemisphere. Ruggles blasted the Federals with sixty-two cannon, making an immense contribution to the Con-

4. *ORN*, XIX, 186.

5. *OR*, XV, 567.

6. William Y. Dixon, Diary, August 16, 1862, William Y. Dixon Papers, Louisiana State University, Department of Archives and Manuscripts, Baton Rouge, Louisiana; Kendall, "Recollections," 1091–92, 1095. Kendall is incorrect on the date of Confederate occupation.

federate successes on April 6, 1862. He then served in district command in Mississippi and Louisiana, before assignment at Port Hudson.[7]

Ruggles hurried to secure Port Hudson. He drew supplies via Williams Bridge and Clinton and commandeered all railroad transportation between Clinton and Port Hudson. Major General John C. Breckinridge had given him full authority to procure any tools, slaves, or other means he might require to construct earthworks. Breckinridge's chief engineer, Captain James Nocquet, reported to Ruggles for temporary duty and within a few days had some of the works ready to receive heavy cannon, which Major General Earl Van Dorn assured Breckinridge would arrive shortly.[8]

The Confederates debated the design of the fortifications. The first proposal called for a fort adjacent to the river, with a uniform line of batteries on that front. The remaining sides would form a semicircle of salient and retiring angles. This design would provide concentrated fire and require only a small garrison, but an investing force would be able to concentrate its fire on so small an area as to make it untenable unless it were constructed with casemates similar to those in a stone fort. The proposal was promptly rejected.

The second proposal was to build a series of lunettes flanking each other at a distance of four hundred yards. These detached works would expose an attacker to a deadly direct, cross, and flanking fire, while at the same time allowing the garrison to sally forth in good order and launch vigorous counterattacks. But strong reserves required between each lunette would have little protection against the enemy's fire.

The third plan consisted of a continuous line of parapet and ditch. This design would provide the best earthworks for withstanding a siege, but the planners concluded that any attacker would be unprepared to conduct a siege and would attempt to storm the position. Consequently, they decided on the second plan.

7. Breckinridge, G.O. No. 18, August 13, 1862, Daniel Ruggles Papers, Perkins Library, Duke University, Durham, N. C.; Ezra J. Warner, *Generals in Gray: Lives of the Confederate Commanders* (Baton Rouge, 1959), 265–66; *OR*, VI, 751; Wiley Sword, *Shiloh: Bloody April* (New York, 1974), 291–92.

8. *OR*, XV, 81, 795, 800, 1220; Breckinridge, G.O. No. 18, August 13, 1862, Ruggles Papers, Duke University.

The first lunette was constructed four miles below Port Hudson on the Baton Rouge road, and six more followed in quick succession. They were to be built as far as Little Sandy Creek. Everyone trusted that the precipitous terrain that stretched from the creek to the Mississippi River, strengthened with felled trees in the ravines, would prove formidable enough to allow a line of infantry to hold that sector. This line of defenses would have stretched eight miles and, according to military experts of the day, to hold it would require a garrison of thirty-five thousand men with a minimum of seventy pieces of artillery.[9]

Following Van Dorn's instructions, Breckinridge divided his forces between Port Hudson and the Comite River so he could guard the roads leading to Camp Moore and Clinton. Leaving his camp on the Comite, Breckinridge accompanied the last of the troops ordered to Port Hudson and took charge.[10]

A Kentuckian, Breckinridge had enjoyed an exceptional political career. Elected vice-president of the United States in 1856 at the age of thirty-five, he made an unsuccessful bid for the presidency in 1860. When Kentucky sided with the North in the fall of 1861, Breckinridge headed south. Though he lacked any military experience, he received a brigadier general's commission the following month. He saw action at Shiloh and Vicksburg before commanding Confederate forces at the Battle of Baton Rouge.

In August, 1862, Confederate armies returned to Kentucky. The authorities in Richmond believed Breckinridge's presence there would contribute more to the war effort than his command of a garrison in Louisiana. Receiving orders to move north with a sizable portion of his men, Breckinridge turned his command back to Ruggles on August 18 and left Port Hudson the next day. The troops moved the following week. Left with scarcely fifteen hundred men at Port Hudson, Ruggles promptly requested reinforcements from Van Dorn.[11]

To prevent the passage of enemy vessels upriver, the garrison needed heavy cannon and experienced artillerists. Ruggles had acquired a forty-two-pounder smoothbore cannon, which he mounted immediately. The gun was manned by former crewmen

---

9. [Wright], *Port Hudson*, 6–7.
10. *OR*, XV, 80–81, 797, 800.
11. Warner, *Generals in Gray*, 34; *OR*, XV, 800–801, 803.

of the *Arkansas*. Those sailors who managed to escape capture following the loss of their vessel, including a few who crossed the river at Port Hudson, had gone to Jackson, Mississippi. There they joined Commander Isaac N. Brown and others of the crew whom sickness and wounds had forced to stay behind. These approximately four hundred men proceeded to Port Hudson to man the river batteries.[12]

A severe shortage of heavy cannon plagued the Confederacy, but fortune smiled on Ruggles with the arrival of the gunboat U.S.S. *Sumter* off Bayou Sara on the morning of August 14. Commodore Porter ordered its commander to remain there and guard the ferry, even though the *Sumter* had severe engine trouble. At 5 P.M. the stock of the anchor parted, and the ship drifted aground. A falling river caused her to careen so that her fore and aft thirty-two-pounders were rendered useless. Francis Marion Mumford, a former second lieutenant in the Confederate service, chanced upon the scene and requested aid from Port Hudson to capture the *Sumter*. When it failed to arrive the following morning, he demanded that the Federals surrender. Bluffing, he "granted" them time to consider. The Federal steamer *Ceres* happened by and made several unsuccessful attempts to free the *Sumter*. Fearful that Confederate artillery would soon arrive, the defenseless sailors abandoned the vessel and escaped on the *Ceres*. The Confederates captured about fifty Negroes, some small arms, and medical stores. Shortly after daylight on the sixteenth, the Union gunboat *No. 7* came in sight, and the Confederates burned the *Sumter*. The Confederates later secured the two thirty-two-pounders and sent them to Port Hudson, where they were mounted by August 29.[13]

Ruggles had yet another reason to celebrate. Following the Battle of Baton Rouge, Union soldiers began to confiscate slaves, plunder private homes, and harass southern sympathizers.

12. *OR*, XV, 779, 785; C. W. Read, "Reminiscences of the Confederate States Navy," *Southern Historical Society Papers*, I (1876), 361; Memphis *Daily Appeal*, August 15, 1862; U. S. Naval War Records Office, *Register of Officers of the Confederate States Navy, 1861–1865* (Washington, D.C., 1931), 23. The correct date for Breckinridge's G.O. No. 20 must be August 14, 1862.

13. *ORN*, XIX, 159; Memphis *Daily Appeal*, August 19, 29, September 1, 1862; "Heroic Deed of Lieutenant Mumford," *Confederate Veteran*, X (1902), 365; "Dr. F. M. Mumford," *Confederate Veteran*, XIX (1911), 444; Booth, *Louisiana Soldiers*, Vol. III, Bk. 1, p. 1090.

Breckinridge complained to the Union commander that further violations "of the rules of civilized war" would force him to "raise the black flag, and neither give nor ask quarter." Breckinridge lacked the resources to impose his will on the enemy, but the Confederate forces remaining on the Comite so vexed the Yankees that they feared a second attack on Baton Rouge. Finally, Butler ordered the Union troops withdrawn to New Orleans and proceeded to remove or destroy all machinery in the town. On August 20 Confederates drove in Union pickets around the city and captured some forty horses and twenty head of cattle. These efforts drew a furious shelling from the Union gunboats. The Federals completed their evacuation of Baton Rouge on the twenty-first.[14] Ruggles now had the breathing space needed to fortify Port Hudson.

Butler had no choice. Limited manpower compelled him to concentrate his forces about New Orleans to secure the city. He strengthened its defenses but could not undertake offensive operations without additional troops. Instead of waiting for reinforcements from the North that did not appear forthcoming, Butler began enlisting Negroes. This fresh source of recruits quickly provided three regiments of infantry and two batteries. These additional troops enabled Butler to detach a brigade west of the Mississippi to secure the La Fourche region. At no time, however, was he able to threaten Port Hudson.[15]

Ruggles had heard rumors of the impending evacuation of Baton Rouge. On August 21 he reported to Van Dorn that if the Federals withdrew, he would "prepare to move toward New Orleans." Ruggles ordered Brigadier General M. Jeff. Thompson, at Ponchatoula, to repair the railroad and rebuild the bridge at Manchac, in preparation for the attack on New Orleans. He also instructed Thompson to advance his scouts toward the Mississippi River to encourage the Federals to evacuate Baton Rouge. Anticipating the withdrawal, the 4th Louisiana started for Baton Rouge at 3 P.M. on August 21 and regained the city on the twenty-third. C. E. Fenner's Louisiana battery arrived at Port Hudson shortly

14. Davis, *Breckinridge*, 324; Caroline E. Whitcomb, *History of the Second Massachusetts Battery (Nims' Battery) of Light Artillery, 1861–1865* . . . (Concord, N.H., 1912), 40; Memphis *Daily Appeal*, October 1, 1862; William DeLoss Love, *Wisconsin in the War of the Rebellion* . . . (Chicago, 1866), 538; *ORN*, XIX, 785; *OR*, XV, 130.

15. Benjamin F. Butler, *Butler's Book* (Boston, 1892), 488, 491, 493, 495.

after the Federal evacuation of Baton Rouge and proceeded there immediately.[16]

Following the evacuation, the *Essex* left Baton Rouge and steamed upriver past Port Hudson that same day. By evening the vessel arrived at Bayou Sara needing fuel but found the stockpile of coal on fire. Angered by this act of arson and the previous wounding of sailors on the *Sumter*, Porter fired two shells into the town but did no damage. The vessel remained anchored overnight and shelled the town the following morning, but the sailors did not attempt to go ashore. Porter sent the wooden gunboat *Anglo-American* off to New Orleans for coal and took the *Essex* to Port Hudson to await the *Anglo-American*'s return. Negro laborers were excavating the water batteries when she came in sight. Although he scanned the bluffs for some time, Porter apparently failed to observe any military activity, and the *Essex*'s guns remained silent. Louisiana Lieutenant Howard C. Wright observed that if the ironclad had "shelled the heights, it would have given the soldiers all the work of building the batteries, as the Negroes would not have stood the fire." Porter gave a different version: "I could discover no guns at this place, but earthworks were in progress, and whilst destroying these I had the misfortune to burst my heavy x-inch gun." The *Anglo-American* failed to arrive at Port Hudson, and the *Essex* returned to Bayou Sara, where Porter ordered all remaining buildings destroyed. When Butler questioned this action, Porter claimed that he burned the town only after citizens had wounded several sailors he had sent ashore.[17]

When the *Anglo-American* returned upstream on August 29, her commander, R. K. Riley, observed earthworks along the bluff and at the waterline. Failing to see any guns, he continued upriver until sighting a second line of earthworks; then he ordered his rifled fifty-pounder to fire. At that moment the Confederates opened fire with two thirty-two-pounders manned by the former crew of the *Arkansas* and eighteen six- and twelve-pounders. This fusillade struck the vessel seventy-three times and wounded the pilot and one sailor. The vessel could not reply because a heavy rain had

16. *OR*, XV, 803, 1032; Dixon, Diary, August 23, 1862, Dixon Papers; Fannie A. Beers, *Memories: A Record of Personal Experience and Adventure During Four Years of War* (Philadelphia, 1889), 233.

17. [Wright], *Port Hudson*, 8; *ORN*, XIX, 181; *OR*, XV, 131–32, 803; Baton Rouge *Weekly Gazette and Comet*, November 19, 1862.

soaked the cartridge in the fifty-pounder and the howitzer lacked ammunition. The vulnerable wooden gunboat had no protection for her machinery, and Confederate fire drove many of the sailors from their posts. But Riley pressed on, feeling it "a matter of urgent necessity" to reach Porter. [18]

The same day, Ruggles received orders to turn over command to Brigadier General William Nelson Rector Beall, leave twenty-five to twenty-eight hundred men at Port Hudson, and take the balance to Mississippi. Born in Bardstown, Kentucky, on March 20, 1825, Beall entered West Point in 1844. An indifferent scholar, he graduated four years later, too late to fight in the Mexican War. He served in both the infantry and cavalry, saw action against Indians and in the disturbances in Kansas in 1856–57, and had attained the rank of captain by the opening of the Civil War. Beall had a sincere attachment for the Union and did not resign until August 20, 1861. He entered Confederate service with the rank of captain of cavalry and served under Van Dorn in Arkansas. Commissioned a brigadier general on April 11, 1862, he had little combat or independent command experience when he took charge at Port Hudson. [19]

By the end of the month barely a thousand soldiers remained at Port Hudson. The garrison consisted of the 30th Louisiana and William R. Miles's Louisiana Legion's infantry; R. M. Boone's Louisiana, Richard T. English's (without guns), J. A. Hoskins', George Ralston's, and Calvit Roberts' Mississippi, and Oliver J. Semmes's Confederate (Regular) batteries; and A. J. Lewis' and C. McLaurin's Mississippi Partisan Ranger companies. Henry Hughes's Mississippi Cavalry Battalion patrolled the surrounding area. [20]

18. *ORN*, XIX, 182–83; P. F. de Gournay, "The Siege of Port Hudson," in "Annals of the War," scrapbook of miscellaneous newspaper clippings, Tulane University, New Orleans, Louisiana. The forty-two-pounders mentioned by de Gournay must have been the thirty-two-pounders captured from the *Sumter*.

19. *OR*, XV, 804; Warner, *Generals in Gray*, 21–22; Fred Harvey Harrington, "Arkansas Defends the Mississippi," *Arkansas Historical Quarterly*, IV (1945), 110; George W. Cullum, *Biographical Register of the Officers and Graduates of the U.S. Military Academy, from 1802 to 1867. Revised Edition, with a Supplement Continuing the Register of Graduates to January 1, 1879* (3 vols.; New York, 1879), II, 222.

20. *OR*, XV, 804, 1212, Vol. XXIV, Pt. 3, p. 706, Vol. XXVI, Pt. 2, p. 587; Dunbar Rowland (comp.), *The Official and Statistical Register of the State of Mississippi* (Nashville, 1908), 853; J. M. Jones, Diary, preface, [J. M.] Jones Collection, Department of Archives, Northwestern Louisiana University, Natchitoches, La.

On September 2 Semmes's and C. E. Fenner's batteries were ordered west of the river, but the latter remained at Baton Rouge. On September 5 J. L. Bradford's Mississippi battery was ordered to Port Hudson. After it arrived, George Ralston's left for duty west of the Mississippi. George F. Abbay's and A. J. Herod's Mississippi batteries quickly followed Bradford's to Port Hudson. A twenty-pound Parrott gun arrived about September 1. Captured in Virginia, it was sent to Miles's Legion as a gift by President Jefferson Davis—a most unusual gesture.[21]

The 12th Louisiana Heavy Artillery Battalion had come from Richmond, Virginia. Confederate authorities selected this unit on the assumption that it could best stand the climate. The commander, Lieutenant Colonel Paul F. de Gournay, had impressed Major General John Magruder during his service on the peninsula around Yorktown, and Magruder wanted de Gournay to raise a regiment of heavy artillery. Five companies made up the original organization. Five more were to be recruited in New Orleans to fill out the regiment, but the city's fall dashed that plan. One company stayed near Richmond, but the remaining four hardy and well-drilled companies arrived at Port Hudson about September 4. For several weeks they had not a single gun to serve.[22]

The Confederates could not deliver large-caliber guns by boat because the *Essex* remained above Port Hudson. Instead, the cannon came by rail to Osyka, Mississippi. From there, they moved over miserable roads through the hilly, piney woods to Clinton and thence by rail to Port Hudson. The slow process of hauling cannon weighing several tons each gave the Confederate artillerists time to construct the necessary earthworks before a gun arrived. They then could place it in position immediately. But the men often became frustrated because of the long delay between completion of the earthwork and the arrival of the gun.[23]

21. *OR*, XV, 841, Vol. XVII, Pt. 2, p. 691; Rowland, *Official and Statistical Register of Mississippi*, 853; S.O. No. 36, September 5, 1862, "Order Book, Withers Artillery," and Colonel William Temple Withers to Lieutenant Colonel James P. Parker, September 4, 1862, Withers Artillery Papers, both in Mississippi Department of Archives and History, Jackson; Claud Estes (comp.), *List of Field Officers, Regiments and Battalions in the Confederate States Army, 1861–1865* (Macon, Ga., 1912), 96, 135; [Wright], *Port Hudson*, 8–10.

22. *OR*, XV, 794, Vol. LII, Pt. 2, p. 334; [Paul F. de Gournay], "D'Gournay's Battalion of Artillery," *Confederate Veteran*, XIII (1905), 31; [Wright], *Port Hudson*, 14; de Gournay, "Siege of Port Hudson."

23. [Wright], *Port Hudson*, 6; Kendall, "Recollections," 1093.

Commodore Porter decided to go downriver to New Orleans for supplies and at the same time ascertain the strength of the Port Hudson batteries. Shortly after 4 A.M. on September 7 the *Essex*, with the *Anglo-American* lashed to her starboard side, came within range, and the Confederates opened fire with two thirty-two-pounders, the twenty-pound Parrott, and some fieldpieces. They did not expect to injure the ironclad. The *Essex* replied with three or four rounds, killing one horse in its paddock at the north end of town and striking an empty house. The affair lasted only a few minutes. One Confederate shot passed through a porthole on the *Essex*; smoke and screams poured out. Although Porter conceded no casualties, southern sources reported from fifteen to more than thirty-two killed and wounded. Two guns on board the *Essex* burst during the engagement, including the ten-inch; Porter attributed its destruction to the shelling of the earthworks at Port Hudson in late August.[24]

The former crew of the *Arkansas* got their revenge against the *Essex*, which a month before had forced them to destroy their vessel above Baton Rouge. The *Essex* had to undergo major repairs at New Orleans; but the Confederates only learned of their success from an article in *Harper's Weekly* several weeks later. Fourteen of their heavy projectiles found their mark, three of them penetrating the ironclad and shattering the twenty-four-inch-thick woodwork. Porter reported: "As nearly as I could judge the enemy had in position from 35 to 40 guns of X-inch, IX-inch, and VII-inch caliber in three batteries. . . . A land force will be necessary to complete the destruction of this fort, which, if allowed to again be restored, would seriously interrupt the free navigation of the Lower Mississippi." The Confederates laughed at Porter's announcement because they had only one gun that large. Lieutenant Wright wrote: "Everything is fair, they say, in love and war. Flights of fancy are legitimate in the former, why not should they be in the latter?"[25]

Beall began to lay out a new line of fortifications more contracted in scope. His design consisted of a continuous parapet and ditch four and one-half miles in length, just over half the length of

24. *ORN*, XIX, 182, 190; [Wright], *Port Hudson*, 8; de Gournay, "Siege of Port Hudson"; Memphis *Daily Appeal*, September 13, 22, 25, 1862; Dawson, *Confederate Girl's Diary*, 236–37.

25. *ORN*, XIX, 182, 190; de Gournay, "Siege of Port Hudson," citing *Harper's Weekly*; [Wright], *Port Hudson*, 8.

the previously adopted plan. A shorter defensive perimeter would allow a smaller garrison to endure a protracted siege more successfully. Beginning on the river a mile and a half below the town, the new line gradually curved northward and away from the river until it encountered Little Sandy Creek, a mile east of town. The first three-quarters of a mile of the new line followed the broken edge of the plateau, taking advantage of the terrain. Then it crossed James Gibbon's and Slaughter's level fields for a mile and a quarter. Another quarter of a mile carried it across a deep crevasse; then three-quarters of a mile through rolling fields, where it ended on a hill overlooking Little Sandy Creek. From here the earthworks would follow the edge of the ridge overlooking Little Sandy Creek wherever possible for about a mile and a half until the defenses intersected the river above Port Hudson. Contemporary military experts believed that eighteen to twenty thousand men could defend such a line. [26]

Construction of the new line proceeded slowly. The breastworks were the weakest allowed by military engineering, built in the crudest manner and revetted with fence rails. The soldiers carried the rails and sometimes helped the small force of Negroes that worked on the fortifications. Beall could not entice the local planters to furnish enough slaves to labor on the works. President Davis rejected his request for a proclamation of martial law, but Beall did receive authorization to call on the citizens in the adjacent counties to contribute the number of slaves needed. Laboring in a desultory manner, the Negroes and soldiers made little progress during the following months. [27]

When Van Dorn moved northward through Mississippi, Ruggles remained at Jackson, Mississippi, in command of that state and eastern Louisiana. On September 11 Ruggles recommended to General Samuel Cooper, adjutant and inspector general, an immediate advance on New Orleans. He proposed throwing twenty thousand men against the city. Aided by the numerous southern sympathizers in New Orleans, this force would have little trouble

26. "Fortification and Siege," 306–307.

27. [Wright], *Port Hudson*, 7–8; John S. Overcash, letter to editor, *Confederate Veteran*, XV (1907), 141; R. T. Martin, "Reminiscences of an Arkansan," *Confederate Veteran*, XVII (1909), 69; Civil War Diary of Andrew Jackson Campbell, December 14, 18, 1862, Tennessee State Library and Archives, Nashville; *OR*, XV, 841–42; "Fortification and Siege," 307.

defeating the fewer than ten thousand Federals, who Ruggles concluded were greatly "demoralized and suffering from the influences of the climate."[28]

The Federals quickly disillusioned Ruggles. On the morning of September 15 they advanced against Ponchatoula. Butler's purpose was to obliterate the bridge at Manchac Pass and thereby safeguard New Orleans against an attack from that direction. This aggressive but fundamentally defensive action shocked the Confederates and forced Ruggles to reexamine his opponent's supposed weaknesses. On the seventeenth he ordered Beall to concentrate his forces at Port Hudson and to leave only one company of infantry, two cannon, and fifteen cavalrymen at Baton Rouge. The following day, after detaching the required number, the 4th Louisiana and Fenner's battery left Baton Rouge for Port Hudson. The only other force Beall could detach was "a small guard at Bayou Sara if expedient." By the twenty-first, light batteries had deployed at Troth's house, three miles below Port Hudson, to prevent the enemy from disembarking at the landing there.[29]

Ruggles also received disheartening news regarding his proposal for an advance on New Orleans. The Adjutant-General's Office notified him on the twenty-third that Major General Richard Taylor, in western Louisiana, had complete authority over any attempt to recapture New Orleans and that Secretary of War George W. Randolph "is at a loss to understand why . . . Ruggles . . . should give publicity through the medium of the telegraph to suggestions which should have been regarded by him as private." The message infuriated Ruggles. New Orleans fell within his jurisdiction, not Taylor's, and no one had informed him of Taylor's instructions regarding that city. Ruggles curtly replied, "If the [telegraph] agents are disloyal the plans of the Government are at their mercy." He added that the secretary's sense of justice should induce him to recall the letter of reproach. He got his letter of apology.[30]

The need for manpower along the Mississippi River led President Davis to order Van Dorn to retain those regiments headquartered in his district that had been recently paroled from Federal prison camps instead of sending them to Tennessee. Davis con-

28. *OR*, XV, 806–807, 817.

29. *Ibid.*, 138, 141, 807, 809; Butler, *Butler's Book*, 489; Dixon, Diary, September 18, 1862, Dixon Papers; Beers, *Memories*, 233.

30. *OR*, XV, 810, 817, 822, 839–40.

cluded, "You will have due care to the safety of Vicksburg, Port Hudson, &c." With Confederate forces within seven miles of Cincinnati, Ohio, and in Maryland as well, this occasion was one of those rare moments when the president had troops to spare.[31]

The first such regiment sent to Port Hudson was the 1st Alabama. The Federals had captured most of the unit at Island No. 10. The women of Mobile provided new uniforms, overcoats, and blankets, but the men lacked muskets when they arrived at Port Hudson on October 4. Van Dorn undoubtedly sent this unit because of its experience with heavy artillery. Three companies immediately began to construct batteries, and three others provided infantry support. The men finally received weapons, which ranged from rifles to flintlocks. The remaining four companies of the 1st Alabama had escaped from Island No. 10 and fought in northern Mississippi. Following Colonel I. G. W. Steedman's request, these companies, including the regimental brass band, rejoined him at Port Hudson on November 5.[32]

On September 30 Lieutenant General John C. Pemberton had received notification to go to Jackson, Mississippi, to relieve Van Dorn. Pemberton was to command the Department of Mississippi and East Louisiana and act in concert with Taylor if an opportunity arose for attacking New Orleans. Before Pemberton arrived, word reached Ruggles at Jackson on October 3 that eight thousand reinforcements had arrived at New Orleans. Ruggles immediately pointed out the need for additional cannon at Port Hudson, and Beall ordered troops there from Ponchatoula. Both men thought the Federals would advance up the Mississippi River. By October 11 Ruggles believed Camp Moore the intended target. When the Yankees landed sixty miles east of Ponchatoula at Bonfouca, Louisiana, Beall asked Ruggles on October 20 to send reinforcements to Covington.[33]

31. *Ibid.*, Vol. XVII, Pt. 2, p. 700; E. B. Long and Barbara Long, *The Civil War Day by Day: An Almanac, 1861–1865* (Garden City, N.Y., 1971), 264.

32. Smith, *Company K*, 37–40; Edward Young McMorries, *History of the First Regiment Alabama Volunteer Infantry C.S.A.* (1904; rpr. Freeport, N.Y., 1970), 48, 51; *OR*, Vol. XVII, Pt. 2, p. 726; [Wright], *Port Hudson*, 14; Robert Partin (ed.), "Report of a Corporal of the Alabama First Infantry on Talk and Fighting Along the Mississippi, 1862–63," *Alabama Historical Quarterly*, XX (1950), 583; Steedman to Pemberton, October 16, 1862, Port Hudson Battlefield Museum, Port Hudson, La.

33. *OR*, XV, 188, 821, 839, 1208, Vol. XVII, Pt. 2, pp. 716–17, 719, 726; Colonel

It now appeared that the Federals were about to begin a serious campaign in southeastern Louisiana, and Pemberton endeavored to strengthen his hold on that region. Assuming command on October 14, he divided the department into three districts a week later. The Third District, assigned to Beall, included that portion of Mississippi between the Big Black and Mississippi rivers and the New Orleans, Jackson and Great Northern Railroad, all Louisiana east of the Mississippi, and the Mississippi counties on the Gulf Coast. Beall's headquarters remained at Port Hudson. Pemberton also renewed the request for additional cannon for Port Hudson.[34]

At the time of its creation Beall's entire district had a mere 3,626 troops. Most of the men garrisoned Port Hudson (2,412) and Ponchatoula (834), with smaller detachments at Baton Rouge, Covington, and Camp Moore. With so few soldiers, many lacking adequate weapons, Beall could offer little resistance against the enemy's impending onslaught. Pemberton promised Beall reinforcements on October 22 and promptly put troops in motion. Roberts' battery apparently rejoined Beall on the twenty-third. The 39th Mississippi and 48th Tennessee reached Port Hudson on the twenty-seventh; the 11th Arkansas came by steamboat the following day; the 49th Tennessee arrived on November 1. Colonel Bart Jones's battalion and the 15th, 16th, 18th, and 23rd Arkansas regiments, consolidated under the command of Colonel Oliver P. Lyles, marched in the same day. The 27th Alabama, three Tennessee artillery companies, and the 9th Tennessee Cavalry Battalion also joined the garrison during this period. The latter, fresh from a Union prison, arrived without horses and served as infantry until the men secured mounts in December. The Tennessee artillery companies lacked cannon. Although sometimes called the 1st Tennessee Artillery Battalion, the unit performed infantry duty. Even more unusual, the captains of the three companies rotated command of the informal battalion. Fragments of regiments that escaped from Forts Henry and Donelson and Island No. 10 earlier in the year arrived to rejoin their released comrades. Recruits for particular units or conscripts assigned to specific commands also provided reinforcements.[35]

A. R. Witt to Ruggles, October 8, 1862 (from Ponchatoula), Daniel Ruggles Papers, Mississippi Department of Archives and History, Jackson.

34. *OR*, XV, 827, 840, Vol. XVII, Pt. 2, p. 749.

35. *Ibid.*, XV, 841–43, 845, 919, 1061; George M. Owens to his wife, Ann,

Additional artillery arrived. By October 24, thirteen heavy guns lined the bluff. The new cannon included one rifled thirty-two-pounder, six rifled twenty-four pounders, and one eight-inch and one ten-inch columbiad, the latter having just arrived on the twenty-first. Two forty-two- and two twenty-four-pounder smooth-bores, an eight-inch shellgun, and a thirty-pound Parrott followed these. The four smoothbores and the shellgun were obsolete and lacked breech sights. [36]

Because of the increased activity in the area Pemberton replaced Beall at the district level with Brigadier General John Bordenave Villepigue. A South Carolinian of French descent, Villepigue graduated from West Point in 1854 and saw service in the dragoons before resigning on March 31, 1861. He soon became colonel of the 36th Georgia Infantry Regiment. Villepigue was assigned to duty on the Gulf Coast, where his successful defense of Fort McRae, near Pensacola, brought him recognition. Bragg appointed him to his staff as chief of engineers and artillery. Appointed brigadier in the spring of 1862, he was transferred to General Pierre G. T. Beauregard's command in Tennessee. Beauregard deemed him "the most energetic young officer available" and placed him in charge

---

October 28, 1862, Owens Papers (xerox copies), in possession of E. Russ Williams, Monroe, La.; J. B. Lindsley (ed.), *The Military Annals of Tennessee* (Nashville, 1886), 547; J. C. Poe (ed.), *The Raving Foe: The Civil War Diary of Major James T. Poe, C. S. A., and the 11th Arkansas Volunteers and a Complete List of Prisoners* (Eastland, Tex., 1967), 53; [Tennessee] Civil War Centennial Commission, *Tennesseans in the Civil War: A Military History of Confederate and Union Units with Available Rosters of Personnel*, 2 pts. (Nashville, 1964–65), I, 30–31, 122, 152, 156, 282, 284; John M. Harrell, *Arkansas* (Atlanta, 1899), 321, Vol. X of Clement A. Evans (ed.), *Confederate Military History*; J. V. Frederick (ed.), "War Diary of W. C. Porter," *Arkansas Historical Quarterly*, XI (1952), 305; Estes (comp.), *List of Field Officers*, 78; M. D. Cannon, *Inside of Rebeldom: The Daily Life of a Private in the Confederate Army* (Washington, D.C., 1899), 71–72; Diary of Campbell, December 15, 28, 30, 1862; Captain Peter K. Stankiewicz to General Samuel Cooper, November 19, 1862, in possession of Gary Hendershott, Little Rock, Ark.; McMorries, *First Alabama*, 50; Morning reports of Captain R. C. Weatherly's Company F of the Miles Legion for the month of October, 1862, Confederate States of America Papers, Perkins Library, Duke University, Durham, N.C.

36. *OR*, XV, 846; Warren Ripley, *Artillery and Ammunition of the Civil War* (New York, 1970), 102; [Wright], *Port Hudson*, 9. Wright is mistaken about the order of arrival of the guns, and apparently the twenty-pound Parrott is listed as a rifled twenty-four-pounder on the October 24 report, which has several errors in the printed version.

of Fort Pillow. Villepigue's skillful defense of that position against superior land and naval forces, coupled with his performance at the Battle of Corinth in early October, clearly demonstrated that he could command at Port Hudson. But on arriving there in late October, he quickly succumbed to a fever. After lingering for several days, he died on the evening of November 9. Beall resumed command of the Third District immediately. The next afternoon he had Villepigue's body escorted to the railroad depot for shipment to South Carolina and ordered all officers to "wear the usual badge of mourning for thirty days."[37] The following week Pemberton inspected the garrison and found no reason to replace Beall.[38]

Another command change occurred on November 24, one that boded well for Port Hudson. President Davis appointed General Joseph E. Johnston to supreme command of all forces in the western theater. Johnston concentrated on the proper transfer of troops between the Mississippi River and Tennessee to defend both successfully. Foreseeing an advance against Port Hudson, he gave that post immediate attention. Beall's fifty-five hundred effective troops could hardly withstand the feared onslaught of twenty-four thousand Federals. Johnston evaluated the situation and met with Davis in Vicksburg in mid-December. Johnston thought he needed another eight to ten thousand troops along the Mississippi; 65 percent of these he earmarked for garrison duty at Port Hudson. Both men agreed that the soldiers required could not come from Tennessee; instead, they looked to Lieutenant General Theophilus H. Holmes in Arkansas to provide them.[39] They looked in vain.

Port Hudson's isolated position demanded a larger garrison. Fifty-eight miles of irregular terrain broken by numerous rivers and streams separated the village from the railroad at Tangipahoa. The twenty-one-mile Clinton and Port Hudson Railroad hardly reduced

37. Taylor (ed.), *Reluctant Rebel*, 53; Warner, *Generals in Gray*, 317–18; *OR*, XV, 843; Beall to Pemberton, October 26, 1862, and Villepigue to Pemberton, October 29, 1862, both in Letters and Telegrams Received, Department of Mississippi and East Louisiana, 1862–65, Record Group 109, National Archives; Smith, *Company K*, 39; Memphis *Daily Appeal*, November 18, 25, 1862. The cause of death was variously reported as typhoid, pneumonia, cholera morbus, and simply fever.

38. *OR*, Vol. XVII, Pt. 2, pp. 750–51.

39. *Ibid.*, XV, 886, 1191, Vol. XVII, Pt. 2, pp. 757–58, 766, 800–801, Vol. LII, Pt. 2, p. 398.

the distance reinforcements would have to march. Moreover, the rolling stock amounted to one locomotive and seven cars; only one was a passenger car, the balance being box- and flatcars. The entire train could accommodate only half a regiment at a time. The roadbed consisted of flat rails on rotten cross-ties, a combination that led to almost scheduled derailments. Some Tennesseans nick-named it the "tri-weekly" road, saying that "the train would go to Clinton one week and try weakly to get back the next." Davis realized that if the Confederate government could build a railroad linking Port Hudson with the line running to Jackson, Mississippi, it would compensate for ten thousand desperately needed men because a mobile reserve could be quickly moved to Vicksburg or Port Hudson when either place became threatened.[40] But the shortage of iron in the South relegated the line to a long list of desirable but unfulfilled projects.

Despite its comparatively isolated location, Port Hudson be-came a bustling commercial port. Louisiana sugar and salt moved east; Virginia tobacco traveled west. Immense profits on sugar shipments that reached the Atlantic states fed speculation. With the speculators came peddlers and sojourners. Friends and relatives of the soldiers lingered about the camps, and Negroes selling food-stuffs made frequent visits. Thus strangers observing the progress of the fortifications came under no suspicion. Occasionally a beau-tiful young woman would appear. The soldiers stared, sighed, and remarked to each other, "Oh! Aren't she a screamer, though!" The officers gladly showed women around and explained every detail of the defenses. At least once, the women proved to be spies, who returned to New Orleans and revealed all to Union authorities.[41]

While the river remained open to the Confederates, one would have expected them to stockpile large stores of provisions at a post as important as Port Hudson. John C. Miller, provost marshal shortly after the occupation, attempted to build warehouses to hold a year's rations for a considerable garrison. Fresh from civilian

40. Jill K. Garrett and Marise P. Lightfoot, *The Civil War in Maury County, Tennessee* (N.p., 1966), 62; *OR*, Vol. XVII, Pt. 2, p. 784; Smith, *Company K*, 38; Mobile *Advertiser and Register*, March 18, 1863; Dawson, *Confederate Girl's Diary*, 231–32; Taylor (ed.), *Reluctant Rebel*, 60–61; Robert McElroy, *Jefferson Davis: The Unreal and the Real* (2 vols., New York, 1937), II, 374.

41. [Wright], *Port Hudson*, 10–12; Jones, Diary, October 12–16, 1862, Jones Collection; Dawson, *Confederate Girl's Diary*, 233–35, 246–47, 261, 279–80.

life, he could not overcome government red tape covering jurisdiction, procedure, and approval that blocked his every move.
During one of Beall's absences, Colonel William R. Miles found
himself in command at Port Hudson. Fearless of bureaucracy and
willing to accept full responsibility for his audacity, he sent agents
out to scour the countryside for provisions and began construction
of storage buildings. Relieved sooner than expected, he too failed
to get the supplies and complete the warehouses. [42]

Improper handling and inferior storage procedures increased
shortages of foodstuffs. Salted pork spoiled after careless placement in the hold of a steamboat. Poorly salted pork that arrived
was issued immediately to the soldiers to prevent a total loss.
Entire boatloads of corn lay for days at the landing until spoiled by
exposure to the weather. A great deal of the corn was stored in open
sheds, where it turned musty and sour. The soldiers became ill
after eating it. Long-horned cattle driven from Texas frequently
swam the Mississippi at Port Hudson, but only those in the worst
condition were left for the garrison. Poor pasture made most of the
animals scrawny by the time they were butchered. The few subordinate officers who voiced complaints were reprimanded by their
superiors. The soldiers generally suffered in silence. An exception
occurred one day in an Arkansas regiment during drill. The colonel
ordered his men to shout "Butler the Beast!" when they executed
a charge. Instead, the men yelled "Bull beef! Bull beef!" The
colonel's horse bolted with him, and the drill came to an abrupt
end. [43]

Rations varied daily and for each individual at Port Hudson. The
most commonly issued were "blue beef" and "corn bread." The
men found the meat repulsive. Chaplain J. H. McNeilly described
it as "nauseating. Poor, gristly blue, gummy, it could be boiled for
hours and never an eye of grease on the water." Sweet potatoes,
pumpkins, and molasses supplemented the regular fare. For soldiers who had never tasted it, sugarcane proved a delightful treat.
Surprisingly, salt, readily available in south-central Louisiana, was
sometimes scarce. The lack of good cooks made the food even less
appealing. Each mess either detailed some of its members or hired

42. [Wright], *Port Hudson*, 12–13; *OR*, XV, 805; Arthur W. Bergeron, Jr., and
Lawrence L. Hewitt, *Miles' Legion: A History and Roster* (Baton Rouge, 1983), ii.

43. Memphis *Daily Appeal*, April 4, 1863; [Wright], *Port Hudson*, 13; Smith,
Company K, 42; McMorries, *First Alabama*, 52.

Negroes to cook. Fortunately, the women in the area often visited the camps and took an interest in culinary duties. One motherly matron pointed out to a novice cook in the 1st Alabama that "it would improve his kettles if he would burn them out." Complimented by the attention, the cook took the first opportunity to remove the excess soot and grease from his utensils. [44]

The soldiers had to tolerate other discomforts. Homesickness undoubtedly headed the list, followed closely by lice. The Confederates nicknamed the latter "graybacks." By boiling their clothes, the troops managed to exterminate the pests. The officers constantly made the men change campgrounds for various reasons, often moving them to an area that lacked adequate drinking water or that flooded whenever it rained. Major inconveniences included repulsive-smelling water unfit to drink, poor shelter, and a short-age of blankets, shoes, clothing, and cooking utensils. The men used fence rails or door shutters to construct beds by placing them between two trestles or benches or simply laying them on the ground. Spanish moss, hay, or cane served for a mattress. [45]

Bad diet and exposure caused most of the sickness. Chills, fever, and mumps plagued the garrison; the death toll mounted daily. The few soldiers who were cared for during their illnesses by women felt extremely fortunate. Beall converted Centenary College at Jackson, Louisiana, into a hospital to handle the overflow from Port Hudson and Clinton, but it soon had a surplus of patients. The soldiers distrusted the attending physicians. One major

44. James H. M'Neilly, "Under Fire at Port Hudson," *Confederate Veteran*, XXVII (1919), 337; McMorries, *First Alabama*, 51; [Tennessee] Centennial Commission, *Tennesseans in the Civil War*, II, 281; Dawson, *Confederate Girl's Diary*, 265; Bell Irvin Wiley (ed.), "The Confederate Letters of Warren G. Magee," *Journal of Mississippi History*, V (1943), 207; Henry Gibbes Morgan to Caroline Morgan, September 24, 1862, Louisiana State University Department of Archives and Manuscripts, Baton Rouge; Smith, *Company K*, 43.

45. George M. Owens to his wife, Ann, October 28, December 25, 1862, Owens Papers; Cannon, *Inside Rebeldom*, 72, 74; Morning reports of Weatherly's Company, October, November, 1862, Confederate States of America Papers; Taylor (ed.), *Reluctant Rebel*, 47, 59; Jones, Diary, December 6, 1862, Jones Collection; Diary of Campbell, December 15, 17, 1862; Wiley (ed.), "Letters of Magee," 207; Dawson, *Confederate Girl's Diary*, 234; Dixon, Diary, October 14, 1862, Dixon Papers; F. L. Allen to brother, December 16, 1862, William M. Allen Correspondence, Merritt M. Shilg Memorial Collection, Louisiana State University Department of Archives and Manuscripts, Baton Rouge.

suffered with a toothache for weeks because "the surgeon enjoys tooth-pulling more than any man I ever saw."[46]

Some of the troops managed to construct suitable winter quarters. They cut magnolia and willow trees and built log barracks; cypress boards covered the roofs. The soldiers built bunks along the walls and provided ventilation by not chinking the cracks between the upper logs; an open door admitted light. Barracks and tents alike had chimneys made of clay and sticks. Partly constructed of wood, the chimneys often caught fire.[47]

The men spent most days drilling, building fortifications, or walking guard duty. Some of the soldiers did courier duty, herded livestock, gathered forage, or hauled supplies. The drill schedule for the 1st Alabama was typical: "Reveille at daybreak with roll-call, inspection of arms and policing of camps; 6 A.M., guard mounting; 9 A.M., non-commissioned offficers drill; 10 A.M., drill in the school of the company; 12 M. dinner; 1 P.M., skirmish drill; 3 P.M., battalion drill; 5 P.M., dress parade; sunset, retreat; 9 P.M., taps."[48] Infantry companies assigned to the artillery drilled at the guns during the hours assigned for company drill. Even though the men found drilling tiresome exercise, it was essential for the inexperienced soldiers at Port Hudson, most of whom were new recruits or fresh from prisoner-of-war camps.[49]

The troops took part in other military activities, some more enjoyable than others. Many units reorganized at the end of one year's service and elected new officers, which pleased the men.

46. Diary of Campbell, December 16, 1862; Lawrence L. Hewitt and Arthur W. Bergeron, Jr. (eds.), *Post Hospital Ledger, Port Hudson, Louisiana, 1862–1863* (Baton Rouge, 1981), v–vi; George M. Owens to his wife, Ann, October 28, November 11, 1862, Owens Papers; Jas. B. Corkern to brother, November 3, 1862, David F. Boyd Papers, Louisiana State University Department of Archives and Manuscripts, Baton Rouge; Wiley (ed.), "Letters of Magee," 207; Dawson, *Confederate Girl's Diary*, 186; [Tennessee] Centennial Commission, *Tennesseans in the Civil War*, II, 74.

47. Smith, *Company K*, 45; Cannon, *Inside Rebeldom*, 72; Taylor (ed.), *Reluctant Rebel*, 62.

48. Smith, *Company K*, 44; Jones, Diary, October 17–20, 27–29, November 4–5, 9–11, 13–15, 17, 23–28, December 3, 5, 11–24, 26–27, 29–31, 1862, Jones Collection; Taylor (ed.), *Reluctant Rebel*, 67; Melmon Marion Butts, Questionnaire, Tennessee State Library and Archives, Nashville; Frederick (ed.), "War Diary of Porter," 306.

49. Smith, *Company K*, 44; McMorries, *First Alabama*, 50; Cannon, *Inside Rebeldom*, 73.

Some soldiers refused to work if they did not get their pay when due, and funds seldom arrived on time. What punishment they received for this disobedience is not known. An occasional court-martial was held to enforce discipline. Although the officers appeared understanding toward their colleagues, they came down hard on the enlisted men, especially deserters. Punishments for the guilty included forfeiture of pay, wearing a ball and chain, and "bucking," or tying the offender's wrists together and slipping them over his knees. A stick or musket was then placed over the arms and beneath the knees; so restrained he sat out his sentence.[50]

The soldiers had little free time to pass. Many sought to supplement their rations by fishing, hunting alligators, or pilfering butter, eggs, and other items. The plentiful molasses encouraged candy makers. Chaplain McNeilly recalled that "all through the camp one could see couples of men pulling the ropes of the candied stuff until it reached the proper color and brittleness, and in the enthusiasm of the pulling they would spit on their hands to get a better hold." They also made candles. Many visited relatives, friends, and local residents. The officers attended balls and banquets at the palatial homes of lovely young women. Many officers also attended church with these women. Regimental chaplains held services for the men on Sundays. The largely Catholic 30th Louisiana and 10th Tennessee had ample priests, but Protestant units lacked chaplains. The Tennesseans loved hearing the laundresses of the 30th Louisiana speak French. One soldier exclaimed to a comrade, "Listen to these women. One of them can give one flutter of her tongue and say more than you can say in a week."[51]

The troops also played games, tried to make money, and drank. Popular games included marbles, cribbage, and "smut," in which the soldiers took turns making a spectacle of themselves by blackening their faces. Some of the men participated in "kangaroo courts." They made up cases during the day and held trials in the

50. Cannon, *Inside Rebeldom*, 71–72; McMorries, *First Alabama*, 49; Frederick (ed.), "War Diary of Porter," 307; Taylor (ed.), *Reluctant Rebel*, 52, 57, 57n; Wiley (ed.), "Letters of Magee," 207.

51. M'Neilly, "Under Fire at Port Hudson," 337–38; Frederick (ed.), "War Diary of Porter," 305–307; Smith, *Company K*, 43; Taylor (ed.), *Reluctant Rebel*, 60–61, 70; McMorries, *First Alabama*, 51; Dawson, *Confederate Girl's Diary*, 232; Dixon, Diary, October 5, 12, 1862, Dixon Papers.

evening. The unsuccessful party to the suit had to treat the crowd to beer, which consisted of corn, molasses, and water mixed in a barrel, a seemingly palatable beverage. Although Louisiana Private Robert D. Patrick drank the brew, he thought it resembled vinegar. Several industrious Tennesseans developed a thriving business selling their Port Hudson "beer." Members of the 49th Tennessee baked and sold round cakes made with flour and mashed sweet potatoes. The soldiers nicknamed them "sweet potato pones." The pushy Tennessee salesmen canvassed the entire garrison. Before long, when the regiment marched out to drill, it met cries of "Here come your sweet 'tater pones." Virtually everyone indulged in beer because of the foul drinking water, and those desiring a stronger beverage drank Louisiana rum, made from the unsold sugar of local planters. Soldiers able to get a jug retailed the beverage for a dollar an ounce and found plenty of customers. Even though many officers enjoyed rum punch during the evenings, provost guards scoured the countryside to locate and destroy the distilleries. Every night gallons of the liquid were confiscated and poured out. Even then some soldiers dipped it up with their cups or drank out of depressions in the ground. Encountering drunken soldiers was common and often resulted in injury to one of the parties.[52]

Reading and writing also occupied much of the soldiers' time. Some of the men enjoyed good novels, and everyone welcomed the arrival of a newspaper, especially the Memphis *Appeal*. Most of the troops wrote letters home, and the men looked forward to receiving a letter from a loved one, especially if accompanied by a package that contained some delicious edible or piece of clothing. Occasionally the soldiers managed to purchase sugar and molasses and send it to loved ones less fortunate back home. The men wrote a daily newspaper called the *Mule*, a satirical account of the officers and men at drill. The *Woodchuck* soon appeared to counter the *Mule*.[53]

52. M'Neilly, "Under Fire at Port Hudson," 337; Frederick (ed.), "War Diary of Porter," 307; Taylor (ed.), *Reluctant Rebel*, 46, 59, 64–65, 70; McMorries, *First Alabama*, 51; Cannon, *Inside Rebeldom*, 74; George M. Owens to his wife, Ann, December 25, 1862, Owens Papers.

53. Frederick (ed.), "War Diary of Porter," 306–307; James H. M'Neilly, "A Good Place to Die," *Confederate Veteran*, XXVI (1918), 45; Thomas W. Skipwith, "A Letter from Port Hudson," *Louisiana Genealogical Register*, XVIII (1971), 68;

Some spent the evening sitting around the fire. They ate roasted potatoes, listened to fiddle music, and swapped lies. Rumors circulated about the ever-impending advance of the enemy's infantry or the expected appearance of a gunboat. Opinions varied regarding the outcome of a land attack against Port Hudson. A few thought the war would end soon, and one private believed that the Democratic party victories in November showed "a diversity of opinion in the North which will be fatal to the successful prosecution of the war." Some of the men simply rested, preferring to do nothing at all.[54]

But the enemy was about to end the comparatively tranquil life at Port Hudson.

George M. Owens to his wife, Ann, November 24, 1862, Owens Papers; Wiley (ed.), "Letters of Magee," 207; McMorries, *First Alabama*, 51.

54. Taylor (ed.), *Reluctant Rebel*, 47, 59–60; McMorries, *First Alabama*, 52; Jones, Diary, November 15, 21, 1862, Jones Collection; Frederick (ed.), "War Diary of Porter," 305–306.

III

Reorganization: December, 1862–February, 1863

Spades are 'trumps.'

—Private M. D. Cannon,
27th Alabama Infantry

During the fall of 1862 the Confederate grasp on the Mississippi River between Port Hudson and Vicksburg appeared unshakable. Eager to wrest control from the enemy, the Union sought new avenues of approach. By October 29 the popular strategy was an expedition to the Texas coast, which Secretary of War Edwin M. Stanton thought would "create a diversion of the enemy's force" and reduce Confederate strength along the Mississippi. Within ten days Stanton's strategy collapsed when the Republican party suffered staggering defeats at the polls. Even the voters in President Lincoln's home state of Illinois repudiated his administration. A letter to Lincoln from Indiana Governor Oliver P. Morton summed up the crisis the president faced:

> The fate of the North-West is trembling in the balance. . . . During the recent campaign it was the staple of every democratic speech, that we of the North-West had no interests or sympathies in common with the people of the Northern and Eastern States . . . that socially and commercially their sympathies are with those of the people of the Southern States rather than with the people of the North and East; that the Mississippi river is the great artery and outlet of all Western commerce; that the people of the North-West can never consent to be separated politically from the people who control the mouth of that river. . . . In some of these arguments there is much truth. . . . The plan I have to suggest is the complete clearing out of all obstacles to the navigation of the Mississippi river.

Lincoln must have taken this recommendation to heart. [1]

On November 8 the president issued orders assigning Major General Nathaniel P. Banks to command of the Department of the Gulf, including Texas, for an advance up the Mississippi. The next day General in Chief Henry W. Halleck sent Banks specific instructions. With the troops already assembled for the Texas expedition, Banks was to proceed to New Orleans immediately and relieve Major General Benjamin F. Butler; additional reinforcements would follow. Halleck made Banks's objective explicitly clear: "The first military operations which will engage your attention on your arrival at New Orleans will be the opening of the Mississippi. . . . The President regards the opening of the Mississippi River as the first and most important of all our military and naval operations, and it is hoped that you will not lose a moment in accomplishing it. . . . The opening of the Mississippi River is now the great and primary object of your expedition." Halleck also provided an enticing incentive to encourage alacrity in Banks: "As the ranking general in the Southwest, you are authorized to assume control of any military forces from the Upper Mississippi which may come within your command. The line of division between your department and that of Major-General [Ulysses S.] Grant is therefore left undecided for the present, and you will exercise superior authority as far north as you may ascend the river." Halleck wanted Grant superseded. [2]

Before his new appointment, Banks's life had been filled with triumphs and defeats. Born in Waltham, Massachusetts, on January 30, 1816, he received little formal education, working instead for his father in a cotton mill. Admitted to the bar at twenty-three, he attempted to enter politics. He campaigned for a seat in the Massachusetts legislature eight times before succeeding. He went on to become Speaker of that body and preside over the state's Constitutional Convention of 1853. That same year Banks won a seat in the U.S. Congress. His success continued, and in 1856 he became Speaker of the House of Representatives, although it took 133 ballots to secure the speakership. His moderate beliefs helped

1. *OR*, Vol. XVII, Pt. 2, p. 302; Morton to Lincoln, October 27, 1862, Edwin M. Stanton Papers, Division of Manuscripts, Library of Congress; Ludwell H. Johnson, *Red River Campaign: Politics and Cotton in the Civil War* (Baltimore, 1958), 23–24.

2. *OR*, XV, 590–91, Vol. XVII, Pt. 2, p. 302; John M. Stanyan, *A History of the Eighth Regiment of New Hampshire Volunteers* . . . (Concord, N.H., 1892), 187.

preserve fairness during bitter slavery debates. He remained as Speaker until elected governor of his native state in 1858. When Banks offered his services to the president in 1861, Lincoln commissioned him a major general. The president's action baffled many West Point graduates, but Lincoln knew Banks could deliver recruits, money, morale, and propaganda. Yet during 1862, Banks's lack of military experience proved costly to the Union. He lost 30 percent of his troops during Stonewall Jackson's Valley Campaign in the spring and barely held his position against Jackson at Cedar Mountain in August. His combat record did not warrant confidence.[3]

It is impossible to determine Lincoln's reasons for selecting Banks to direct so important an undertaking. One student of Lincoln as commander in chief concluded, "Why he thought Banks could command it is a mystery. . . . The appointment of Banks was a case of Lincoln misreading his man." Possibly the president chose Banks because he wanted someone who shared his moderate view on slavery in Louisiana. And Banks had been instrumental in raising the troops initially intended for Texas. Because these soldiers would now be diverted to Louisiana, Lincoln possibly thought it best for Banks to retain command of them.[4]

But despite Banks's past failures, Lincoln needed someone to replace Butler. Nicknamed "Beast" because of his stern occupation of New Orleans, Butler had offended a majority of its citizens, especially the foreign consuls. Several European governments had bitterly protested his treatment of their representatives, and Lincoln was on the verge of having to relieve him to avoid an international incident. The president also distrusted Butler's ability to command an expedition of the magnitude he now envisioned moving up the Mississippi.[5]

Unaware of the impending arrival of Banks, Butler remained idle and awaited reinforcements. The Union navy, however, continued to patrol the Mississippi. On the morning of November 16

---

3. Ezra J. Warner, *Generals in Blue: Lives of the Union Commanders* (Baton Rouge, 1964), 17–18.

4. T. Harry Williams, *Lincoln and His Generals* (New York, 1952), 188; Fred Harvey Harrington, *Fighting Politician: Major General N. P. Banks* (1948; rpr. Westport, Conn., 1970), 86.

5. Williams, *Lincoln and His Generals*, 188; Winters, *Civil War in Louisiana*, 148.

four vessels approached Port Hudson from downriver on a reconnaissance mission. The Confederates held their fire to conceal
their strength, yet the naval commander reported: "The fortifications of Port Hudson are now made, by the peculiar advantages
of situation, capable of resisting more effectually than Vicksburg
the passage of any vessel or fleet." The fleet shelled sugar houses
and private residences along the west bank before returning to New
Orleans.[6]

Rear Admiral David Glasgow Farragut, commander of the West
Gulf Blockading Squadron, was also in charge of naval operations
along the lower Mississippi. Born in Tennessee on July 5, 1801, he
entered the navy as a midshipman at the age of nine. Before his
thirteenth birthday he had commanded a prize ship, fought in one
of the bloodiest encounters in the history of the U.S. Navy, and
been captured by the British. Following the War of 1812, Farragut
remained in the navy. By 1861 he had attained the rank of captain
and had served in various capacities, usually ashore.

Stationed at Norfolk, Virginia, when the Civil War erupted,
Farragut soon found it necessary to make a choice between the
warring sections. Despite his birth in Tennessee and relatives in
Louisiana, Farragut's state loyalty was to Virginia. He had spent
nearly forty years at Norfolk, where he had twice married. But
Farragut had worn the United States uniform more than fifty years.
And on the bloody decks of the *Essex* during an engagement with
the British he came to revere the flag of an undivided nation. His
duty to the national government remained undiminished, yet it
was with sadness that he made the choice. "God forbid," he said,
"that I should have to raise my hand against the South!"[7]

Shortly after he learned of Virginia's secession Farragut told his
wife that he intended to remain loyal. "This act of mine may cause
years of separation from your family; so you must decide quickly
whether you will go North or remain here." She decided to go
north, and the family moved to New York. Farragut applied at once
for active service, but he had to endure many weary months of

6. *ORN*, XIX, 350–51, 353; Baton Rouge *Weekly Gazette and Comet*, November
19, 1862; Taylor (ed.), *Reluctant Rebel*, 57.

7. A. T. Mahan, *Admiral Farragut* (1892; rpr. New York, 1916), 4, 8, 25, 44, 106,
109; Charles Lee Lewis, *Famous American Naval Officers* (rev. ed.; Boston, 1948),
228.

waiting. The Navy Department was suspicious of officers of southern birth.[8]

Finally, he was selected to command the squadron that would attack New Orleans. It was the opportunity he had waited for all his life. He sailed aboard the *Hartford* for the Mississippi Gulf Coast on February 2, 1862. Leading the mightiest fleet ever assembled by the United States, Farragut passed the forts guarding New Orleans on April 24. Continuing up the Mississippi River, he reached the city the next day. Following the surrender of New Orleans, Farragut steamed upriver. When Union efforts to capture Vicksburg proved unsuccessful, Farragut returned to New Orleans. Although the commission was not confirmed until January 9, 1863, President Lincoln appointed him rear admiral on July 16, 1862, making him the first admiral in U.S. history. During the fall of 1862 he busied himself with directing the blockade. By mid-November Farragut had secured all the Gulf ports except Mobile, Alabama. Unable to acquire the necessary land forces with which to attack Mobile, Farragut returned to New Orleans, anxious to move against Port Hudson.[9] Undoubtedly, Farragut correctly realized that the troops he needed for operations against Mobile would not be available until Federal forces occupied Port Hudson and Vicksburg.

Believing the navy could break the Confederate blockade of the lower Mississippi at Port Hudson, Farragut requested the army's assistance. Major General Butler agreed, hoping to halt the flow of Texas beef eastward. But he lacked manpower, and additional troops did not appear forthcoming. On November 29 he wrote Halleck: "For the want of a sufficient land force . . . I have been compelled to postpone a projected attack upon the position. It might have been taken by five regiments four weeks since had I had troops sufficient to hold it."[10]

Despite Butler's failure to lend support, Farragut did not remain idle. The *Essex, Kineo, Katahdin,* and *Winona* made a reconnaissance upriver, arriving below Port Hudson at 2 P.M. on December

8. Lewis, *Naval Officers,* 229; Mahan, *Farragut,* 112–13.

9. Mahan, *Farragut,* 123, 126, 165, 193, 197, 200; Lewis, *Naval Officers,* 215–39; *ORN,* XIX, 661.

10. *OR,* XV, 602–603; *ORN,* XIX, 372, 384; Benjamin F. Butler, *Private and Official Correspondence of Gen. Benjamin F. Butler During the Period of the Civil War* (5 vols.; Norwood, Mass., 1917), II, 466.

12. The ships anchored off the upper end of Prophet's Island for the night. A Confederate cavalry company crossed the river at Port Hudson and moved down the west bank to a point opposite the vessels. Early the next morning a Negro, whom the rebel captain had paid $20, signaled from the bank. The sailors thought the black man was a runaway slave seeking refuge. A rowboat left the *Kineo* to pick him up, but when it came within thirty yards of the shore the cavalrymen fired a volley of musketry that perforated the boat. The squadron opened on the levee. Both sides suffered minimal casualties. The *Kineo* and *Katahdin* steamed downstream at 10 A.M., but the *Essex* and *Winona* remained at anchor.[11]

During the night three guns of Boone's battery crossed the river and took position behind the levee opposite the *Winona*. Two companies of the 1st Alabama lined the east bank levee below Prophet's Island. At first light Boone's Louisianians opened fire from 250 yards. Within seconds, the *Winona* replied. Her sailors slipped the anchor cable hoping to obtain a better firing position. The vessel drifted upon a sandbar, however, which rendered useless all but one gun. Federal Lieutenant Winfield S. Schley recalled that "for ten or fifteen minutes this disadvantage continued, while a storm of projectiles from artillery and musketry swept the ship." The *Winona* finally slid free, maneuvered her broadside guns toward the enemy, and blasted the levee with eleven-inch shells for over an hour. But the Confederates bested their stronger opponent. Boone's six- and twelve-pounders peppered the *Winona*, striking her twenty-seven times. The ironclad *Essex* finally interposed herself between the combatants to save the *Winona* from further destruction. Lashed together, the two vessels dropped down out of range stern first. They then turned about, and the *Winona* secured to the opposite (port) side of the ironclad. But the ordeal aboard the *Winona* had not yet ended. Just below the island the Alabamians opened fire. The sailors gave weak reply while the vessels passed. The *Winona* continued downstream to the docks in New Orleans for major repairs.[12]

11. *ORN*, XIX, 777–78; Memphis *Daily Appeal*, December 17, 1862; Misc. Doc., November 16 [?], p. 20, First Alabama Infantry Regiment, Military Records Division, Alabama Department of Archives and History, Montgomery; F. L. Allen to brother, December 16, 1862, Allen Correspondence.

12. Winfield Scott Schley, *Forty-Five Years Under the Flag* (New York, 1904), 38–39; Smith, *Company K*, 45; *ORN*, XIX, 408, 778; Misc. Doc., November 16 [?],

That same day, December 14, 1862, Banks arrived in New Orleans. The transition of command from Butler to Banks went smoothly. Farragut "promised a hearty and cordial co-operation," and the new army commander returned it. Banks promptly dispatched troops to reoccupy Baton Rouge. Farragut furnished vessels to provide covering fire for the army's landing because he wanted to secure Baton Rouge before undertaking a naval expedition against Port Hudson. [13]

The Union convoy arrived off Baton Rouge early on the morning of December 17. The *Essex* fired about a dozen shells over the town, enough to drive off about five hundred infantrymen with their two fieldpieces. Shortly after 9 A.M., sailors from the *Richmond* landed and hoisted the U.S. flag over the imposing state capitol. The *Essex* served as a wharf boat for the infantry, who disembarked by noon. The 22nd Maine had the honor of being the first army unit to go ashore. That same day Brigadier General William N. R. Beall notified Lieutenant General John C. Pemberton, "Fourteen gunboats and sloops are at Baton Rouge this morning. The Essex has started up." Beall informed his superior later that day that "between 6,000 and 7,000 of the enemy [were] at Baton Rouge." [14] This faulty information appeared in the Vicksburg *Whig* on the eighteenth, and everyone expected a simultaneous land and naval attack on Port Hudson. But Brigadier General Cuvier Grover, Union commander at Baton Rouge, had no intention of launching an attack. Instead, he feared a Confederate assault on his forty-five hundred "effective"—but undrilled—troops and pleaded for reinforcements. Meanwhile, the Yankees occupied and strengthened the fortifications they had abandoned in August. [15]

Grover did not intend to be caught napping. He kept his men constantly on the alert. The "long roll" sounded almost every

---

p. 20, First Alabama Infantry Regiment, Military Records Division; Memphis *Daily Appeal*, December 17, 1862.

13. *OR*, XV, 609, 613, 624, 1096–97; *ORN*, XIX, 409, 414–15.

14. *OR*, XV, 901; *ORN*, XIX, 415, 711, 762, 779; Beers, *Memories*, 233; Memphis *Daily Appeal*, January 8, 1863; William E. S. Whitman and Charles H. True, *Maine in the War for the Union: A History of the Part Borne by Maine Troops in the Suppression of the American Rebellion* (Lewiston, 1865), 508.

15. Memphis *Daily Appeal*, December 19, 1862; *OR*, XV, 191, 1184; Richard Irwin, *History of the Nineteenth Army Corps* (1893; rpr. Baton Rouge, 1985), 61.

morning long before dawn. The troops tramped heavily to the breastworks and waited until daylight for an attack that never came. One sergeant major recalled standing in line, "waiting a possible onslaught by the enemy, unable to see more than a few yards in our front owing to the heavy, thick mist which usually prevailed from midnight to sunrise, chilled through by the damp, cold night air and heavy dew which fell like light rain, and when dismissed to our quarters we felt far from comfortable." Bugler James K. Ewer remembered that the soldiers "began to think the enemy was not coming at all."[16]

Eventually the men adjusted to the routine of garrison duty. The troops learned discipline and took pride in their proficiency at drill. The officers constantly inspected the guns and ammunition of individual units and guard detachments. Unfortunately, rapid weather changes and the general inactivity of the soldiers led to severe sickness and death; the majority of the troops had only recently joined the army and were unaccustomed to the rigors of life in the field. The garrison reorganized almost daily with the arrival of new officers and units. Major General Christopher C. Augur replaced Grover in command at Baton Rouge.[17]

Having learned on his arrival that the Port Hudson garrison numbered about twelve thousand men, Banks had intended an immediate attack. But he began to hesitate on the morning of December 18 when a supposedly reliable rebel captain told him that new conscripts had brought to twenty-three thousand the

16. William F. Tiemann (comp.), *The 159th Regiment Infantry, New-York State Volunteers, in the War of the Rebellion, 1862-1865* (Brooklyn, 1891), 18-19, Frederick Phisterer (comp.), *New York in the War of the Rebellion, 1861 to 1865* (3rd ed., 5 vols; Albany, 1912), V, 3867; James K. Ewer, *The Third Massachusetts Cavalry in the War for the Union* (Maplewood, Mass., 1903), 53–54, Roster, p. xxxv.

17. Henry Warren Howe, *Passages from the Life of Henry Warren Howe . . .* (Lowell, Mass., 1899), 40–41; *The Twenty-Fifth Regiment Connecticut Volunteers in the War of the Rebellion . . .* (Rockville, Conn., 1913), 17–19, 32; Major C. R. Dimon to Lieutenant W. S. [?] Payne, December 28, 1862, Charles A. R. Dimon Papers, Southern Historical Collection, University of North Carolina Library, Chapel Hill; Francis Winthrop Palfrey, *Memoir of William Francis Bartlett* (Boston, 1878), 58–59, 67; Colonel Halbert E. Paine, G.O. No. 6, January 22, 1863, Box 24, Folder 3, New Hampshire Civil War Records, New Hampshire Division of Records Management and Archives, Department of State, Concord, N.H.; Whitman and True, *Maine in the War*, 502, 508; Henry T. Johns, *Life with the Forty-ninth Massachusetts Volunteers* (Pittsfield, Mass., 1864), 143; *ORN*, XIX, 765, 767; *OR*, XV, 1104, LIII, 549.

number of soldiers at Port Hudson and that a division of Confederates from California was marching for the Mississippi. More reasons for delay followed. Banks believed he needed time to discipline Butler's troops, many of whom were demoralized because of the graft and corruption that had permeated Butler's regime; he lacked cavalrymen, horses, and mules. And though in the last few days of 1862 Banks received detailed intelligence describing the Confederate defenses and stating that only fifteen thousand men garrisoned Port Hudson, Banks had already turned his attention to the nonmilitary problems that plagued an army of occupation. Farragut's disgust with Banks's failure to advance grew and spread to others. Colonel Sidney A. Bean wrote in his diary that under Butler, "much was accomplished with small means. Now nothing is accomplished with great means. Butler's little finger is thicker than Banks' loins."[18]

Had Banks acted instead of overestimating his opponent and doubting his own troops' capabilities, he might have taken Port Hudson in a matter of days. His caution proved costly. Although some of the soldiers agreed that his troops needed more training, the majority expected—and wanted—an immediate advance. A seasoned private wrote his father from Baton Rouge, "We are still here (probably to give the rebels time to complete their fortifications) for I can see no other reason."[19]

Butler's small force had dictated a firm rule in occupied Louisiana. But no such restriction hampered Banks, who had brought thousands of soldiers with him. Banks inaugurated a more lax policy to conciliate the ardently disaffected citizens, nurture any seeds of loyalty, and forge a workable structure of state and federal government. John C. Palfrey, assistant engineer on Banks's staff, thought little of his methods: "Social gayety was attempted, indulgencies granted, restrictions relaxed, salaried offices distributed, reconstruction encouraged, and the seed sown for a luxuriant

18. Love, *Wisconsin in the War*, 550; *OR*, XV, 614, 619, 626, 1096, 1149; Winters, *Civil War in Louisiana*, 138; Robert L. Kerby, *Kirby Smith's Confederacy: The Trans-Mississippi South, 1863–1865* (New York, 1972), 24; *ORN*, XIX, 420; Charles Lee Lewis, *David Glasgow Farragut: Our First Admiral* (Annapolis, 1943), 166.

19. M. [Morris] Fyfe to father [James Fyfe], January 11, 1863, Fyfe Family Papers, Archives Division, State Historical Society of Wisconsin, Madison; Harrington, *Fighting Politician*, 118–19; *Memorials of William Fowler* (New York, 1875), 20.

crop of carpet-bag government."[20] Banks believed that many of Butler's cronies were interested only in "stealing other peoples' property" and so clamped down on their flourishing trade with the rebels. He also endeavored to gain territory in southern Louisiana to secure cotton for European and northern mills.[21]

The last week of 1862 passed in relative quiet for the Federals at Baton Rouge. The *Essex* reconnoitered the Port Hudson fortifications on Christmas Eve. The Confederates did not open fire. The sailors spotted one steamer anchored close under the bluff and a new battery mounting six or seven guns. Christmas came and went for the Union soldiers, the absence of milk, tea, coffee, eggs, flour, and salt meat their only hardship, the accidental burning of the state capitol on the twenty-eighth their only excitement. Cavalry skirmished on the twenty-ninth, and the *Essex* went upriver and shelled the woods below Port Hudson. Refugees entered the city from the surrounding countryside, driven by hunger or "conscript hunters" seeking men for the Confederate army. Activity centered around the levee. The Baton Rouge *Weekly Gazette and Comet* reported "vessels belching forth their contents until the whole front of the city presented one mass of barrels, boxes, bags, trusses of fodder, mules, negroes, stalwart knights of valor and death, the rolling of drums, the shrill bugle sounds, the heavy lumbering of cannon, and the fizzing of steam. The like has not been witnessed here. A deserted city crowded in one day."[22] By December 31 Banks had 31,253 officers and men present for duty. One-third of his force occupied Baton Rouge.[23]

---

20. John C. Palfrey, "Port Hudson," in *The Mississippi Valley, Tennessee, Georgia, Alabama, 1861–1864*. Vol. VIII of *Papers of the Military Historical Society of Massachusetts* (Boston, 1910), 25; Cullum, *Biographical Register*, II, 447.

21. Banks to wife, January 16, 1863, N. P. Banks Papers, Essex Institute, Salem, Mass.; Palfrey, "Port Hudson," 25.

22. Baton Rouge *Weekly Gazette and Comet*, December 31, 1862; [George Canaday Harding], *The Miscellaneous Writings of George C. Harding* (Indianapolis, 1882), 332; *ORN*, XIX, 430, 762–63; *A Memorial of Lt. Daniel Perkins Dewey, of the Twenty-fifth Regiment Connecticut Volunteers* (Hartford, 1864), 47–48; Grover to [Banks], December 29, 1862, Letters Sent, December, 1862–August, 1863, Department of the Gulf, Record Group 393, National Archives; S. C. Corkern to brother [Dr. J. McKinney], January 1, 1863, Jeptha McKinney Papers, Merritt M. Shilg Memorial Collection, Louisiana State University Department of Archives and Manuscripts, Baton Rouge; Diary of Campbell, December 29, 1862.

23. *OR*, XV, 627.

By early January, 1863, officials in Washington daily expected news of Banks's capture of Port Hudson. Then Banks would need only to link up with Grant for an assault on Vicksburg. But to accomplish his mission, Banks saw few options. He lacked the land and water transportation to join Grant directly. Moreover, if he moved the bulk of his forces to join Grant, he would leave Confederate armies intact on both sides of the river between New Orleans and Vicksburg—and an inadequate Federal garrison at New Orleans. Banks also ruled out a direct assault on Port Hudson for, at least in his opinion, want of troops. He finally decided to detach the required garrisons, disperse the Confederates west of the Mississippi, and march for the Red River. From there, Banks could join Grant if water transportation became available, or he could move down the Mississippi against Port Hudson.[24]

Banks notified Halleck on January 15 that his purpose west of the Mississippi was "control of the water communications and approaches to the Red River, which will become of great importance to us as soon as we are prepared to move against Port Hudson." He requested additional troops, especially cavalry. Repeating his plea three days later, he added mounted artillery to his list of needs. By February 12 Banks's revised plan called for cutting Port Hudson's supply line west of the river and advancing from Baton Rouge to the rear of the Confederate garrison, cutting off supplies from the east. This would force the Confederates to surrender or to abandon their fortifications and fight in the open. Banks again requested horses and mules on February 19.[25] The consequence of Banks's decision, however, was to provide additional time for the garrison at Port Hudson to strengthen its fortifications and receive reinforcements. And his opponents were quick to take advantage of this unexpected opportunity.

The Confederates had not been idle after the Union landing at Baton Rouge. On December 19 the men marched to the positions along the breastworks that they would defend against an attack.

24. Edward G. Bourne *et al.* (comps.), *Sixth Report of Historical Manuscripts Commission: With Diary and Correspondence of Salmon P. Chase*, Vol. II of *Annual Report of the American Historical Association for the Year 1902* (Washington, D.C., 1903), 343–44; *OR*, XVII, Pt. 2, p. 531; Palfrey, "Port Hudson," 28–29.

25. *OR*, XV, 240–41, 647, 1099–1100; Banks to Halleck, January 18, 1863, Letters Sent, December, 1862–August, 1863, Department of the Gulf, Record Group 393.

Leaves of absence virtually ended, and the soldiers speeded up work on the fortifications. Beall ordered a battalion from Port Hudson to Clinton to thwart any Union raid in that direction.[26]

The imminent threat brought a new commander—Major General Franklin Gardner. Born in New York City on January 29, 1823, he received an appointment to West Point from Iowa. Graduating seventeenth in the class of 1843 (Grant finished twenty-first), Gardner won two brevets for gallantry during the Mexican War. He entered the regular Confederate States Army on March 16, 1861, as a lieutenant colonel of infantry. Not bothering with the formality of resigning from the U.S. Army, he was dropped from its rolls on May 7. During 1862 he commanded a cavalry brigade at the Battle of Shiloh, was promoted to brigadier general, and led an infantry brigade in the Confederate invasion of Kentucky. Appointed major general in December, Gardner received Port Hudson as his first command at his new rank. Though New Yorkers, both he and his sister had married into the Mouton family of Louisiana. His brother, however, fought for the North, and his father, retired Colonel Charles K. Gardner (former adjutant general of the army during the War of 1812), worked in the Treasury Department in Washington.[27]

The garrison knew of Gardner's assignment but not when he would arrive, and when he stepped off the train on December 27, no one greeted him. He inquired directions to Beall's headquarters and walked there to announce himself. The soldiers learned his identity the next day, when, accompanied by Beall, he made a detailed inspection of the garrison.[28]

Gardner immediately put his engineering knowledge to work to correct defects he found in the defenses during his tour. Redesigning the river defenses, he clustered the heaviest guns to enable the batteries to support each other with a more concentrated field of fire. The artillerymen constructed their own works, and they took pride in their labor. Rejecting gabions and sandbags, they built the new parapets entirely of packed earth, revetted with green sod. Gardner also built roads from various points to the breastworks, taking advantage of the terrain to protect the movement of troops,

26. Diary of Campbell, December 19, 20, 28, 1862; J. W. Harmon Memoir, 1861–65, Civil War Collection, Tennessee State Library and Archives, Nashville.
27. Warner, *Generals in Gray*, 97; *OR*, Vol. XVII, Pt. 2, p. 796.
28. [Wright], *Port Hudson*, 15.

artillery, and ammunition. With qualified engineers scarce, Gardner gleaned from his command men capable of supervising the construction of fortifications. Private Henry Ginder, for example, had worked on the U.S. Coast Survey for five years before enlisting in Fenner's Louisiana battery. When Gardner learned of his experience, he transferred Ginder to the engineer corps and promoted him to first lieutenant. Acting Chief Engineer Frederick Y. Dabney had charge of fortifying the post after Gardner assumed command. Shortages of axes, spades, and pickaxes slowed construction, but the troops worked steadily on the breastworks even on Sundays. On January 4, 1863, Alabama Private M. D. Cannon wrote in his diary: "Spades are 'trumps' to-day, although it is the Sabbath." Overseers also worked gangs of Negroes, but Gardner replaced the overseers with soldiers and increased the number of Negro laborers. [29]

The new commander instituted other changes. The machinery and tools in the arsenal and all medical supplies at Clinton were moved to Port Hudson. Residents vacated houses to provide storage space. A military officer took charge of Mr. Troth's mill, and construction started on a government mill for the garrison. Another officer ran a government shoe shop Gardner established. Upset by the laziness of the fatigue detail charged with moving corn from the landing to the top of the bluff, Gardner detailed a field officer to superintend. He further notified the chief quartermaster, "I do not wish to either superintend this work myself or be oblidged to repeat this order." Gardner ordered five officers from each depleted regiment to return to their local communities in search of deserters and fresh recruits. He requested more heavy cannon and ammunition for the large-caliber guns already on hand. [30]

29. Cannon, *Inside Rebeldom*, 75; [Wright], *Port Hudson*, 9, 15–16; Gardner, G.O. No. 9, January 12, 1863, General and Special Orders, Port Hudson, La., 1862–63, Third Military District, Department of Mississippi and East Louisiana, Chap. II, Vol. 198, Record Group 109, National Archives; John Dimitry, *Louisiana*, Vol. X of Clement A. Evans (ed.), *Confederate Military History* (Atlanta, 1899), 428; Frederick Y. Dabney, Special Requisition, January 4, 1863, Roll 104, Microcopy 258, Compiled Service Records of Confederate Soldiers Who Served in Organizations Raised Directly by the Confederate Government, National Archives; Gardner to Lieutenant Colonel Wingfield, January 24, 1863, Chap. II, Vol. 8, Record Group 109; *OR*, XV, 913.

30. [Gardner] to Major Bennett, January 6, 1863, [Gardner] to Beall, January 6,

Gardner's ability to recognize the weaknesses of the garrison and his willingness to act promptly and decisively to correct them made him instantly popular with his troops. A junior officer pointed out the value this impression would have during the coming months:

> Human nature is capricious, and likes and dislikes are readily conceived by soldiers of an officer, who will often fail or succeed according to the esteem and confidence he enjoys with his command. First impressions are apt to be lasting, and the first impression a general creates upon assuming a command usually continues. It was well that Gen. Gardner was popular at first sight, for his hold upon the confidence and good will of his men steadily increased and was one of the great influences which resulted in holding Port Hudson so long.

The men concluded that the appointment of an officer of Gardner's rank and ability to command the Third District meant that the Richmond authorities had finally recognized Port Hudson's importance. Beall retained direct command of the garrison. [31]

Gardner quickly appraised his situation and gathered accurate intelligence about his opponent. Scouting parties reconnoitered on both sides of the river and destroyed any cotton that might fall into enemy hands. Gardner unsuccessfully sought the cooperation of Major General Richard Taylor, commander of western Louisiana, in the defense of the lower Mississippi. Brigadier General Henry Hopkins Sibley, who commanded Taylor's troops adjacent to the river, declined to defend Port Hudson from the west bank. Instead, he asked Gardner to bolster his command with infantry and cavalry. Pemberton supported Gardner's refusal to send reinforcements, but Gardner felt compelled to station two companies of cavalry across the river to protect his signal stations. One of Gardner's staff informed General Joseph E. Johnston that Port Hudson's new commander expressed utmost confidence in his ability to defend the bastion without reinforcements. [32]

1863, Chap. II, Vol. 8, Gardner, S.O. No. 9, January 6, 1863, Gardner, S.O. No. 12, January 9, 1863, Gardner, S.O. No. 25, January 23, 1863, Gardner, S.O. No. 45, February 12, 1863, Chap. II, Vol. 198, all in Record Group 109; Diary of Campbell, January 28, 31, 1863; Taylor (ed.), *Reluctant Rebel*, 95; *OR*, XV, 914.

31. [Wright], *Port Hudson*, 15–16; [Gardner] to Beall, January 6, 1863, Chap. II, Vol. 8, Record Group 109.

32. Lee H. Farrar to Cousin Maggie, March 7, 1863, Lee H. Farrar Letters (copies), Confederate Collection, Tennessee State Library and Archives, Nashville;

On December 29, 1862, with Union soldiers marching on Vicksburg and apparently ready to advance on Port Hudson, Pemberton requested fresh troops from Johnston. He wanted to relieve some of his exhausted soldiers from the trenches around Vicksburg and send them to Port Hudson. Before the day had ended, however, a comparatively small portion of his command, about fourteen thousand men, had decisively repulsed more than thirty thousand Federals at the Battle of Chickasaw Bayou. And his fears regarding Port Hudson were groundless. Johnston correctly denied the request; his information did not support the need for additional troops at Port Hudson, and with the Federals advancing in middle Tennessee, reinforcements were not available. But Pemberton repeated his request the following day. Finally, Johnston asked for Gardner's opinion.[33]

The disagreement between Johnston and Pemberton stemmed from their opposing views on defensive strategy. Pemberton believed in a static defense that emphasized holding Vicksburg and Port Hudson to the last. Johnston supported a mobile defense based on an active field army that could regain lost positions instead of risking the capture of thousands of troops in a fortified post. Each man stood fast, with President Davis supporting Pemberton, until Union operations ended the debate.[34]

Pemberton apparently disobeyed Johnston's instructions and sent Brigadier General John Gregg's infantry brigade and a field battery by steamboat to Port Hudson during the first week of 1863. A private recalled that when the vessel arrived at Port Hudson, the steamer "was minus all its mirrors, knives, forks, spoons, blankets, and rations."[35] The arrival of reinforcements led Gardner to reorganize the garrison into three brigades. The 1st Brigade, commanded by Gregg, occupied the right wing. It contained the 1st Battalion, 3rd, 10th, 30th, 41st, 50th, and 51st Tennessee, 7th Texas, and 9th Louisiana Battalion. Hiram M. Bledsoe's and

[Gardner] to Major Akin, January 11, 1863, [Gardner] to Captain Stockdale, January 12, 1863, [Gardner] to Sibley, January 12, 1863, Chap. II, Vol. 8, Record Group 109; *OR*, XV, 921–23, 943, 971, Vol. XVII, Pt. 2, pp. 823, 837.

33. *OR*, XV, 920–21, Vol. XVII, Pt. 2, p. 820; Long and Long, *Civil War Day by Day*, 301.

34. Jones, *Confederate Strategy*, 128–29, 149.

35. Herschel Gower and Jack Allen, *Pen and Sword: The Life and Journals of Randal W. McGavock, Colonel, C.S.A.* (Nashville, 1959), 84; *OR*, XV, 921, 926, Vol. XVII, Pt. 2, pp. 826–28.

Hoskins' batteries also formed part of the command. Brigadier General Samuel Bell Maxey occupied the center with the 2nd Brigade. The 10th Arkansas, 4th, 30th, and Miles's Louisiana Legion, Colonel W. A. Quarles's consolidated regiment (42nd, 46th, 48th, and 53rd Tennessee), Colonel J. E. Bailey's consolidated regiment (49th and 55th Tennessee) and Boone's, Roberts', and Fenner's field batteries made up this brigade. Beall's 3rd Brigade held the left and consisted of Colonel R. H. Crockett's consolidated regiment (1st Battalion, 14th, 16th, 17th, 18th, and 23rd Arkansas), Colonel John L. Logan's consolidated regiment (11th and 15th Arkansas), Colonel J. M. Simonton's consolidated regiment (6th Battalion, 27th and 49th Alabama), Colonel William B. Shelby's consolidated regiment (1st and 39th Mississippi), and Abbay's, Bradford's, and Herod's field batteries. Two companies of infantry and three light batteries provided an informal reserve.[36]

Gardner's new brigadiers ranked among the best in the Western Department. Thirty-four-year-old Gregg had moved from his native Alabama to Texas in 1852. A distinguished legal career led to his election to the Provisional Confederate Congress in 1861. He resigned his seat that same year to recruit the 7th Texas Infantry Regiment and became its colonel. The regiment surrendered at Fort Donelson in February, 1862. After his exchange, Gregg gained promotion to brigadier, to rank from August 29, 1862. He commanded his brigade in northern Mississippi and at the Battle of Chickasaw Bayou on December 27, just a week before its reassignment to Port Hudson.

A Kentuckian by birth, thirty-seven-year-old Maxey graduated from West Point in 1846. After serving with distinction in the Mexican War, he resigned from the army in 1849 to begin a career in law. In 1857 he moved to Texas and entered politics. Following the bombardment of Fort Sumter, he gave up his seat in the state senate to become colonel of the 9th Texas Infantry Regiment. Promoted to brigadier in 1862, he commanded a brigade in eastern Tennessee before his transfer to Port Hudson.[37]

36. *OR*, XV, 934–35, Vol. XXIV, Pt. 3, p. 613; Gardner, S.O. No. 11, January 8, 1863, Gardner, S.O. No. 16, January 13, 1863, Gardner, S.O. No. 19, January 16, 1863, Chap. II, Vol. 198, Record Group 109; Warner, *Generals in Gray*, 216; Misc. Doc., Forty-Ninth Alabama Infantry Regiment, Military Records Division, Alabama Department of Archives and History, Montgomery.

37. Warner, *Generals in Gray*, 118–19, 216; O. M. Roberts, *Texas*, Vol. XI of Clement A. Evans (ed.), *Confederate Military History* (Atlanta, 1899), 235.

The cavalry and heavy artillery remained separate from the three brigades. The 9th Louisiana Battalion Partisan Rangers furnished courier details. Gardner concentrated most of his mounted troops (six unattached companies, Hughes's battalion, and Lieutenant Colonel George Gantt's 9th Tennessee Battalion Cavalry) at Olive Branch. The camp, under Gantt's command, lay sixteen miles east of Port Hudson and ten miles south of Clinton on the Plank Road, which ran from Baton Rouge to Clinton. William T. Garland's battalion and T. C. Rhodes's company picketed the approaches from Baton Rouge to Tangipahoa. Two companies of the 1st Mississippi Cavalry occupied Ponchatoula. Gardner needed an efficient cavalry commander experienced in gathering intelligence and posting pickets in the enemy's presence. He requested the promotion and transfer of Colonel James Hagan, but his plea fell on deaf ears. The heavy artillery consisted of the 12th Louisiana and 1st Tennessee Heavy Artillery battalions and the 1st Alabama Infantry. Gardner retained Lieutenant Colonel Marshall J. Smith for his chief of heavy artillery. Smith, appointed to that position by Beall, would prove a valuable addition to Gardner's staff. A former graduate of the U.S. Naval Academy and a veteran naval officer, Smith knew heavy cannon. Just over eleven thousand men were present for duty in the entire district.[38]

In one respect Gardner disappointed his men. He failed to assault Baton Rouge or even to annoy the enemy. Undoubtedly influenced by the frustration of garrison duty, his troops believed that the arrival of reinforcements, coupled with the inactivity of the Yankees, would result in aggressive action on their part. Weeks passed, and expectations of an advance proved vain. A Tennessee major thought, "This place will be like Fort Donelson. May the troops have skill enought to evacuate, but I don't think the general

38. *OR*, XV, 934–35, 943, 948–49, 965, 1181, Vol. XXIV, Pt. 3, p. 613; L. B. Butler to E. S. Jefferies, January 17, 1863, William Terry and Family Papers, W. J. Martin to Lemanda, January 24, 1863, Lemanda E. Lea Papers, Merritt M. Shilg Memorial Collection, both in Louisiana State University Department of Archives and Manuscripts, Baton Rouge; Lee H. Farrar to Cousin Maggie, March 7, 1863, Farrar Letters; [Gardner] to Cooper, January 15, 1863, Chap. II, Vol. 8, Gardner, S.O. No. 15, January 12, 1863, Chap II, Vol. 198, both in Record Group 109; Dimitry, *Louisiana*, 587; Beal [*sic*] to Cooper, February 28, 1863, Louisiana Historical Association Collection, Manuscript Department, Special Collections Division, Tulane University Library, New Orleans, La. (hereinafter cited as LHA Collection). Lieutenant Colonel Wilbourn temporarily commanded Hughes's battalion.

has or cares." Rumors circulated that Pemberton held Gardner in check out of jealousy, apparently because Pemberton insisted that all paperwork, even individual leaves of absence, pass through his headquarters. Both men spent their time strengthening Port Hudson to withstand the impending Federal onslaught.[39]

During the second week of January, Pemberton and Johnston's inspector-general, Colonel Charles M. Fauntleroy, inspected Port Hudson. Although Pemberton wanted to build an interior line of redoubts, he told Johnston, "I think everything will be in good condition in one week." Fauntleroy, however, took a more critical view: he saw poor placement of powder magazines; corn accumulated at the landing lost to the rising river; insufficient storage for food already on hand; the troops' pay in arrears; the presence of "a number of women and children . . . remaining in spite of his [Gardner's] recommendations to remove—persons who have come to occupy the houses made vacant by owners removed away"; and "lack of discipline and instruction among the troops, with the very general inefficiency of the officers of the command."[40] These problems had existed before Gardner's arrival, and he took steps to correct them. He especially had trouble conducting business with area residents because they had not yet been paid for their services to Breckinridge and Ruggles.[41]

Gardner imposed a rigid schedule that left little free time for the troops. Soldiers on fatigue duty labored from 7:30 A.M. to noon and from 1:00 to 5:30 P.M. They unloaded steamboats, herded cattle, or cared for hospital patients. Some troops performed guard, picket, or scouting duty. Various staff departments, including commissary, quartermaster, ordnance, and engineer, received detachments. These men hauled supplies or worked at the gristmill, arsenal, or earthworks. Details rotated daily among the brigades to allow for drill.[42]

39. Diary of Campbell, February 8, 12, 1863; [Wright], *Port Hudson*, 16–17; Jas. B. Corkern to brother [Dr. J. McKinney], January 23, 1863, McKinney Papers.

40. *OR*, XV, 943–45, Vol. XVII, Pt. 2, p. 833; Gardner, G.O. No. 19, February 20, 1863, Chap. II, Vol. 198, Record Group 109.

41. [Gardner] to [Pemberton], February 14, 1863, Chap. II, Vol. 8, Record Group 109.

42. "Roster," January 9–April 6, 1863, Chap. I, Vol. 166, Gardner, S.O. No. 5, January 2, 1863, Gardner, G.O. No. 9, January 12, 1863, Gardner, S.O. No. 38, February 5, 1863, Chap. II, Vol. 198, all in Record Group 109; Dixon, Diary, January 2, 8, 11, 19, 22, 25, 29, February 10, 18, 22, March 4, 1863, Dixon Papers; Jones,

Soldiers who managed to escape a work detail had to drill. Each morning they took position along the breastwork and remained there for thirty minutes to familiarize themselves with the area. This routine would minimize confusion in case the enemy advanced. Drill consumed the next two and a half to three hours, after which the troops returned to camp for lunch. Drill resumed at 2:00 P.M. and continued until 4:00.[43]

Other aspects of life at Port Hudson changed little under Gardner. Steamers delivered spoiled meat and damaged flour. The river continued to rise and constantly washed away corn, sugar, molasses, meal, and other supplies that officers carelessly left at the landing. Livestock quickly broke down because of their diet of inferior corn and insufficient fodder and the strain of hauling supplies up the bluff. Criticism of the neglect of subsistence stores continued. Rations of "very tough," "slimy old blue" beef and "damaged" cornmeal predominated. Texas cattle still arrived enfeebled. One private reported, "They have a log in the slaughter-pen, and kill only those [beeves] that are unable to step over it," adding, "If any of them can step over a common-sized fence-rail they deceive their looks." Louisiana Private Robert D. Patrick declared, "I have been living almost like a dog for the last six weeks . . . never since I have been in the army have I fared so badly and in truth I have been almost starved." At times the commissary substituted ears of corn for meal. Patrick thought this "pretty low down." The soldiers sifted the coarse meal in crudely perforated tin pans to make distasteful bread. Some of the soldiers also received, although with mixed feelings, wet brown sugar and rice. Private Cannon said, "Of all the sickening messes human beings ever had to eat, sugar and rice are the most detestable." The mere sight of sugar brought on "heaving and retching, but with a vain effort, for there is nothing in my stomach to vomit." Cannon dreamed of the repulsive food and never again ate rice, even though he, like others, preferred rice over the beef, bread, and sugar. The men needed vegetables, but supplemental rations brought exorbitant prices: flour, $100 a barrel, bacon, 60 cents a pound; sweet potatoes, $4 per bushel; butter, $2.50 a pound, eggs, $1.50 a dozen;

Diary, January 1–12, 14–15. 17–23, 25–28, February 12–22, 1863, Jones Collection; Little Rock *Arkansas Gazette*, October 25, 1936, mag. sect., 1.

43. Cannon, *Inside Rebeldom*, 78–79; Diary of Campbell, January 24, 1863.

one turkey, $5; one goose, $1.50; and lard, $1 a pound. The overwhelming desire for more and different rations, coupled with poverty, forced some soldiers to steal from neighboring plantations. A Tennessee soldier wrote his wife, "I wisht this state would sink so as the soldiers was out of it the people of this state has no respect for soldiers attall they make us pay" outrageous prices. [44]

The shortage extended to other items. Substitutes for coffee came into general use, among them parched rye, wheat, sweet potatoes, corn, and especially sugar. One doctor used cherry tree bark for bitters. Spoons were the only table cutlery. The soldiers depended on loved ones at home for clothing. When available, soap brought $5 a bar and candles $1 each. Boots went for $40 and shoes averaged $12.50. A watch sold for $212.50. Although these prices reflected the discounted value of Confederate currency, inflation seldom affected the soldiers at Port Hudson because currency was scarce and their pay was always in arrears. [45]

Poor food and shelter caused increased sickness during early 1863. Although some had built comfortable quarters, Tennessee Lieutenant R. B. Crockett wrote his cousin, "We are living in a swamp and drinking water out of a Mud hole." The region experienced its coldest weather in twenty-five years; this environment bitterly affected the soldiers, especially those from the Gulf states. Fevers, chills, diarrhea, and jaundice were common. Fortunately, few men were sick enough to need hospitalization. Smallpox struck Miles's Legion and the 41st Tennessee, but most of the garrison's soldiers had been vaccinated. Smallpox victims were hospitalized

44. Cannon, *Inside Rebeldom*, 76–77, 81; Diary of Campbell, February 11, 1863; Taylor (ed.), *Reluctant Rebel*, 81–82, 88–89, 91–93; *OR*, Vol. XXIV, Pt. 3, p. 634; Douglas Southall Freeman (comp.), *A Calendar of Confederate Papers with a Bibliography of Some Confederate Publications* (Richmond, Va., 1908), 357; John W. Robison to [wife], February 20, 1863, John Wesley Robison Papers, W. J. Brigham to Mary Brigham [mother], January 24, 1863, Brigham Family Papers, both in Tennessee State Library and Archives, Nashville; Memphis *Daily Appeal*, January 16, 1863; [Gardner] to Gant [*sic*], January 20, 1863, Chap. II, Vol. 8, Record Group 109.

45. Albert Theodore Goodloe, *Confederate Echoes: A Voice from the South in the Days of Secesssion and of the Southern Confederacy* (Nashville, 1907), 271–72; Diary of Campbell, January 8, February 13, 1863; Cannon, *Inside Rebeldom*, 77, 84; Lee [H. Farrar] to Cousin Maggie, March 11, 1863, Farrar Letters; W. J. Brigham to Mary Brigham [mother], January 24, 1863, Brigham Family Papers; Memphis *Daily Appeal*, January 23, February 10, 1863; Taylor (ed.), *Reluctant Rebel*, 71–72; J. W. Robison to [wife], [n.d.], Robison Papers.

outside the fortifications. Sick cavalrymen packed Olive Branch Church. Gardner had moved the hospital from Magnolia to Woodville, Mississippi, so patients could travel by boat to Bayou Sara and from there by rail to Woodville, instead of overland in a wagon to Magnolia. Patients often suffered the effects of bad drugs after the original illness had ended. Private Patrick believed that "I am suffering now from the treatment of ignorant, sap-headed physicians."[46] Many did not survive treatment. Death rolls appeared in the newspapers; burials became a common sight. A local reporter described a private's funeral parade:

> a rough pine coffin drawn in a mule team, and followed by eight men and a corporal, with reversed arms, and perhaps some half dozen men who knew and loved the man whose remains are to be committed to the earth. . . .
>
> Quietly and silently the firing party fall into line by the side of the grave—the coffin is laid before them—arms are presented as a token of respect, the necessary command to load at will, is given; three vollies are fired and the comrades of the deceased shoulder arms and with rapid steps march back to their encampment.

Opportunity seldom allowed such military honors or even a monument to mark the grave.[47]

Homesickness increased with time, and mail became more sporadic. Dreams of the past filled the soldiers' sleep. Private Patrick frequently thought "of the happy hours of my boyhood and then I wish myself a hermit, away from the cares and ambitions, the strife, and the jarrings of the active world, with no seductions of dissipation, neither prolonged stimulants, nor the late hours of passion."[48] A few tried to hire temporary substitutes to secure

46. Taylor (ed.), *Reluctant Rebel*, 82, 88; R. B. Crockett to cousin, February 9, 1863, Farmer Family Papers, 1838–89, Tennessee State Library and Archives, Nashville; Frederick (ed.), "War Diary of Porter," 308; Cannon, *Inside Rebeldom*, 76, 78; Baton Rouge *Weekly Gazette and Comet*, January 21, 1863; Hewitt and Bergeron (eds.), *Post Hospital Ledger*, vi; Little Rock *True Democrat*, March 25, 1863; Diary of Campbell, January 27, February 7, 1863; [Gardner], S.O. No. 15, January 12, 1863, Chap. II, Vol. 198, Record Group 109; Lee H. Farrar to Cousin Maggie, March 7, 1863, Farrar Letters; *OR*, XV, 943.

47. Memphis *Daily Appeal*, February 6, 1863; Vicksburg *Daily Whig*, February 13, March 19, 1863; Smith, *Company K*, 47–48.

48. Taylor (ed.), *Reluctant Rebel*, 84–85, 100; Frederick (ed.), "War Diary of Porter," 309; Lee H. Farrar to Cousin Maggie, March 7, 1863, Farrar Letters; Diary of Campbell, January 9, 1863.

furloughs. A photographer opened a studio in nearby Jackson, where a soldier could have his image taken to send to his sweetheart. Friends often had to hand-carry letters to and from home, especially if money or gifts were included. These letters helped ease the absence from home. Private Cannon wrote, "While they [at home] are suffering the privations and hardships incident to war, [they] are still cheerful and live in hopes that we will finally be victorious and be reunited again."[49]

Though they enjoyed less leisure time under Gardner, the men took advantage of any respite. While some washed clothes or simply lounged around camp, others sought more stimulating relaxation. A Tennessee captain visited Miles's Legion to witness his first cockfight and was disappointed by its brevity. Drinking increased dramatically, and Gardner extended his prohibition to Clinton and Olive Branch. Nevertheless, the soldiers got drunk and brawled. Major William F. Pennington, a barkeeper before the war, attempted to break up one such fight; his sound thrashing at the hands of the brawlers thoroughly entertained the enlisted men. Intoxicated soldiers were usually placed in the guardhouse, but one soldier literally drank himself to death.[50]

The officers lived somewhat better. A few boarded their wives nearby. Sick officers often stayed in private homes. The healthy ones often visited nearby plantations, where they danced and flirted with young women, everyone sublimely ignorant of the darker days ahead. Whatever tension remained after dancing was relieved by petty squabbles among themselves, by taking it out on their men, or by forgetting with a bottle of liquor.[51]

49. Cannon, *Inside Rebeldom*, 79; W. J. Brigham to John Brigham [father], January 24, 1863, W. J. Brigham to Mary Brigham [mother], February 15, 1863, Brigham Family Papers; Jones, Diary, January 24, 1863, Jones Collection.

50. Cannon, *Inside Rebeldom*, 81, 85; Jones, Diary, February 10, 11, 23, 1863, Jones Collection; S. R. Simpson, Diary, March 7, 1863, Captain S. R. Simpson Papers, Tennessee State Library and Archives, Nashville; [Gardner] to Lieutenant Colonel [Paul Lynch] Lee, February 21, 1863, [Gardner] to Lieutenant Colonel Gantt, February 21, 1863, Chap. II, Vol. 8, Record Group 109; Taylor (ed.), *Reluctant Rebel*, 84, 87, 102; Booth, *Louisiana Soldiers*, Vol. III, Bk, 2, p. 103.

51. Diary of Campbell, January 3, 23, 26, 29, February 7, 8, 9, 1863; Dawson, *Confederate Girl's Diary*, 321, 330–31; Frederick (ed.), "War Diary of Porter," 310; Lee [H. Farrar] to Cousin Maggie, March 11, 1863, Farrar Letters; Charles P. Roland, *Louisiana Sugar Plantations During the American Civil War* (Leiden, 1957), 129; Gardner, S.O. No. 13, January 10, 1863, Chap. II, Vol. 198, Record Group 109;

Civilians, particularly women, suffered great hardships. With so many men off fighting, the mistress generally ran the plantation. Both armies had stripped the countryside for miles, forcing civilians to trade with the enemy for ordinary supplies. Mrs. Francis Collins East hid her preserves under a hedge when some Yankee foragers approached her plantation. The soldiers tried to behead her chickens and turkeys with their swords, and when the fowl sought to escape under the hedge, the soldiers found her hiding place. They carried off their booty, including every jar of preserves, and laughed as they departed. Relatives fleeing Federal occupation required shelter, sick soldiers needed care, and travelers wishing to avoid the Federals sought civilian hospitality. The demands became so great on one woman in the area that she finally set aside two rooms for her unexpected guests. Women also smuggled much-needed drugs through enemy lines, and they often brought important information about the enemy with them.[52]

Civilians in Baton Rouge and especially the Confederate signal corps stationed across the river observed enemy movements. They did an exceptional job of gathering and transmitting information. Gardner received accurate, detailed reports almost daily. B. F. Burnett and another person known only as "+——" managed to get letters from the city delivered to Gardner.[53]

The Federal navy posed a threat which Gardner and his colleagues could seldom thwart. The *Essex* steamed in sight about every ten days, lobbing shells into either bank and at the batteries. Southern cavalry occasionally replied with a few minié balls, but

---

W. J. Brigham to Mary Brigham [mother], February 15, 1863, Brigham Family Papers.

52. Memphis *Daily Appeal*, February 7, 1863; *ORN*, XIX, 841; Assistant Surgeon J. J. Overstreet to [Gardner], January 27, 1863, Letters and Reports, Port Hudson, La., 1862–63, Third Military District, Department of Mississippi and East Louisiana, Entry 138, [Gardner] to Captain English, January 20, 1863, Chap. II, Vol. 8, both in Record Group 109; Mrs. S. G. Miller, *Sixty Years in the Nueces Valley, 1870 to 1930* (San Antonio, 1930), 1, 200; Roland, *Louisiana Sugar Plantations*, 63; Diary of Campbell, December 22–24, 1862; Taylor (ed.), *Reluctant Rebel*, 95.

53. *OR*, XV, 942–43, 958, 972, 981, 990, 1008; J. W. Claton to Gardner, January 21, 1863, Geo. Blood to Sir, February 25, 1863, M. S. Bowman to [Gardner], January 19, February 17, 27, 1863, Paul W. Collens to [Gardner], January 21, March 9, 1863 (two letters), B. F. Burnett to [Beall and Gardner], December 12, 29, 1862, February 1, 21, 24, 1863, Reports from "+——," January 30, February 5, 8, 26, 1863, Entry 138, Record Group 109.

Confederate cannon remained silent. Gardner had no desire to divulge the specific location of his heavy guns.[54]

A select group of Confedrate officers and men formed a special detail that constructed rafts and torpedoes. The rafts might obstruct the passage of enemy vessels, but the torpedoes had a more deadly purpose—the destruction of a vessel, especially the *Essex*. A Mr. Stewart, who successfully destroyed a Union ironclad in the Yazoo River, took charge of torpedo construction at Port Hudson. He planted several of them, each containing a barrel of powder, in the Mississippi River below Port Hudson. An unusual floating torpedo was attached to a log. Adding a cotton bale to attract the enemy's attention, the Confederates released the disguised bomb and allowed it to drift downstream.

But the crew of the *Essex* managed to stave off disaster. Thanks to information provided by a Negro, the sailors succeeded in removing four of the infernal machines during a single voyage. And because of the vigilant patrols of the *Essex*, none of these torpedoes ever damaged a Union vessel.[55]

When the torpedoes failed to destroy the *Essex*, the Confederates tried bribery. The first lieutenant aboard the *Essex* offered to turn her over to the Confederates at the first opportune moment for three hundred bales of cotton. Pemberton ordered Gardner, "Buy her at any price. I will guarantee payment." Before the transfer could take place, the Federals arrested the lieutenant for treason.[56]

The Federal navy upriver proved more dangerous than the *Essex*. The *Queen of the West* had run the Vicksburg batteries in broad daylight on February 2. She quickly cleared the Mississippi and Red rivers of Confederate transports, disrupting the flow of foodstuffs to Port Hudson. On the night of the thirteenth the *Indianola* ran past Vicksburg. Before she could join the *Queen of the West*, however, her commander learned that the Confederates had sunk that vessel on the fourteenth. The *Indianola* lingered about the

54. *ORN*, XIX, 763–66; Cannon, *Inside Rebeldom*, 78–79, 81.

55. Kendall, "Recollections," 1095; Cannon, *Inside Rebeldom*, 78; Taylor (ed.), *Reluctant Rebel*, 80; Partin (ed.), "Report of a Corporal," 588; Memphis *Daily Appeal*, February 28, March 9, 1863.

56. *OR*, Vol. XXIV, Pt. 3, p. 645, XV, 269; B. F. Burnett to [Gardner], February 1, 1863, Entry 138, Record Group 109.

mouth of the Red River for three days before beginning a slow ascent of the Mississippi.[57]

While Confederates fitted out a naval expedition up the Red River to confront first the *Queen of the West* and afterward the *Indianola*, Gardner began assembling his own one-vessel navy. Gardner had detained the *Dr. Beatty* at Port Hudson when word arrived that the *Queen of the West* had passed Vicksburg. He had both decks of the frail side-wheeler protected from stem to stern with cotton bales and placed in command Lieutenant Colonel Frederick B. Brand, a former officer of the U.S. Navy. Gardner empowered Brand to select four captains, eight lieutenants, sixteen noncommissioned officers, and two hundred privates. Brand also had his choice of cannon but Gardner insisted that he include the twenty-pound Parrott gun. Gardner granted Beall the privilege of providing half the crew from his brigade, giving preference to soldiers with naval experience. Because this expedition promised the first chance for excitement since the men had arrived at Port Hudson, volunteers were plentiful, and Brand got a choice pick. Boone's battery provided two more cannon and the accompanying artillerymen. Miles's Legion and the 4th Louisiana provided most of the infantry contingent. At least three thousand soldiers assembled on the bank to witness the departure of the *Dr. Beatty* on February 19. One private recalled that "the deafening acclamations of these and those on board marked this as one of the most memorable incidents of Port Hudson."[58]

57. James Russell Soley, "Naval Operations in the Vicksburg Campaign," in Robert Underwood Johnson and Clarence Clough Buel (eds.), *Battles and Leaders of the Civil War* (4 vols.; 1887–88; rpr. New York, 1956), III, 564–65; *OR*, Vol. XXIV, Pt. 1, p. 338; [Gardner] to R. Taylor, February 8, 1863, Chap. II, Vol. 8, Record Group 109; Diary of Campbell, February 3, 5, 7, 1863; Francis Vinton Greene, *The Mississippi* (New York, 1882), 111.

58. McMorries, *First Alabama*, 53; Soley, "Naval Operations," 565; Gardner to Smith, February 2, 1863, Louisiana Historical Association Collection; Gardner to [Pemberton], February 5, 1863, [Gardner] to R. Taylor, February 8, 1863, [Gardner] to Brand, February 13, 1863, [Gardner] to Beall, February 14, 1863, Gardner to Gregg, February 14, 1863, Gardner to Maxey, February 19, 1863, Chap. II, Vol. 8, Gardner, S.O. No. 40, February 7, 1863, Gardner, S.O. No. 47, February 14, 1863, Gardner, S.O. No. 48, February 15, 1863, Chap. II, Vol. 198, all in Record Group 109; U.S. Navy Department, *Dictionary of American Naval Fighting Ships* (8 vols.; Washington, D.C., 1959–81), II, 516; Dixon, Diary, February 13, 1863, Dixon Papers; Diary of Campbell, February 7, 1863; Bergeron and Hewitt, *Miles' Legion*,

The *Dr. Beatty* joined the C.S.S. *Webb* and the refloated, Confederate-manned *Queen of the West* on February 22. The flotilla then steamed after the *Indianola*, which it overtook thirty miles south of Vicksburg on the evening of the twenty-fourth. Believing that only surprise would achieve victory over the formidable *Indianola*, renowned as the strongest ironclad on the Mississippi, the Confederates attacked under cover of darkness. The *Webb* and *Queen of the West* rammed the *Indianola* until they disabled her. Brand then ran the *Dr. Beatty* alongside the sinking vessel and shouted "Board her, boys! board her!" At that moment the *Indianola's* commander cried, "For god's sake don't shoot any more! I've surrendered!" Brand jumped aboard, claimed his opponent's sword, and had the *Indianola* towed downstream until she finally sank in ten feet of water. The crew of the *Dr. Beatty* escaped without a single injury and returned to Port Hudson on the twenty-sixth. [59]

A Yankee trick, however, was to deprive the South of the *Indianola*. While Confederates labored to raise the vessel, Union Acting Rear Admiral David D. Porter built a dummy "ironclad" of barrels atop a coal barge. Passing the Vicksburg batteries, the sham approached the *Queen of the West* upstream of the *Indianola*. Deceived, the captain of the *Queen* fled south with his vessel, stopping only to warn the men working on the *Indianola*. The false ironclad ran aground two miles above the *Indianola*, but the officer in charge of repairing that vessel, Lieutenant Charles H. Frith, chose to blow up the ironclad instead of risking her recapture by the Federals. [60] The addition of the *Indianola* to the Confederate flotilla would have provided the South with a chance to maintain a hold on the Mississippi River between Port Hudson and Vicksburg. Without her, it was merely a question of time before control of that waterway was lost forever.

The capture of the two Union vessels once more opened the rivers to safe travel. Provisions began arriving at Port Hudson

37; Cannon, *Inside Rebeldom*, 79–80; A. P. Richards, *The Saint Helena Rifles*, ed. Randall Shoemaker (N.p., 1968), 9; Taylor (ed.), *Reluctant Rebel*, 94.

59. Memphis *Daily Appeal*, March 11, 1863; *OR*, Vol. XXIV, Pt. 1, p. 363–64; Bergeron and Hewitt, *Miles' Legion*, 7.

60. Soley, "Naval Operations," 565; Memphis *Daily Appeal*, March 11, 1863; Bergeron and Hewitt, *Miles' Legion*, 57; *OR*, XXIV, pt. 1, 370, 397.

almost every day, and the garrison no longer had to rely on supplies hauled overland. Apparently the limited number of wagons and often washed-out railroads could barely transport the minimum requirements of the garrison. When a steamer arrived on February 24 with a cargo that included hogs and bacon, the men of every regiment rejoiced. [61]

Beyond the naval activities, the soldiers had little to excite them except the attractive young women who frequently visited the post. The men on picket duty skirmished every day or two. Captain T. R. Stockdale secured three much-needed wagons by posing as a Yankee officer, an easy task because he had been born and educated in Pennsylvania. A saboteur tried to spike the heavy cannon. When caught, the man confessed that the Federals had promised him $50,000 if he succeeded. Gardner even decommissioned the *Dr. Beatty* because it was no longer needed as a vessel of war. [62]

A flag of truce arrived from the Federals on February 7. The Yankees asked if Gardner would follow the cartel of exchange. Hesitant, Gardner finally agreed after masking his batteries with tree branches. The Union vessel carried the prisoners to Vicksburg, the point of exchange, but on February 22 Gardner insisted that they move the place of exchange to a point between Port Hudson and Baton Rouge, selected by the Confederates. The first such exchange occurred three days later, when the *General Quitman* arrived unexpectedly at Port Hudson with Yankee prisoners captured in Texas. Gardner retained the officers and sent the balance to Baton Rouge. [63]

Three newspapers opened offices in the village. The Pointe Coupee *Echo* moved its office to Port Hudson and began publishing the last week of December. Within two months it became the *Tri-Weekly News*. The *Chronicle* commenced operations that same

61. Diary of Campbell, February 4, 17, 19–20, 1863; *OR*, XV, 985; [Gardner] to [Pemberton], February 28, 1863, Chap. II, Vol. 8, Record Group 109; Cannon, *Inside Rebeldom*, 81–83.

62. Taylor (ed.), *Reluctant Rebel*, 95; Memphis *Daily Appeal*, February 23, March 11, 1863; Gardner S.O. No. 71, March 10, 1863, Chap. II, Vol. 198, Record Group 109.

63. [Gardner] to Gantt, February 7, 1863, Chap. II, Vol. 8, Record Group 109; Diary of Campbell, February 10, 1863; Taylor (ed.), *Reluctant Rebel*, 89; Jos. Hibbert, Jr., AAG, to Major N. G. Watts, C.S.A. and agent for the exchange of prisoners of war, February 22, 1863, Entry 2134, Record Group 393; Baton Rouge *Weekly Gazette and Comet*, February 25, 1863; *ORN*, XIX, 453.

week. The Port Hudson *Courier* started publication during the first week of January, apparently with a morning and evening edition. The shortage of paper in the Confederacy may have occurred first at Port Hudson. The *Chronicle* consisted of one short column on each side of a small piece of brown wrapping paper. An issue of the *Evening Courier* appeared on one side of a slip of paper only two inches by six. [64]

Rumors spread by these and other newspapers proved more interesting than the truth. The most common speculations were whether the Yankees would advance against Port Hudson. Other rumors told of the Confederate capture of Nashville; a Union regiment issued uniforms identical to those worn by Louisiana Confederates; Kentucky and Indiana joining the Confederacy; Confederate reinforcements transferred from Virginia to Tennessee; and peace in the near future. Corporal John Wesley Powers wrote: "There has been a good deal of talk about Peace of late, and some pretty large Bets being made that there would be Peace in the course of four or six months." Powers disagreed, thinking peace impossible "unless the conduct of the war was drastically changed" and the black flag hoisted. Another rumor focused on mutiny among the Federals at Baton Rouge, which the Confederates heard about firsthand. [65]

Numerous Yankee deserters from Baton Rouge had entered Confederate lines. All of them told of the division of opinion in Banks's army regarding Lincoln's Emancipation Proclamation. They objected to having to salute Negro officers, opposed Negro equality or supremacy, and disdained Negro fighting abilities. The Memphis *Appeal* quoted Banks as saying: "My army had gone to hell, and it is useless to deny it." [66]

The dissension in the Federal ranks brought abounding confi-

64. Memphis *Daily Appeal*, December 22, 1862, January 31, February 18, 1863; Baton Rouge *Weekly Gazette and Comet*, January 14, March 4, 1863; Opelousas *Courier*, February 21, 1863; Port Hudson *Evening Courier*, January 3, 1863; Diary of Campbell, January 8, 1863.

65. Partin (ed.), "Report of a Corporal," 585; Memphis *Daily Appeal*, January 13, 24, 28, February 5, 7, 12, 23, 24, March 6, 1863; Diary of Campbell, January 1, 23, February 3, 1863; Frederick (ed.), "War Diary of Porter," 309; Cannon, *Inside Rebeldom*, 77; Taylor (ed.), *Reluctant Rebel*, 72.

66. Memphis *Daily Appeal*, February 7, 1863; Taylor (ed.), *Reluctant Rebel*, 101; Jones, Diary, March 6–8, 1863, Jones Collection; Lee H. Farrar to Cousin Maggie, March 7, 1863, Farrar Letters; Goodloe, *Confederate Echoes*, 270.

dence to Port Hudson. One private thought that if the Yankees advanced, "they will be one of the worst whipped set of men that ever was." Sarah Morgan, a young woman staying at a plantation just beyond the Confederate fortifications, wrote in her diary: "They are confident that our fifteen thousand can repulse twice the number. Great God!—I say it with all reverence—if we could defeat them! *If* we could scatter, capture, annihilate them! My heart beats but one prayer—victory!"[67]

The Confederates longed for a fight. Finally, reliable intelligence arrived on February 24 that the Yankees would soon attack. Rain delayed their advance, but the weather broke on March 2, and all were sure that sunshine would bring the assault. One Arkansas soldier wrote the editor of the Little Rock *True Democrat*: "Before the ides of March shall have passed, the weapons of the soldiers of liberty will be crossed with the followers of Abraham the first."[68]

67. Jno. A. Morgan to sister, March 8, 1863, John A. Morgan Papers, Louisiana State University Department of Archives and Manuscripts, Baton Rouge; Booth, *Louisiana Soldiers*, Vol. III, Bk. 1, p. 1050; Taylor (ed.), *Reluctant Rebel*, 93; Dawson, *Confederate Girl's Diary*, 328.

68. Little Rock *True Democrat*, March 25, 1863; Frederick (ed.), "War Diary of Porter," 310; Taylor (ed.), *Reluctant Rebel*, 97–100; *OR*, XV, 990.

IV

Final Preparations: March, 1863

The time has come, there can be no more delay.
—Rear Admiral David Glasgow Farragut,
West Gulf Blockading Squadron

The Federal fleet above Vicksburg had failed miserably. Between that city and Port Hudson the river lay open, a situation the authorities in Washington would no longer tolerate. The loss of the *Queen of the West* and *Indianola* led Rear Admiral David Glasgow Farragut to place himself directly in charge of closing the river to Confederate traffic. The admiral told a subordinate, "The time has come, there can be no more delay. I must go—army or no army."[1]

Farragut had considered action in January without the army's cooperation; by late February, when he asked Major General Banks to support him, the general reluctantly agreed. He had no choice. President Lincoln thought Banks should have advanced immediately after he assumed his new command, and through General in Chief Henry W. Halleck, he repeatedly urged Banks on. Lincoln wanted to send Banks to Texas and replace him with Major General Benjamin F. Butler in January, 1863. The president even ordered Butler to the Gulf theater in February to examine the situation.[2] Banks must have realized that he had to move or lose his command.

---

1. Mahan, *Admiral Farragut*, 211; *ORN*, XIX, 644, 906.
2. Lewis, *Farragut*, 166; Palfrey, "Port Hudson," 30; *OR*, XV, 656–57, 671, 690, 1104–1106, 1109–11, LIII, 547–48.

The campaign opened in late February, when Federal forces advanced from Indian Village toward Morganza. Major General Gardner dispatched Colonel William R. Miles with his legion, the 4th Louisiana, and Fenner's battery by steamboat to drive back the enemy and cut the levees. The expedition left on the twenty-sixth, with the band playing "La Marseillaise." It landed at the Hermitage, about three miles above Port Hudson, and marched ten miles, the last three in a heavy rainstorm. The larger Yankee force fled before it, and finding no enemy, the Confederates returned the next day. [3]

Rain and last-minute Federal preparations granted the Confederates time to make some final adjustments of their own. On February 22 Lieutenant General Pemberton ordered Albert Rust's brigade to move immediately by train for Port Hudson. Some twenty-eight hundred members of the brigade entered the garrison on March 3. While marching through Clinton, the column was observed by several women. One of them cried out, "These are the ones to whip the Yankees. Kill a half dozen for me boys." One soldier broke into a smile "but thought her patriotic zeal had got a little higher than was necessary." The 6th Mississippi and Rust's three batteries followed a few days later. The 1st Texas Battalion Sharpshooters took an easier path by steamboat down the Red River. The Texans joined the garrison on March 6. [4]

Port Hudson's new brigadier boasted military experience. Born in Virginia in 1818, Albert Rust moved to Arkansas as a young man, became an attorney, and entered politics. He served in the state and national legislatures for twelve years between 1842 and 1861. A huge, muscular man, his best-known political act was a street brawl with Horace Greeley, editor of the New York *Tribune*. Leading the 3rd Arkansas, Colonel Rust fought under Robert E. Lee in western Virginia before his promotion to brigadier in early 1862.

3. *OR*, XV, 990–91; Gardner, S.O. No. 58, February 25, 1863, Chap. II, Vol. 198, Record Group 109; Taylor (ed.), *Reluctant Rebel*, 96–98; Dixon, Diary, February 26, 1863, Dixon Papers.

4. Harmon Memoir, Civil War Collection; *OR*, XV, 1005, Vol. XXIV, Pt. 3, p. 639; H. Grady Howell, Jr., *Going to Meet the Yankees: A History of the "Bloody Sixth" Mississippi Infantry, C.S.A.* (Jackson, Miss., 1981), 144; Muster and Pay Roll of Captain B. D. Martin's Company A of the [1st Texas] Battalion of Sharp Shooters, February 28–April 30, 1863, in possession of Philip B. Eckert, Baton Rouge, La.

He led a brigade at the Battle of Corinth in October before the transfer of his command to Port Hudson.[5]

Gardner continually strove to strengthen his position. On March 8 he cut the east levee to prevent the Federals from landing immediately below Port Hudson. All quarantined troops except smallpox victims were moved inside the fortifications. Work continued on the breastworks, with one-inch planks replacing fence rails. Shipments of corn, cattle, and hogs gave Gardner a three-day supply of corn and thirty days' rations of meat on hand.[6]

On March 9 Yankee cavalry attacked the pickets at Monte Sano bridge. Everything indicated an advance. Gardner reported that fresh troops landing at Baton Rouge on the seventh and eighth brought his opponent's strength to thirty thousand men; Pemberton replied: "The odds are large against, but I . . . believe you will whip their demoralized army." Confidence abounded among the enlisted men within the garrison. An Alabama corporal summed it up best: "When Old Banks makes an attack on this place he will get a worse whiping than he ever had in Virginia."[7]

The constant threat to river traffic forced west-bound travelers to seek passage at Port Hudson, and an occasional famous visitor provided diversion for the soldiers. On his way to assume command of the Trans-Mississippi Department, Lieutenant General Edmund Kirby Smith with his family and staff stopped at Port Hudson on March 4. Major General Sterling Price, accompanied by his staff, reached Port Hudson on the tenth. Many in the garrison had fought under "Old Pap," as they familiarly called him. Price spoke that night to a cheering crowd of ten thousand and announced his impending return to Missouri. Some Arkansas troops

5. Warner, *Generals in Gray*, 266; Harrington, "Arkansas," 111; Mark M. Boatner III, *The Civil War Dictionary* (New York, 1959), 354.

6. *OR*, XV, 271; [Gardner] to Dr. J. W. Jones, March 8, 1863, Chap. II, Vol. 8, [Gardner], S.O. No. [none], March 9, 1863, Entry 138, both in Record Group 109; Frederick Y. Dabney, Special Requisition No. 40, March 10, 1863, Roll 104, Microcopy 258.

7. *OR*, XV, 269, 271–72, 280; Partin (ed.), "Report of a Corporal," 587–88; I. N. Hicks to C. C. Dunn, March 12, 1863, Melrose Collection, Department of Archives, Northwestern Louisiana University, Natchitoches, La.; R. A. Medearis to father, March 12, 1863, xerox copy in possession of David R. Perdue, Pine Bluff, Ark.

serenaded Price and Gardner the following night, when Gardner assured his men that the Yankees would advance within the week. [8]

On March 13 Gardner deployed. Gregg's brigade held the right of the breastworks, Maxey's the center, and Beall's the left. Rust's brigade formed an advance guard about a mile in front of the fortifications. Company E, 12th Louisiana, took a position two miles in front of Rust, and a detachment of the 35th Alabama, under Sergeant William G. Whitefield, moved downriver adjacent to the *Essex*, with orders to fire on any boat attempting to land. Though they could have peppered thirty "blue coats" on the upper deck of the ironclad, the men held their fire. Rust kept the 6th Mississippi and a battery at Troth's house to cover the approach from Troth's landing, and Gardner had a small detachment observing Springfield Landing. [9]

Gardner's plan called for Rust's men to engage the Federals and draw them onward until they were committed to a frontal assault. When that assault ended in a repulse, Rust's brigade would form a reserve while the other three brigades counterattacked. The plan was sound if Banks could be enticed into attacking. [10]

Banks's preparations began in early March. Reinforcements constantly arrived at Baton Rouge. Everyone struck tents, packed baggage, and prepared rations. The troops believed that the long-awaited move against Port Hudson had finally begun. A sergeant wrote, "All are in good spirits and anxious to move," but more than a few soldiers dreaded the impending battle. [11]

On the night of March 8 Banks arrived to issue marching orders

8. R. A. Medearis to father, March 12, 1863, Perdue Collection; Memphis *Daily Appeal*, March 6, 1863; Kerby, *Kirby Smith's Confederacy*, 29; Warner, *Generals in Gray*, 246; Cannon, *Inside Rebeldom*, 84.

9. [Wright], *Port Hudson*, 17; "Reminiscences of R. J. Tabor," *Southern Bivouac*, III (1885), 420; William G. Whitefield, "Movements of 35th Alabama Regiment near Edwards Depot, Mississippi, January & February 1863," and A. T. Goodloe, "William G. Whitefield," both in Thirty-Fifth Alabama Infantry Regiment, Military Records Division; *OR*, XV, 271; Howell, *Going to Meet the Yankees*, 145. Howell's placement of Troth's landing on the west bank is incorrect.

10. [Wright], *Port Hudson*, 17.

11. Howe, *Passages from Howe*, 40, 135; Diary of Private James Very Waters, Company A, 50th Massachusetts Infantry, March 8, 1863, in possession of Maurice Garb, Baton Rouge, La.; Homer B. Sprague, *History of the 13th Infantry Regiment of Connecticut Volunteers, During the Great Rebellion* (Hartford, 1867), 101; Johns, *Forty-ninth Massachusetts*, 159–60.

to the troops. On the tenth he sent the 25th Connecticut to occupy a line north of Monte Sano Bayou to protect the men working on the bridge on the Bayou Sara road. After a West Point engineer despaired of the task, Connecticut Sergeant William Webster repaired the bridge, assisted by Negroes of the 3rd Louisiana Native Guard. Cavalry detachments occupied positions four miles from Baton Rouge on the Clinton and Greensburg roads. The Federal troopers ordered out the Clinton road skirmished with the 25th Connecticut in the darkness. The mistake cost the life of at least one infantryman. On March 12 and 13, Company K, 42nd Massachusetts, laid a pontoon bridge across Monte Sano Bayou. But the wait for the navy left some units in constant readiness from March 9 to 13. One Union soldier concluded, "Nothing ever seemed to be done at the time designated. And . . . we reached the unmilitary conclusion that an order to move to-day meant to-morrow or the day after." [12]

The delay left Banks free to deal with a new—and imaginary—enemy. He heard on March 4 that a multitude of Confederates, including several Virginia and Georgia regiments, had just arrived at Camp Moore. "It is probable from this," Banks wrote Farragut, "and the reports from the Northern papers, that the Army of [Northern] Virginia is moving toward the Mississippi." [13] He asked the admiral to post a gunboat near Pass Manchac to block an enemy advance on New Orleans and ordered the bridges over the Comite River destroyed to prevent the Confederate horde at Camp Moore from striking his exposed flank and rear when he advanced on Port Hudson. The expedition, commanded by Colonel T. E. Chickering, burned Bogle's amd Roberts' bridges, but Confederate pickets blocked the destruction of Strickland's. Chickering then returned to Baton Rouge, his men fatigued by the lengthy march through the

12. Luther Tracy Townsend, *History of the Sixteenth Regiment, New Hampshire Volunteers* (Washington, D.C., 1897), 76; William B. Stevens, *History of the Fiftieth Regiment of Infantry Massachusetts Volunteer Militia in the Late War of the Rebellion* (Boston, 1907), 65, 276; [Banks] to Bissell, March 9, 1863, Bissell to [Banks], March 12, 1863, [Banks] to Commanding Officer, Company F, 2nd Rhode Island Cavalry, March 10, 1863, [Banks] to Commanding Officer, Company B, 2nd Rhode Island Cavalry, March 10, 1863, [Banks] to Captain Smith, Company B, 2nd Rhode Island Cavalry, March 11, 1863, Record Group 393; *Twenty-Fifth Connecticut*, 6, 21; Charles P. Bosson, *History of the Forty-Second Regiment Infantry, Massachusetts Volunteers, 1862, 1863, 1864* (Boston, 1886), 354.

13. *ORN*, XIX, 650; *OR*, XV, 1110.

knee-deep mud and mire. Banks greeted the footsore men when they entered the city, many with custom-made boots slung over their shoulders. One barefooted young fellow saluted the general when he passed, and Banks accosted him, asking, "Well, my boy, don't you find those boots rather harder to march in than government shoes?" The youth replied in the affirmative and moved on.[14]

Farragut arrived at Baton Rouge on March 11. He had intended to run the batteries on the night of the seventh but had to wait for the *Essex* to complete repairs. Banks insisted that a naval force remain at Baton Rouge to protect his transports after the admiral passed Port Hudson, and Farragut needed the *Essex* for this task. On the twelfth Banks staged a grand review, the first for his new command. His honored guests included Farragut and several naval officers. On horseback, they slowly accompanied Banks along the lines. The admiral's son Loyall recalled jumping several ditches, "which the navy men declared had been dug for their especial benefit; but it was a subject of deep congratulation to the sailors that only one man went off, and he was an aide to Banks."[15] A corporal commented, "Winnowing the air may be graceful work for the wings of a swallow, but not for the elbows of a commodore." The soldiers thought it a rare treat to see Farragut. When the admiral, riding a bob-tailed horse, passed the 24th Connecticut, the regimental band struck up "I bet my money on the bob-tailed nag." The troops ached from standing through the entire ceremony in heavy marching order, but Banks, mounted on a coal-black stallion, nevertheless impressed his command.[16]

14. Ewer, *Third Massachusetts Cavalry*, 60–62; *ORN*, XIX, 650; Banks to Chickering, March 9, 1863, Record Group 393; *OR*, XV, 263–64. Ewer's statement that the second attempt to destroy Strickland's bridge succeeded is incorrect.

15. Loyall Farragut, "Passing the Port Hudson Batteries," in James Grant Wilson and Titus Munson Coan (eds.), *Personal Recollections of the War of the Rebellion: Addresses Delivered Before the New York Commandery of the Loyal Legion of the United States, 1883–1891*, 1st ser. (New York, 1891), 316; *ORN*, XIX, 652, 709; Robert Means Thompson and Richard Wainwright (eds.), *Confidential Correspondence of Gustavus Vasa Fox, Assistant Secretary of the Navy, 1861–1865* (2 vols.; New York, 1920), I, 327; Irwin, *Nineteenth Corps*, 77.

16. James K. Hosmer, *The Color-Guard: Being a Corporal's Notes of Military Service in the Nineteenth Army Corps* (Boston, 1864), 81; J. F. Moors, *History of the Fifty-second Regiment Massachusetts Volunteers* (Boston, 1893), 59; Johns, *Forty-ninth Massachusetts*, 157; Albert Plummer, *History of the Forty-eighth Regiment M.V.M. During the Civil War* (Boston, 1907), 25; Loyall Farragut, "Farragut at Port Hudson," *Putnam's Monthly and the Reader*, V (October, 1908), 47.

Banks sent out two probing detachments on March 13. Colonel E. L. Molineux led the 159th New York, three companies of the 26th Maine, and two guns of the 2nd Massachusetts Battery up the Plank Road. After driving off Confederate pickets in a sharp skirmish, they took up a position at Cypress Bayou bridge. The 48th and 53rd Massachusetts boarded transports and, accompanied by the gunboat *Albatross* and the *Essex*, steamed upstream to Springfield Landing. Disembarking, the Federals waded through waist-deep water to the bluff and forced Confederate signalmen to flee. The infantrymen, escorted by eighteen troopers of Company C, 1st Louisiana (U.S.) Cavalry, moved cross-country to the Baton Rouge and Bayou Sara road, where they scattered the Confederate pickets. They drove in several head of cattle when they returned, via the road, to Baton Rouge. Along the march, the Federals took time to visit some of the local residents. Surprisingly, they left most unharmed, but they did pillage a Mrs. Susan Newport's deserted house.[17]

Banks made his final dispositions on March 13. He tried to make it appear that his was more than just a diversionary force, merely intended to aid Farragut's passage, which the admiral scheduled for the morning of the fourteenth or the following day. But Banks's deployment illustrated his fear of an enemy strike on his exposed flank. The main column—Grover's, William H. Emory's, and Augur's divisions—would advance up the Bayou Sara road. Detachments would leave at intersecting roads and proceed to the Plank Road, searching out any Confederate force threatening the Union right. When they reached the Plank Road, these units would link up and, while a detachment destroyed Strickland's bridge, the balance would march toward Clinton. A portion of Grover's division would move west and join forces disembarking at Springfield Landing. A reserve of at least three thousand men under Colonel Chickering would remain at Baton Rouge.[18]

17. Tiemann (comp.), *159th New-York*, 23; Thomas P. Kettell, *History of the Great Rebellion . . .* (3 vols.; New York, 1863), II, 750; Henry A. Willis, *Fitchburg in the War of the Rebellion* (Fitchburg, 1866), 77, 239; Plummer, *Forty-eighth Regiment*, 26; Company C, 1st Louisiana Cavalry, Muster Roll, March and April, 1863, Compiled Records Showing Service of Military Units in Volunteer Union Organizations, Roll 67, Microcopy 594, National Archives; Jennings, *Plains*, 59–60.

18. *OR*, XV, 692, LIII, 550–51; Ewer, *Third Massachusetts Cavalry*, 64, 64n; *ORN*, XIX, 768.

Grover's division led off on the afternoon of the thirteenth. His troops marched with streaming colors to strains of inspiring martial music. They crossed Monte Sano Bayou and proceeded some three miles beyond. One sergeant major thought it an easy march, the road "in splendid condition, soft to the feet, yet without a particle of dust."[19]

Emory's division followed Grover's at 7 P.M. These men found the march tiresome, the weather unpleasantly warm, and the road extremely dusty. Two hours later the soldiers received orders to secure all tinware and to talk in whispers, for fear the enemy would hear them coming. A Massachusetts private was struck that "in Louisiana, one must hunt very hard in order to discover a pebble, so that a [wagon] train can move with but little noise, an advantage of great importance to an army on the move."[20] When Emory's men halted at midnight near White's Bayou, many collapsed on the ground. But fear did not stop the hungry from building campfires. The soldiers had learned that because the plantation where they camped belonged to a "Union man," they could take only the top fence rails for firewood. This soon became a standing order in Banks's army, and the troops remembered that each regiment took only the top rails, "*as they found them.*"[21] The Yankees concluded that the southerners had shown "commendable foresight, [having] put up rail fences about ten feet high, and often ten or twelve rails in one pannel."[22]

The Federals continued their advance on the morning of March 14. At 3 A.M. the long roll sounded for Augur's troops. Two hours later the soldiers moved out in fine spirits, with hearty cheers and

---

19. Moors, *Fifty-second Massachusetts*, 78–79, iii; Banks to Grover, March 13, 1863, Record Group 393; Sprague, *13th Connecticut*, 102.

20. Frank M. Flinn, *Campaigning with Banks in Louisiana, '63 and '64 and with Sheridan in the Shenandoah Valley in '64 and '65* (Lynn, Mass., 1887), 19, 68; George W. Powers, *The Story of the Thirty Eighth Regiment of Massachusetts Volunteers* (Cambridge, Mass., 1866), 52; Henry A. Willis, *The Fifty-third Regiment Massachusetts Volunteers: Comprising Also a History of the Siege of Port Hudson* (Fitchburg, 1889), 69; Adjutant General, *Massachusetts Soldiers, Sailors, and Marines in the Civil War* (9 vols.; Norwood, Mass., 1931–37), IV, 21.

21. Henry B. Maglathlin, *Company I, Fourth Massachussetts Regiment, Nine Months Volunteers, in Service, 1862-3* (Boston, 1863), 27; Powers, *Thirty Eighth Massachusetts*, 53; Claudius W. Rider Diary, March 13, 1863, Rider Collection, New-York Historical Society, New York; Flinn, *Campaigning with Banks*, 19.

22. Johns, *Forty-ninth Massachusetts*, 167.

singing. But when Banks rode through portions of the column, the men fell silent. When he moved past Colonel William F. Bartlett, the colonel remembered marching down a Virginia road the year before when Major General George B. McClellan "passed along through the army, and for miles and miles the cheers were deafening."[23] By the time the division bivouacked in the afternoon, the heat was oppressive. For many it was their first march; they fell along the roadside, exhausted by the burdens they bore. A Massachusetts private believed "marching is our *work*; every thing else is play in comparison. Carry a . . . knapsack . . . an overcoat and two blankets, and a ten-pound gun with sixty rounds of cartridges, and haversack filled with food, and canteen holding a quart of water, and you have a load that will bow you over."[24]

After halting for the day, most troops foraged about for supplemental rations. One private "shot lots of cows calfs pigs hens &c for the fun of it." Colonel Bartlett observed that soldiers "not only steal poultry and other live meat, but in some cases even go into the houses and take the food off the table, and steal jewelry and other valuables." The colonel thought such pillaging would demoralize the army, and he imposed restraints; the men resented them but believed that he would shoot violators and take the consequences.[25]

Emory's men roused at three that morning. They then stood, sat, or lay in line, allowed to change position for comfort, for four hours before the division marched. Unlike Augur's troops, Emory's men cheered as Banks rode past. Halting for a ten-minute rest each hour, the soldiers marched until 3 P.M. They had walked only seven wearisome, sun-baked miles—the heat of the day purportedly reached 100 degrees in the shade. They soon discarded their "bulletproof" iron vest linings. Blankets, overcoats, and knapsacks covered the roadside as the soldiers changed to light marching order.

23. Palfrey, *Memoir of Bartlett*, 73–74; Stevens, *Fiftieth Massachusetts*, 66; Adjutant General, *Massachusetts Soldiers, Sailors, and Marines*, IV, 472.

24. Johns, *Forty-ninth Massachusetts*, 165–67; Orton S. Clark, *The One Hundred and Sixteenth Regiment of New York State Volunteers . . .* (Buffalo, 1868), 55; Journal of Private Elbridge Sweetser, Company E, 50th Massachusetts Infantry, March 14, 1863, Earl Hess Collection, U.S. Army Military History Institute, Carlisle Barracks, Pa.; Adjutant General, *Massachusetts Soldiers, Sailors, and Marines*, IV, 481.

25. Diary of Waters, March 14, 1863, Garb Collection; Palfrey, *Memoir of Bartlett*, 59–60.

A career officer, Lieutenant William L. Haskin, decried the "volunteers," complaining that "more clothing was thrown away during that short march than would suffice to clothe the whole Confederate garrison of Port Hudson for a year." Thirst forced men to drink from puddles covered with green scum. The troops bivouacked in a cane field on Mrs. A. D. Alexander's plantation, more than six miles from the Confederate fortifications. Shortly after nightfall the men heard conflicting orders and wondered about the cause of all the activity. Nobody knew, but some speculated that it was part of their "discipline"; others resented Banks for failing to take them into his confidence. Colonel H. E. Paine's brigade finally moved out. Advancing through Grover's division and turning eastward, the brigade marched about a mile down the Springfield Landing road. The men slept with their weapons that night, ready to assault. [26]

Grover's division began a slow advance at 7 A.M., preceded by cavalry and skirmishers. The heat bore on Grover's men as it did Augur's and Emory's. The division halted at noon about six miles from the Confederate fortifications. [27]

Colonel John S. Clark, a member of Banks's staff, refused to sit idle and rode off for the outpost toward Springfield Landing. About 3:30 that afternoon, three cavalrymen of Company B, 2nd Rhode Island Cavalry, rode up to headquarters and reported Clark and their captain dead after reconnoitering beyond the Federal pickets with a handful of men. The colonel's party had halted at a damaged bridge, about three miles from Port Hudson, noting, "The——— 'rebs' have been here." And they were still there, for Company E, 12th Louisiana, lay in the woods along the road. The Federals heard

26. William L. Haskin (comp.), *The History of the First Regiment of Artillery from Its Organization in 1821, to January 1st, 1876* (Portland, Me., 1879), 547; Townsend, *Sixteenth New Hampshire,* 77–78, 82; Powers, *Thirty Eighth Massachusetts,* 53–54; James F. Dargan, *My Experiences in Service, or a Nine Months Man* (Los Angeles, 1974), Bk. 2; "Baton Rouge to Port Hudson; Showing, Position of 19*th* Army Corps, Maj. Gen. N. P. Banks Com'd'g. On the 14*th* of March 1863," Map Z218, Record Group 77, National Archives. Hereinafter cited as Map Z218; *Champion Map of Baton Rouge, Louisiana* (Charlotte, N.C., n.d.); Flinn, *Campaigning with Banks,* 21; Stanyan, *Eighth New Hampshire,* 190–91; *OR,* XV, 337; Willis, *Fifty-third Massachusetts,* 70.

27. Sprague, *13th Connecticut,* 102; Moors, *Fifty-second Massachusetts,* 69, 75; Hosmer, *Color-Guard,* 89–90; Diary of Aldis, March 14, 1863, Wm. H. Aldis, Jr., Papers, New-York Historical Society, New York.

the command "Fire!" and Clark yelled "right about." The Confederates' first volley swept the road. A few Yankees escaped uninjured, but one poor fellow's foot got caught in the stirrup when he fell from his horse. The frightened animal dragged him off down the road and out of sight. The Confederates captured most of the party, including the captain. But the report of the colonel's death proved premature. His horse shot from under him, Clark broke his left leg below the knee in the fall but survived. [28]

Banks responded with a reconnaissance in force; the 91st New York, 52nd Massachusetts, and a squadron of cavalry. The infantry double-quicked most of the first two miles. They passed the Federal surgeons working on Colonel Clark—the first sight of bloodshed for most. Their pace slowed when they approached the Confederate picket post, where they found campfires burning and placards nailed to trees bearing various greetings, including "Yanks, beware! this is a hard road to travel." The 91st New York halted there, but the remainder of the troops continued until reaching a point less than a mile from the line of lunettes southeast of Port Hudson. The Federals then withdrew a mile or so and encamped for the night. Darkness and fear enveloped the men as they huddled together. Lieutenant Colonel David Hunter Strother, an aide-de-camp to Banks, thought, "A dozen horse attacking them would have thrown the whole body into confusion." [29]

Late that night, two guns of Ormand F. Nims's battery passed through the camp of the 52nd Massachusetts and unlimbered. The lieutenant in charge repeatedly asked the guide the direction and distance to Port Hudson. The guide finally said the fortifications lay far beyond the range of the cannon, but the gunners elevated the pieces anyway and fired a few shells in the direction indicated. The artillerymen then hitched up and returned to their camp. [30]

28. "Reminiscences of Tabor," 420; Cecil D. Eby, Jr. (ed.), *A Virginia Yankee in the Civil War: The Diaries of David Hunter Strother* (Chapel Hill, 1961), 155; Sue Lyles Eakin and Morgan Peoples, *"In Defense of My Country...": The Letters of a Shiloh Confederate Soldier, Sergeant George Washington Bolton, and His Union Parish Neighbors of the Twelfth Regiment of Louisiana Volunteers (1861–1864)* (Bernice, La., 1983), 23; Map Z218; *Champion Map; OR,* XV, 254; Moors, *Fifty-second Massachusetts,* 79.

29. Moors, *Fifty-second Massachusetts,* 69, 79; Eby (ed.), *Virginia Yankee,* 156–57.

30. Moors, *Fifty-second Massachusetts,* 69; Whitcomb, *Second Massachusetts Battery,* 44.

Banks had intended to land siege guns at Ross's Landing and move them within range of Port Hudson, but imperfect maps, a damaged bridge, Confederate skirmishers, and approaching darkness stopped him. Other portions of Banks's plan proved more successful. Brigadier General Cuvier Grover opened communication with Springfield Landing at 2 P.M., and the Federals finally destroyed Strickland's bridge, though ironically, troops could ford the Comite River two hundred yards above it. At 7 A.M. Colonel Molineux's forces advanced up the Plank Road. Within just two miles the Federals encountered resistance, but one artillery piece dispersed the Confederate pickets. Advancing cautiously, Union skirmishers spotted a queer-looking obstruction in the road, resembling a cannon. Closer examination proved it a ''Quaker gun,'' made of an old boiler. Clearing it from the road, the Federals marched to the bridge spanning Redwood Creek, where the Confederates, supported by artillery, opened fire. The Yankees destroyed the bridge and withdrew several miles. Molineux's forces had reached a point that would have allowed him time to warn Banks had there been any rebels on hand to attack the general's exposed flank.[31]

Confederate cavalry skirmished with the Federal advance. Armed with everything from shotguns to Maynard rifles, and numbering fewer than two thousand in all, the southerners hardly faced a fair contest. They did mange to keep the Federal cavalry near its infantry support and stop Yankee marauders from plundering civilians. The 9th Louisiana Battalion Partisan Rangers engaged in particularly sharp skirmishing about a half mile south of Plains Store.[32]

Rust fared no better than the Confederate cavalry. During the afternoon and evening he tried in vain to entice an attack from Banks. Failing, Rust asked permission to turn Banks's right flank and rear while Gardner sallied forth with his other three brigades in a frontal assault. Gardner's refusal disheartened the troops, but they did not hold him responsible.[33]

31. Irwin, *Nineteenth Corps*, 78–79; Captain R. L. Dunham, AAG, to [Banks], March 14, 1863, 11 A.M., Record Group 393; Tiemann (comp.), *159th New-York*, 24; Map Z218.

32. New Orleans *Daily Picayune*, July 30, 1905, Pt. 3, p. 11; Memphis *Daily Appeal*, March 31, 1863; Jennings, *Plains*, 60.

33. [Wright], *Port Hudson*, 17.

Banks felt confident on the afternoon of the fourteenth. He sent word to Farragut shortly after one o'clock that his command had reached Barnes's Crossroads and occupied the road to Ross's Landing "on the flank and rear of the rebel batteries." He asked when the admiral intended to open fire and concluded, "We shall be ready this evening." Farragut had postponed the passage that morning because of fog. Elated that the army could divert the Confederates and anxious to get under way, Farragut changed his timetable. Instead of passing during the predawn hours on the fifteenth, he decided to proceed at first dark that evening.[34]

But the bulk of the land forces had stopped their advance that afternoon. And instead of resuming the march when he learned of Farragut's change of plans at 5 P.M., Banks sent word to the admiral that he could expect no diversion that evening. Banks's assistant adjutant general, Lieutenant Colonel Richard B. Irwin, summed up the army's performance: "The change of hour left us little more than spectators and auditors of the battle between the ships and the forts."[35]

34. *OR*, XV, 261–62; *ORN*, XIX, 768; Irwin , *Nineteenth Corps*, 79.

35. Richard B. Irwin, "The Capture of Port Hudson," in Robert Underwood Johnson and Clarence Clough Buel (eds.), *Battles and Leaders of the Civil War* (4 vols.; 1888; rpr. New York, 1956), III, 590; *Nineteenth Corps*, 79; Mahan, *Admiral Farragut*, 213; *OR*, XV, 654.

V

Fighting the Fleet: March 14, 1863

"There is no use in trying to dodge God Almighty."
—Rear Admiral David Glasgow Farragut,
West Gulf Blockading Squadron

On Friday, March 13, Rear Admiral Farragut prepared to run the Port Hudson batteries. His crews spent the day readying their ships, and by early afternoon Farragut had inspected each vessel. Knowing the fire from the batteries crowning the bluff could cripple or even destroy his fleet, he decided to chance an uncertain navigation around the bend just before dawn instead of improving Confederate aim by running the gauntlet in broad daylight. "The best protection against the enemy's fire," Farragut believed, "is a well-directed fire from our own guns."[1]

At 4 P.M. Farragut signaled his fleet to get under way from Baton Rouge. Thirty minutes later the *Hartford* started upstream, followed by the *Monongahela*, *Richmond*, *Kineo*, and *Mississippi*. After steaming fifteen miles the *Hartford* dropped anchor at 7:30 near Prophet's Island, alongside the *Albatross* and the *Essex*. The remainder of the fleet anchored astern. After towing two mortar boats to the head of the island, the *Genesee* anchored near the *Hartford*. Because of the supposed invulnerability of the ironclad *Essex*, Farragut assigned her to protect the wooden vessels in case of a surprise attack by any Confederate ship.[2]

During the voyage and throughout the night and following day,

---

1. *ORN*, XIX, 665, 669, 709.
2. *Ibid.*, 709, 768; Harrie Webster, *Some Personal Recollections and Reminiscences of the Battle of Port Hudson* (N.p., n.d.), 7.

the crews filled shells with powder and attached cartridges to them. On the suggestion of Captain James Alden, the sailors white-washed the decks and gun carriages so they could better see the ropes and gun gear during the night passage. This contrivance silhouetted the stands of grape and canister like black hats against snow, drawing astonishment from all. The sailors took down all surplus spars, unscrewed and stowed below all brass railings and other ornaments, secured splinter nettings, and sprinkled sand about the gun carriages to provide a foothold and also to soak up any blood. Shallow, square wooden boxes containing reserve saw-dust lined the deck behind the cannon. Reverend Thomas S. Bacon of Christ Church in New Orleans, a guest aboard the *Richmond*, thought the boxes resembled "the spittoons one used to see in country barrooms." Where possible, the crews protected the en-gines with cotton bales, the boilers with bunkers of coal. The crew of the *Hartford* rested the lower yards athwartships on the ham-mock nettings and suspended chain cables from the extreme ends of the yards on each side to thwart attack from the Confederate cotton-clad steamers. The sloops of war (*Hartford*, *Richmond*, and *Monongahela*) had chain coiled vertically in front of the boilers, as they had during the passage of Forts Jackson and St. Philip. The crew of the *Richmond* moved one nine-inch Dahlgren from the port side to the poop deck so that it could fire to the starboard side. Farragut attached a trumpet to a tube running from the mizzentop to the wheel of his flagship (the *Hartford*) so that the pilot, sta-tioned in the top to see over the fog and smoke, could communicate more efficiently with the helmsman astern. On the *Mississippi* the crew strapped howitzers securely in the fore- and maintops so that flashes from their muzzles would delude the aim of the enemy; besides, firing from such heights, they might inflict more damage on the Confederates.[3]

3. Thomas Scott Bacon, "The Fight at Port Hudson. Recollections of an Eye-witness," *Independent*, LIII (1901), 591; *ORN*, XIX, 666, 768; *ibid.*, ser. II, Vol. I, pp. 99, 149, 192–93; Webster, *Battle of Port Hudson*, 8–9; John S. C. Abbott, "Heroic Deeds of Heroic Men," IV; "Siege and Capture of Port Hudson," *Harper's New Monthly Magazine*, XXX (1865), 428; R. F. W. [Robert F. Wilkinson] to friends, April 17, 1863, Wilkinson Papers, New-York Historical Society, New York; Far-ragut, "Passing the Port Hudson Batteries," 315; James W. Kesler, "Loss of the U.S.S. *Mississippi*," *United Service*, XII (1885), 651.

At five in the morning the fleet moved up to the head of Prophet's Island, where the *Essex*, *Sachem*, and six mortar boats lay at anchor. Fog forced Farragut to postpone the passage. He called his commanders to the *Hartford* for a conference at 10 A.M. Commander Charles H. B. Caldwell of the *Essex* told the others what faced them. The five Confederate vessels—clearly visible in the distance—particularly intrigued the Union officers. Farragut ordered the mortar boats to check the range of their thirteen-inch mortars. When their shells fell short of the enemy's batteries, the mortar boats moved half a mile upstream. The Confederates paid little attention to the projectiles; nobody was injured. The gunboat *Sachem* steamed up near the Confederate batteries to draw their fire, but the Confederates did not wish to divulge the positions of their guns. His preparations complete, Farragut ordered his commanders back to their vessels. He returned their salute with a wide smile.[4]

To pass Port Hudson, the admiral adopted a somewhat novel tactic—one that has particular advantages when the enemy lies on only one side. Because the port guns were useless, a large ship had a smaller gunboat lashed well aft on her port side. The gunboat, protected by her larger consort, could pull the ship should it run aground or become disabled. To equalize the speed of the pairs, Farragut assigned the fastest gunboat (*Genesee*, capable of nine knots at best) to the slowest ship (*Richmond*). He paired the *Albatross* and the *Hartford*, each averaging eight knots.

About midafternoon Farragut received Banks's dispatch stating that the army could move immediately on Port Hudson by land. The admiral replied that he hoped to have passed the batteries by midnight. At dusk Farragut signaled for the gunboats to take their assigned stations. By 8 P.M. every crew was ready. The air felt moist and heavy on that calm, dark evening. A stubborn fight threatened, and each man realized the importance of the occasion. A sailor aboard the *Hartford* remembered it being "as quiet as death."[5]

4. *ORN*, XIX, 666, 768–69, 872; Partin (ed.), "Report of a Corporal," 589; Smith to Gardner, March 15, 1863, Louisiana Historical Association Collection, Manuscript Department, Special Collections Division, Tulane University Library, New Orleans; John C. Parker, "With Farragut at Port Hudson: A First Person Account by Lt. John C. Parker, USN," *Civil War Times Illustrated*, VII (November, 1968), 45.

5. William T. Meredith, "Admiral Farragut's Passage of Port Hudson," in A.

Farragut signaled to get under way at 9 P.M., but the *Mississippi* and *Monongahela* failed to take their positions. Nervous and impatient, the admiral paced the quarterdeck. One button of his double-breasted frock coat held it about his shoulders, and his uniform cap was pressed far down on his forehead. Occasionally he fondled the strap holding the night-glass slung over his right shoulder. Nearly an hour later the tug *Reliance*, with loudly-puffing, high-pressure engines and flaring lights, pulled alongside the *Hartford* with a message from Banks: the army would provide no diversion. Irritated by the tug, which the admiral believed had attracted the enemy's attention, Farragut muttered, "He had as well be in New Orleans or at Baton Rouge for all the good he is doing us." The tug went down with orders for the vessels to close up, and shortly after ten o'clock the fleet headed north.[6]

Slowly, and for a short time quietly, they slid upstream, the *Hartford*, with the *Albatross* lashed alongside, in the lead. Next came the *Richmond* with the *Genesee*, then the *Monongahela* with the *Kineo*, and finally the *Mississippi*. A side-wheeler with big paddle boxes extending some twenty feet on each side and no consort, the *Mississippi* had the least chance of passing the batteries. Farragut placed her where she would not hinder the advance of the fleet if disabled. Under orders not to fire until the Confederates did, the *Essex* and *Sachem* stayed with the mortar boats to cover the advance. The sailors on the latter vessels must have waited impatiently for the battle. Anchored behind the head of Prophet's Island almost three miles below the closest Confederate battery, they would pay for any glory they won that night in sweat, not blood. But their comrades steaming northward toward the foe must have felt more dread.

Indeed, Farragut's son Loyall noted the anxiety among the crew of the *Hartford*. They stood by their guns with arms bared, while

Noel Blakeman (ed.), *Personal Recollections of the War of the Rebellion: Addresses Delivered Before the Commandery of the State of New York, Military Order of the Loyal Legion of the United States* (New York, 1897), II, 120, 122; ORN, XIX, 666, 668, ser. II, Vol. I, pp. 30, 99; Webster, *Battle of Port Hudson*, 4, 12. The evidence proves that Farragut must have received Banks's communication about 2:30, rather than 5:00 P.M., as he claimed.

6. Mahan, *Admiral Farragut*, 213; ORN, XIX, 666, 709; H. D. Smith, "With Farragut on the Hartford," in George Morley Vickers (ed.), *Under Both Flags: A Panorama of the Great Civil War as Represented in Story, Anecdote, Adventure, and the Romance of Reality* (Chicago, 1896), 31–32.

officers cautioned subordinates in low, earnest tones. The marines lay ready to assist either in working the tackle or in repelling boarders. Farragut seemed worried about Loyall; he gave his son useful suggestions about how to stanch a wound or use a tourniquet. [7]

Alerted by the mortar firing and the unusual number of ships visible throughout the day, Confederate gunners awaited the fleet's passage. On the evening of the thirteenth, Companies A and C, Pointe Coupee (Louisiana) Artillery, replaced Fenner's battery, which had covered Troth's landing. The next battery to the north consisted of Lieutenant J. Watts Kearny's twenty-pound Parrott. Then came the nine heavy batteries containing seventeen cannon, all of which fired *en barbette*. Lieutenant Colonel Marshall J. Smith commanded the big guns. Colonel I. G. W. Steedman commanded the right (northern) wing (Batteries 1–3 and 5) under Smith, and Lieutenant Colonel Paul F. de Gournay commanded the left (southern) (Batteries 4 and 6–9). The hot-shot battery (No. 7) had an oven to bring numerous solid shot to a white heat. Wads of wet hay or hemp prevented premature ignition. Smith personally checked to see that the ammunition was properly arranged beforehand in every battery and gave detailed instructions to each gunner. [8]

About 11:20 P.M. the *Hartford* passed a light on the west bank, and a lookout there fired a warning rocket. Immediately, Lieutenant Colonel de Gournay fired the first round. The eight-inch shell from Battery No. 9 exploded over the *Albatross*, and the battle began. De Gournay moved from battery to battery shouting commands, but the deafening roar of cannon drowned out his voice, so the batterymen loaded and fired as rapidly as possible, without further guidance. Only the forty-five-pound Sawyer gun could reply from the *Hartford*, but the *Essex*, the *Sachem*, and the mortar

7. Edwin Stewart, "Address on Admiral Farragut," in A. Noel Blakeman (ed.), *Personal Recollections of the War of the Rebellion: Addresses Delivered Before the Commandery of the State of New York, Military Order of the Loyal Legion of the United States*, n.s., IV (New York, 1912), 167; *ORN*, XIX, 666, 669; Webster, *Battle of Port Hudson*, 10; Farragut, "Passing Port Hudson," 317.

8. *OR*, XV, 272, 1027, 1033; George S. Waterman, "Afield—Afloat," *Confederate Veteran*, VI (1898), 390–91; de Gournay, "Siege of Port Hudson"; [Frederick Y. Dabney], "The Sinking of the Mississippi," *Confederate Veteran*, XXXII (1924), 181; George Dewey, *Autobiography of George Dewey: Admiral of the Navy* (New York, 1913), 94.

boats joined in the return bombardment. The sailors thought their mortar fire had paralyzed the enemy at the lower batteries because the reply there was less intense than from the upper batteries. In truth, the Confederates simply had fewer guns in the lower batteries.[9]

As the ships passed through, the Confederates lit piles of pitch pine along the west bank, throwing the Union fleet into vivid relief and—the sailors unanimously concluded—giving the enemy an immense advantage. As Assistant Engineer Harrie Webster of the *Genesee* wrote, "the illumination of the river showed with all needful accuracy the position of each ship, her lead-colored sides and outlined rigging affording excellent targets for the gunners on the bluffs, beneath which we seemed to be crawling at a snail's pace."[10] Lieutenant Colonel Smith disagreed. He claimed—probably correctly—that only one fire was ignited and that the limited illumination from the single blaze proved of little benefit to his gunners. The Federals had an unobstructed view of the bonfires, however, whereas the southerners had to peer through the curtain of cannon smoke between the bluff and the vessels; this difference undoubtedly accounts for the discrepancy in opinion.[11]

When the *Hartford* came abreast of the lower Confederate batteries, she opened with a full broadside. The cannon could not fire simultaneously, however, without straining the ship. Instead, the gunners discharged the forward cannon first, then along the line "as fast almost as the ticking of a watch."[12] Loyall Farragut ducked when a shot whistled by. The admiral grabbed his shoulder: "Don't duck, my son," he said, "there is no use in trying to dodge God Almighty."[13]

Now both sides fired rapidly, and smoke from the cannon and

9. *ORN*, XIX, 666, 692, 694, 709; *OR*, XV, 1027; [Wright], *Port Hudson*, 18; Meredith, "Farragut's Passage," 121; McMorries, *First Alabama*, 54. The specific times mentioned in the text are based on a comparison of the individual source with the starting time of the initial firing (11:20 P.M.).

10. Webster, *Battle of Port Hudson*, 10, 13; Kendall, "Recollections," 1108–1109; Dewey, *Autobiography*, 88; Meredith, "Farragut's Passage," 122.

11. Smith to Gardner, March 15, 1863, LHA Collection; de Gournay, "Siege of Port Hudson."

12. Webster, *Battle of Port Hudson*, 12; Frank Moore (ed.), *The Rebellion Record: A Diary of American Events with Documents, Narratives, Illustrative Incidents, Poetry, etc.* (12 vols; New York, 1861–71), VII, 452.

13. Smith, "With Farragut," 33.

bonfires grew so dense that it nearly blinded all. An officer stationed himself at the prow of each vessel and transmitted directions through a line of men to the helmsman at the stern. The fleet hugged the eastern shore just under the enemy guns to avoid running aground on the shoal that jutted out from the west bank at the bend. In doing so, the ships hovered just below the range of many of the Confederate guns, which had to fire over the edge of the bluff. They passed so close, in fact, that the yards brushed against overhanging tree limbs and the voices of Confederates could be heard. The sailors taunted the men on the bluff to "shoot their damned old batteries." And the Confederates did just that when the vessels moved upstream enough to allow their fire to clear the bluff and strike the ships.[14]

The first shell had brought a halt to the card games within the garrison. The long roll sounded and officers rushed about ordering their men to fall in. The two-thirds of the infantrymen who had remained in camp hurriedly formed ranks and moved to the breastworks, taken aback by the night attack. Officers had the horses moved out of range. Private Robert D. Patrick received orders to take a trunk containing at least $50,000 and valuable papers half a mile north of town to protect it from enemy shells. After a hazardous journey, Patrick found at his destination that "the shells fell just as thick or thicker there than they did at my quarters."[15] The heavy artillerymen ignored the mortar shells and did not have to worry about the high-flying projectiles from the fleet, which passed over their heads.[16]

When the bombardment began, alert Union soldiers in the rear of Port Hudson woke the sleeping to witness the rare sight. A Massachusetts private recalled,

> We were only to see the flashes, hear the reports, and watch the flight of the mortar shells as they took their flight upward, at an angle of

14. Mobile *Advertiser and Register*, April 2, 1863; Irwin, *Nineteenth Corps*, 79.

15. Taylor (ed.), *Reluctant Rebel*, 104–105; McMorries, *First Alabama*, 53; Waterman, "Afield—Afloat," 391; Lindsley (ed.), *Military Annals*, 448; Simpson, Diary, March 14, 1863, Simpson Papers; *OR*, XV, 944, 1151; Map of Port Hudson and Its Defenses, drawn by Major J. de Baun (9th Louisiana Battalion Partisan Rangers), Camp Moore State Commemorative Area, State of Louisiana Office of State Parks, Department of Culture, Recreation and Tourism, Tangipahoa, Louisiana.

16. "Fortification and Siege," 310; C. W. Trice, "The Battleship Mississippi," *Confederate Veteran*, XXV (1917), 112.

forty-five degrees, with the rapidity of lightning. Small globes of golden flames were seen sailing through the pure ether; not a steady, unfading flame, but coruscating like the fitful gleam of a fire-fly, now variable, and anon, invisible like a flying star of the sixth magnitude. The terrible missile, a thirteen-inch shell, nears the zenith. Up, and still up, higher and higher. Its flight now becomes much slower, till, on reaching its utmost altitude, its centrifugal force becoming counteracted by the earth's attraction, it describes, it may be, ere it reaches terra firma, a grand parabola. [17]

The noise of the bombardment, louder than any peal of thunder, carried to the outskirts of New Orleans. Recalling Milton's description of battle in *Paradise Lost*, members of the 52nd Massachusetts trembled for Farragut and his fleet, but the Federals took comfort in the apparent destruction raining down on the enemy. [18]

The incoming shells from the fleet no less impressed their targets, many of whom came under fire for the first time. The Confederate infantrymen hugged their trenches and watched what was possibly the finest pyrotechnic display ever to take place in North America. To a Tennessee private, "the whole atmosphere appeared to be full of the screaming, exploding heavy bombs. The man who would say he could look with complacency and ease on such a scene has no regard for the truth. It was terrific." [19]

Concussions from blazing cannon and exploding shells shook the earth. Projectiles uprooted huge trees or splintered them to pieces. Often the large shells buried themselves in the soft, sandy earth before exploding. Then from the ground came a flash of light and a boom, as if the shot originated underground. A shell-burst looked dangerous at first, and the men would drop to the ground. Standing on a parapet, Private John T. Goodrich spotted a thirteen-inch mortar shell coming straight at him: "I jumped about twenty feet to get out of the way, to learn later that the old screeching shell

17. Flinn, *Campaigning with Banks*, 22–23; Plummer, *Forty-eighth M.V.M.*, 28.

18. L. A. Gallup, *et al.*, *Roster, Muster Roll—and—Chronological Record of The Twenty-Sixth Regiment, Connecticut Volunteers* . . . (Norwich, Conn., 1888), 7; Moors, *Fifty-second Massachusetts*, 70; Clark, *One Hundred and Sixteenth New York*, 57.

19. Thomas R. Myers' Memoirs, March 28, 1916, p. 2 (typescript copy in author's possession); M'Neilly, "Under Fire at Port Hudson," 338; Lindsley (ed.), *Military Annals*, 448; Harmon Memoir, Civil War Collection; [Tennessee] Centennial Commission, *Tennesseans in the Civil War*, II, 299.

fell something like a fourth of a mile from me." The men soon learned that fragments from shells exploding directly overhead carried beyond them. By withstanding the shelling without a man killed, "the Forty-first [Tennessee] Regiment never afterward seemed to have any fear of cannon on land or water," according to its lieutenant colonel.[20]

Panic seized many within the garrison. Several women who had come to Port Hudson to visit their husbands fled north through the woods. Ignorant of the terrain, one woman and a child fell into Little Sandy Creek and drowned. Many of the Negroes who remained in camp, mostly cooks and teamsters, were likewise terrified. Running through the woods terror-stricken, one Negro tripped over a stump and broke his neck. Chaplain J. H. McNeilly witnessed a fleeing Negro:

> Some one called to him: "Tom, it's time for you to be praying."
>
> He accepted the suggestion and flopped down on his knees and began. . . .
>
> Just then his eye caught sight of one of the big shells from the mortar boats soaring up into the heavens with its burning fuse until it seemed just over his head: He didn't wait to finish . . . he started again on the run, and in his blind terror he struck his forehead against a projecting pole of a cabin, his neck was broken, and he fell dead.

A few civilians did remain calm. Fully exposed to flying shot and shell, several Irish women, married to men in Company E, 12th Louisiana Heavy Artillery Battalion, sat on the powder magazine behind the battery. Cheering their husbands on, they called: "Jemmie, why don't you hurry with the cartridge," and "Mike, hurry with the shell."[21] Four miles northeast of town at Linwood plantation, six women huddled at a second-floor window to witness the shelling. Sarah Morgan thought she

> had heard a bombardment before; but Baton Rouge was child's play compared to this. . . . Such an incessant roar! And at every report the

20. Lindsley (ed.), *Military Annals*, 510; John T. Goodrich, "Humorous Features as Well as Tragedies," *Confederate Veteran*, XVI (1908), 126; Natchez *Weekly Courier*, March 25, 1863; Albert Theodore Goodloe, *Some Rebel Relics from the Seat of War* (Nashville, 1893), 203; [Tennessee] Centennial Commission, *Tennesseans in the Civil War*, II, 173; M'Neilly, "Under Fire at Port Hudson," 338.

21. Natchez *Weekly Courier*, March 25, 1863; M'Neilly, "Under Fire at Port Hudson," 338; Taylor (ed.), *Reluctant Rebel*, 105; de Gournay to [Gardner], September 12, 1863, LHA Collection.

house shaking so. . . . That dreadful roar! . . . From the window . . . we can see the incessant flash of the guns. . . . and silently wondered which of our friends were lying stiff and dead, and then, shuddering at the thought, betook ourselves to silent prayer. I think we know what it is to "wrestle with God in prayer"; we had but one thought. Yet for women, we took it almost too coolly. No tears, no cries, no fear, though for the first five minutes everybody's teeth chattered violently.

The bombardment woke Clinton and was distinctly audible along the railroad leading to Jackson, Mississippi.[22]

Lieutenant Colonel Smith had stationed himself at Battery No. 4 to await the foe. He had served under Farragut before the war and intended to give him a warm reception. The *Hartford* passed Smith so closely that he could have struck the officers on her poop deck with a pistol shot. Instead he double-loaded an eight-inch and ten-inch columbiad to pay his respects to his former commander; he personally trained the ten-inch gun on the *Hartford*, but when he gave the order to fire, both friction primers failed. Replacing them, again Smith gave the order to fire. Once more, both primers misfired, and the *Hartford* passed unscathed. Defective primers plagued the garrison, and the gunners had to resort to port fires or slow matches. But when the gunners raised them to the powder vent to ignite the piece, they also revealed their positions in the darkness.[23]

As the *Hartford* proceeded upstream, the gunners scanned the bluff for a muzzle flash or a port fire. When Farragut sighted one he would shout, "That's your sort, boys, now's your time!" and the gunners would quickly discharge their cannon. When the smoke became so thick that the pilot could not see, Captain James S. Parker ordered his men to cease fire to allow the smoke to clear. When it did, the pilot suddenly discovered that the treacherous, five-knot current had turned the ship toward shore directly under the batteries. Before the helmsman could change course the *Hartford* touched shore. Fearing the enemy would disembark, sharpshooters lining the bluff quickly brought their muskets to bear. Despite the ten-minute ordeal, the vessel escaped with little dam-

22. Dawson, *Confederate Girl's Diary*, 337–38; Taylor (ed.), *Reluctant Rebel*, 104.

23. Smith to Gardner, March 15, 1863, LHA Collection; *OR*, XV, 1027; Notebook of Lieutenant William Trask (xerox copy in author's possession); Waterman, "Afield—Afloat," 390; de Gournay, "Siege of Port Hudson."

age because the Confederates either failed to lower their cannon far enough to hit it or were prevented from doing so by the *Hartford's* proximity to the bluff. Possibly the howitzers firing from the *Hartford's* top deceived them because the opposing guns rested on nearly the same elevation.[24]

Struggling to free the vessels, the *Albatross* reversed engines while the *Hartford* continued forward. Every man on the deck of the two vessels watched breathlessly. Farragut, impatient, shouted, "Back! back on the *Albatross!*" (Loyall repeated his father's order and received a lecture afterward for officiousness.) The maneuver succeeded, and the two vessels continued upstream. A voice rang out, "Ram on the port bow, sir!" and another ordered, "Man the port battery, and call away the boarders!" Farragut seized his cutlass and started forward, saying, "I am going to have a hand in this myself."[25] The ram proved an illusion. Ruins of an old building, coupled with the reflection from burning logs, had misled the nervous lookouts.[26]

The *Hartford* continued upriver after firing a final broadside. By 12:15 A.M. the two vessels had passed the last of the shore batteries. For the next two miles the *Hartford* fired the nine-inch Dahlgren and thirty-pound Parrott mounted on the poop deck. Within thirty minutes both vessels were beyond the range of the enemy guns. Unable to close with the faster Confederate steamers, which chose to flee instead of doing battle, Farragut dropped anchor.[27]

Unknown to the admiral, the Confederate fleet—except for the *Queen of the West*—consisted of four steamboats making last-minute deliveries of corn, a scarce commodity at Port Hudson. Two vessels had remained at the wharf, still being unloaded, when the bombardment began. A private viewed the sight aboard the transports, where "all was confusion, the shrieks of the women,

24. Farragut, "Passing Port Hudson," 318; *ORN*, XIX, 666, 671; E. B. Potter *et al.* (eds.), *Sea Power: A Naval History* (Englewood Cliffs, N.J., 1960), 304; A. T. Mahan, *The Gulf and Inland Waters* (New York, 1883), 135; Waterman, "Afield—Afloat," 391; McMorries, *First Alabama*, 54, 56; Charles S. Foltz, *Surgeon of the Seas . . .* (Indianapolis, 1931), 262.

25. Farragut, "Passing Port Hudson," 319; *ORN*, XIX, 666.

26. Smith, "With Farragut," 34.

27. Meredith, "Farragut's Passage," 123; *ORN*, XIX, 666, 671, 707, 709, 711; *OR*, XV, 277.

the shouts of the officers to their crews, and the glare of light from the cabins and furnaces, contrasted strangely with the death-like stillness and darkness of the batteries on the bluff." Immediately after the steamers left the wharf for safer waters upstream, Gardner galloped up to Battery No. 1. Lights on the vessels caught his eye, and he shouted to Captain J. F. Whitfield, "Why don't you fire on those boats?" Private John C. Hearn failed to recognize the commanding general and replied, "They are our transports, you infernal thief." Gardner acted as though he had not heard the remark and rode on.[28]

The admiral now faced a new worry. Signal rockets had failed to elicit a response from the five missing vessels, and as the admiral stood with his arm on his son's shoulder, a sailor could see "the expression of anxiety and woe in the old hero's face" in the flare's light.[29] Where was the rest of his fleet?

Downstream, between 11:20 and 11:30 P.M., the men aboard the *Richmond* watched the fire of the mortar boats overhead while the helmsman struggled to avoid ramming the *Hartford*. A reporter on the *Richmond* thought "Farragut seemed to be so enamored with the sport in which he was engaged as to be in no hurry to pass by." Repeatedly, Lieutenant Edward Terry called for the engines to stop to avoid a collision. The crew of the eighty-pound Dahlgren rifle stationed on the bow had to fire cautiously to avoid striking the *Hartford*.[30]

The smoke from the *Hartford*, coupled with that from the bonfires and Confederate batteries, made visibility even worse on the *Richmond*. The gun captains passed the order: "Boys, don't fire till you see the flash from the enemy's guns." Above the roar of battle the men aboard the *Richmond* could hear the cries for help from a marine who had fallen off the *Hartford*. Terry shouted, "Man overboard, throw him a rope." But no one could help, and the victim's screams grew faint as he floated downstream.[31]

While the *Richmond* pushed ahead through the smoke, an offi-

28. Smith, *Company K*, 49–50, 83, [139, 143]; *OR*, XV, 271.

29. Meredith, "Farragut's Passage," 123–24; Farragut, "Passing Port Hudson," 319.

30. Moore (ed.), *Rebellion Record*, VII, 452; *ORN*, XIX, 673.

31. Moore (ed.), *Rebellion Record*, VII, 452–53; L. P. Brockett, *Battle-Field and Hospital: or, Lights and Shadows of the Great Rebellion . . .* (N.p., n.d.), 228; Mahan, *Gulf and Inland Waters*, 136.

cer on the forward topgallant shouted, "Ready with the port-gun." But before the gunners could fire, Terry yelled, "Hold on, you are firing into the *Hartford!*" A second later the muzzle flash of the *Hartford*'s guns revealed its spars and rigging. When the *Richmond* reached a point about halfway through the gauntlet, the smoke cleared momentarily to reveal the Confederates running a cannon to the edge of the bluff. They pointed it sharply downward and fired it almost point-blank at the *Richmond*. The *Richmond* stood helpless, her cannon unable to elevate enough to hit those on the bluff. The Confederates raked her deck with grape and canister. The sailors replied weakly with double-shotted guns.[32]

Enraged over the *Hartford*'s successful passage, the Confederates mercilessly pounded the *Richmond*. A shell entered the port of the forward starboard gun and exploded directly beneath it, the concussion reeling the ship. Fragments splintered the gun carriage, dented the barrel, and struck the boatswain's mate, cutting off one arm and both legs. With his dying breath he shouted, "Don't give up the ship, lads!"[33] Seconds later a rifled solid shot passed under No. 8 gun port and tore through the bulkhead. A twelve-pounder shell ripped through the side between gun ports 11 and 12, took off the head and arm of one marine, half the head of another, and wounded some twelve or thirteen more with splinters. When it passed through the bulwark, it exploded. The largest fragment plowed up the deck and twisted the brass rods that protected the lower cabin's skylight. Continuing its flight, it shivered a stanchion that supported the poop deck and punched a hole in the captain's office, where it dropped to the floor, spent. Blood now covered the entire front of the office, some twenty feet from where the marines fell. Much of the rigging and every waist boat sustained damage. One shot went through the mainmasthead and another struck the starboard bow only two feet above the waterline.[34]

Captain Alden and Lieutenant Commander A. B. Cummings stood on the bridge. Cheering his men through his trumpet, Cummings directed them to fire "in rapid succession from bow to

32. Moore (ed.), *Rebellion Record*, VII, 453; John Truesdale, *The Blue Coats, and How They Lived, Fought and Died for the Union* (Philadelphia, 1867), 469; Webster, *Battle of Port Hudson*, 13.

33. Brockett, *Battle-Field and Hospital*, 229; ORN, XIX, 674.

34. ORN, XIX, 674–75, 769; Moore (ed.), *Rebellion Record*, VII, 454–55.

stern." But the trumpet fell, smashed, when a large-caliber conical shot passed over the starboard gangway, taking off the lieutenant's foot just above the ankle and knocking Alden down with the windage before passing through the smokestack. The captain escaped injury, but Cummings, gushing blood, screamed: "Put a tourniquet on my leg, boys. Send my letters to my wife. Tell her that I fell in doing my duty!" On his way below, blood streamed from his shattered leg. While the surgeons amputated below the knee, he told them, "If there are others worse hurt, attend to them first." Moments later a shell exploded under the stern and threw water thirty feet high. The ship quivered, equipment fell overboard, and the cabin windows shattered.[35]

Disaster struck when the *Richmond* turned the point about 12:35 A.M. A solid shot fired from a six-inch rifle came through the starboard side and destroyed the starboard safety-valve chamber and damaged the port safety valve. Instantly, dense volumes of vapor enveloped the ship. The scream of escaping steam penetrated the air; steam pressure plummeted to nine pounds, and vapor extinguished the port fire. Some determined sailors tried to haul fire from the furnace of the starboard boiler; First Assistant Engineer Eben Hoyt penetrated the hot steam several times while overseeing and trying to gauge the damage. Comrades finally led him away, exhausted and fainting. First Class Firemen Matthew McClelland, Joseph E. Vantine, and John Rush and Second Class Fireman John Hickman fell in to help. Relieving each other every few minutes, these four men, "acting courageously in this crisis . . . persisted in penetrating the steam-filled room in order to haul the hot fires of the furnaces and continued this action until the gravity of the situation had been lessened." All four received the Congressional Medal of Honor.[36]

Even with the aid of the *Genesee*, the *Richmond* could make no headway against the current. Both vessels had to turn back. The mortally wounded Cummings heard the escaping steam, and, told that a shot had disabled the vessel, cried, "I would rather lose the

35. Moore (ed.), *Rebellion Record*, VII, 454–55; Brockett, *Battle-Field and Hospital*, 230, 232; *ORN*, XIX, 673, 676–77; Bacon, "Fight at Port Hudson," 593; Webster, *Battle of Port Hudson*, 13–14.

36. U.S. Senate, *Medal of Honor Recipients, 1863–1963* (Washington, D.C., 1964), 465, 508–509, 558–59, 599; *ORN*, XIX, 673, 678; Brockett, *Battle-Field and Hospital*, 232.

other leg than go back." The dense smoke confused the crew; many on board did not realize that the ship had reversed course. At least four gunners on the *Richmond* mistook the flashes of the *Mississippi's* cannon for those of the Confederates and fired at her.[37]

Lashed to the *Richmond*, the *Genesee* could fire only three of her guns; Confederate riflemen peppered her from the west bank. The sailors replied with the port battery. The *Genesee* passed up nearly unharmed, but the destruction inflicted on her consort was obvious. The head of the decapitated marine, splinters, and other debris from the *Richmond* fell on the *Genesee's* quarterdeck. When the two ships rounded the turn, the *Richmond* lost power; the *Genesee* could not tow her against the current. Only by skillful maneuvering could the *Genesee* turn her consort downstream, but in her caution to avoid collision with the *Monongahela* or *Mississippi* below, she ran the *Richmond* aground on the west bank. The *Richmond's* top hamper smashed through the branches of the trees lining the river.

Just as the *Genesee* swung the *Richmond* back into the current, a ten-inch solid shot struck the former at the waterline. After disabling the port steerage, the shot passed through the ship and exploded a shell that had just been hoisted from below. The explosion set the ship on fire directly over an open hatch that led to the shell locker and magazine. Miraculously, the crew managed to extinguish the fire before a flaming splinter could ignite the magazine. Meanwhile, the carpenter plugged the hole in the ship's hull. Without further incident, both vessels then dropped downstream, defeated. Had the *Genesee* not been lashed to the *Richmond*, the Confederates probably would have destroyed the latter. The two vessels sustained little damage while returning to a point west of Prophet's Island, where they dropped anchor about 1 A.M.[38]

The *Monongahela* engaged the lowest Confederate battery about 11:30. In reply to musketry, her consort, the *Kineo*, fired shrapnel and grape into the west bank, immediately silencing the Confederates there. An hour later, as the *Monongahela* passed the heaviest of the shore batteries, she grounded on the point opposite. The

37. ORN, XIX, 672, 677, 769; Bacon, "Fight at Port Hudson," 598n; Eby (ed.), *Virginia Yankee*, 161; Dewey, *Autobiography*, 90.

38. ORN, XIX, 678–79; Webster, *Battle of Port Hudson*, 4, 13–16; Moore (ed.), *Rebellion Record*, VII, 454.

impact tore loose the *Kineo*, and she too grounded. For almost half an hour, the Confederate fire played havoc with the grounded *Monongahela*. It disabled two thirty-two-pounder broadsides and an eleven-inch pivot gun. A shot destroyed the bridge, killed three men, and severely wounded the captain. A shell-burst knocked Acting Master's Mate Henry B. Rome overboard. After swimming ashore, he managed to board the *Kineo*. That vessel freed herself and, assisted by the reversed engines of the *Monongahela*, succeeded in swinging the latter off. Farragut's plan of lashing two vessels together no doubt saved the *Monongahela*.[39]

The *Monongahela* then cast off from her consort and proceeded upstream. But the crank pin of the forward engine had overheated while backing off the sandbar. The chief engineer had to stop the engines, finding it impossible to cool the pin by applying water. Unable to maneuver against the current, the vessel appeared doomed. She drifted into the eddy opposite Battery No. 7, within thirty yards of the bluff. A Confederate officer noticed that the vessel "could not extricate herself. She was being carried around and around in an apparently helpless condition." The crew's only solace was the Confederates' inability to lower the muzzles of their cannon enough to blast the vessel. One sailor taunted, "Now let me see you strike me from those hills, God damn you!" In reply, batteries north and south of the ship zeroed in. A shell smashed through the forecastle, and grape swept the decks from the mizzenmast forward; sharpshooters peppered away. The withering fire brought from the defiant soul who had shouted the oath, "For God's sake don't shoot any more! We are sinking!" But the vessel's commander made no sign of surrender, and the Confederates answered the plea for pity with twelve double charges of grape and canister. The *Monongahela* had ceased firing, and finally, someone aboard screamed, "Cease your firing; I surrender." The Confederates complied, but before they could secure their prize, the *Monongahela* escaped the eddy and drifted downstream. Confederates speculated about the fate of the ship, but all agreed that if she survived, it was because they ceased fire. She continued to drift southward until she dropped anchor abreast of Prophet's Island.[40]

39. *ORN*, XIX, 686–88; Meredith, "Farragut's Passage," 122.

40. [Dabney], "Sinking of the Mississippi," 181; Memphis *Daily Appeal*, March 20, 1863; *ORN*, XIX, 687–89; Waterman, "Afield—Afloat," 393; J. Wes Broom to [Miss G. A. Brigham], March 27, 1863, Brigham Family Papers; Smith to Gardner,

Just before the *Kineo* ran aground, a thirty-two-pounder shot split her rudderpost. The commander sent a man over the stern, but he could not repair it. The absence of the pilot, who had been stationed on the *Monongahela*, coupled with a useless rudder, made it extremely difficult for the *Kineo* to aid her consort. Only by alternating the motions of her engines could she get in position to assist the *Monongahela*. Once that ship got free, the *Kineo* ceased fire and dropped downriver. Her engines failed as she neared the head of Prophet's Island, where now, she, too, anchored.[41]

Last in line, the *Mississippi* passed the lower batteries unscathed. When the *Richmond* drifted between her and the Confederate guns, her crew mistook the vessel for the enemy and nearly fired into their comrades before her officers intervened. Unable by this time to see the *Monongahela*, Captain Melancton Smith ordered the pilot to "go ahead fast," hoping to close with the column. When the pilot thought his ship had passed the shoal point, he shouted, "Starboard the helm! Full speed ahead!" As the crew congratulated themselves on reaching the turn, their vessel grounded and heeled over to port, just above the *Monongahela*. Smith ran in the port guns to return the *Mississippi* to an even keel and reversed the engine. He increased steam pressure from thirteen to twenty-five pounds, the greatest the boilers would bear, and for thirty-five minutes the engine strained to back the vessel into deep water.[42]

The sailors could not free the *Mississippi*, now the principal target of the Confederates. Shot and shell riddled the doomed ship. Some of the men jumped overboard to escape but drowned. Amid this holocaust Smith remained cool. He lit a cigar with steel and flint and remarked to Lieutenant George Dewey (future admiral and hero of the Spanish-American War): "Well, it doesn't look as if we could get her off." "No, it does not!" said Dewey. "Can we save the crew?" Smith asked. "Yes, sir!" replied Dewey. Smith ordered "the port battery to be spiked and, with the pivot gun, to be thrown overboard, but the latter was not accomplished before

---

March 15, 1863, LHA Collection; Assistant Surgeon J. S. Gardner to Major David French Boyd, March 24, 1863, David F. Boyd Papers; Partin (ed.), "Report of a Corporal," 590; Natchez *Weekly Courier*, March 25, 1863.

41. *ORN*, XIX, 693–94.

42. Dewey, *Autobiography*, 92; *ORN*, XIX, 680–81; Moore (ed.), *Rebellion Record*, VII, 453, 455; Mahan, *Gulf and Inland Waters*, 137.

I deemed it most judicious and humane to abandon the vessel, as the enemy had obtained our range and we were exposed to the falling and cross fire of three batteries, their shot hulling us frequently." Confederate hot shot ignited a fire in the forward storeroom. The sailors continued firing, however, as if confident of victory, until other crewmen helped the disabled above deck.[43]

One boat took the seriously wounded downriver while two others began ferrying the remaining men ashore. The latter returned slowly, their oarsmen afraid to go back after reaching safety. Dewey, fearing the crews would not return at all the next time, jumped into one boat. Later in life he thought this "the most anxious moment of my career. What if a shot should sink the boat? What if a rifle bullet should get me? All the world would say that I had been guilty of about as craven an act as can be placed at the door of any officer. . . . If the ship should blow up while I was away and I should appear on the reports as saved, probably people would smile over my explanation." When they landed, he shouted, "Now, all of you except four get to cover behind the levee. Those four will stay with me to go off to the ship." The men "obeyed one part of my command with great alacrity . . . all but one scrambled over the levee in a free-for-all rush. The one who remained standing was a big negro, the ship's cook. . . . When I called out, shaming them, in the name of their race, for allowing a negro to be the only one who was willing to return to save his shipmates, I did not lack volunteers." Dewey often said afterward that he "lived five years in an hour" during the passage of Port Hudson, "about four and a half of the years I was absent with the boats."[44]

On board ship, Smith ordered the engineers to destroy the machinery. Although the sailors might be captured ashore, Smith ordered all small arms thrown overboard. Before abandoning the vessel, he had the yeoman check the fire below deck. As he did so, three shots passed through the hull and entered the storeroom. Water poured in and extinguished the flames. After other seamen started four new fires aft, two shells tore through her, exploded, and ignited some turpentine and oil. The flames spread quickly, and a master's mate reported that the fire had reached the entrance

43. Moore (ed.), *Rebellion Record*, VII, 455–56; Dewey, *Autobiography*, 93–95; *ORN*, XIX, 681. Smith's report is incorrect regarding the cause of the fire.

44. Dewey, *Autobiography*, 85, 96–98.

to the magazine. With little time left, Smith told Dewey, ''We must make sure that none is left aboard alive.'' Dewey described it as

> a search whose harrowing memory will never fade from my mind. We went up and down the decks, examining prostrate figures to make sure that no spark of life remained in them, haste impelling us in the grim task on the one hand, and, on the other, the fear that some poor fellow who was still unconscious might know the horror of seeing the flames creep up on him as he lay powerless to move. Meanwhile, we kept calling aloud in the darkness that this was the last chance to escape. As a result of the thorough search, we found one youngster, little more than a boy, who was so faint that he could scarcely speak. We pulled him out from under the body of a dead man, in the midst of a group of dead who had been killed by the bursting of a shell.

Smith, preceded by Dewey, sadly took leave of his ship—the last man ever to stand on her deck.[45]

They rowed away from the *Mississippi*, and Smith, having no desire to surrender his sword and pair of fine revolvers, threw them overboard. Dewey, at the tiller, determined to reach a vessel downstream instead of risking capture ashore. About 1:15 A.M. they came alongside the *Essex*. After informing Caldwell that most of the *Mississippi*'s crew had landed on the west bank, Smith continued south in the rowboat and pulled up to the *Sachem*. When he learned that the *Richmond* lay below, he boarded the *Sachem* and proceeded to the *Richmond*. After delivering Smith, the *Sachem* headed upstream, but her propeller fouled when she struck a raft. She had to drop anchor to avoid drifting down and colliding with the *Richmond*. The *Essex* promptly crossed to the west bank and under a murderous fire conveyed the stranded sailors on board the ram.[46]

When flames enveloped the *Mississippi*, the bluff erupted in cheers. To one observer, ''a wild, enthusiastic delirium seemed to pervade the mind of every one.''[47] One Confederate lieutenant

45. *Ibid.*, 98–100; ORN, XIX, 681; Moore (ed.), *Rebellion Record*, VII 455; Brockett, *Battle-Field and Hospital*, 234.

46. Dewey, *Autobiography*, 101–102; ORN, XIX, 692, 694–95; Truesdale, *Blue Coats*, 475.

47. Mobile *Advertiser and Register*, April 2, 1863.

thought, "It was a beautiful sight to see the enemys fleet on fire before our eye."[48]

Shortly after 3 A.M. the abandoned *Mississippi* slid off the shoal, swung around with the current, and floated downstream. The heat reached the friction primers in her loaded port guns, which now faced the Confederates. A dying ship, manned by a dead crew, the *Mississippi* fired a final broadside at the enemy. When Engineer Webster, aboard the *Genesee*, first sighted the burning *Mississippi*,

> the fire was already crawling up the rigging.
>
> From every hatch the flames were surging heavenward, and it seemed but a question of minutes when the good old ship must blow up.
>
> Every mast, spar, and rope was outlined against the dark background of forest and sky, and it was a sad, and at the same time, a beautiful spectacle. . . .
>
> Majestically, as though inspired with victory, the ship, which by this time was a mass of fire from stem to stern, from truck to water-line, floated past the fleet, down past Profit's Island, down into the darkness of the night.[49]

When the burning hulk approached the fleet below, panic ensued. The *Essex*, fearing the explosion of the *Mississippi*'s magazine, quit rescuing those sailors on shore and hastened across the river. The mortar fleet hoisted anchor and headed downstream. Although the *Sachem* and *Richmond* moved out of the *Mississippi*'s path, Alden worried about her port broadside guns discharging into the *Richmond*. Smith assured Alden that the "port guns had all been discharged." Apparently shells exploding on deck gave the contrary appearance. After the *Mississippi* drifted past, the *Essex*, now assisted by the *Genesee*, *Sachem*, and unarmed *Reliance*, resumed picking up the *Mississippi*'s survivors.[50]

Union soldiers thought the drifting *Mississippi* was Confederate ironclads chasing Farragut's wooden vessels downstream. At five minutes past five that morning, Connecticut Captain Homer B. Sprague saw the heavens "lit from horizon to horizon with a

---

48. Diary of R. H. Hughes, March 17, 1863, R. H. Hughes Collection, U.S. Army Military History Institute, Carlisle Barracks, Pa.; List of Confederate officers sent to New Orleans aboard the *Zephyr* on July 13, 1863, Record Group 393.

49. Webster, *Battle of Port Hudson*, 16–17; Waterman, "Afield—Afloat," 393–94.

50. Moore (ed.), *Rebellion Record*, VII, 456; *ORN*, XIX, 679, 692, 695, 770; George G. Smith, *Leaves from a Soldier's Diary* . . . (Putnam, Conn., 1906), 42.

fiery splendor. The stars sank in an ocean of flame. For ten seconds the lurid glare filled the sky; then came a moment of dense blackness; and then, a crash so loud and deep that the earth shook for a hundred miles, and it seemed as if all the thunder of the past five hours had been concentrated in one terrific peal." It was as noonday. A lieutenant witnessed the scene from Baton Rouge, five miles to the south. When the light died out, he "tried to look into the faces of my comrades, but all was silence and darkness, no one moved or spoke. The scene had stupified them. They were smitten with awe."[51] Federals on guard duty on the outskirts of New Orleans saw the flash of light from the explosion, and the concussion rocked houses more than twenty miles away. By 5:30 on the morning of March 15 the *Mississippi*, flagship of Commodore Matthew C. Perry during the Mexican War and the Japan expedition, was gone. Only her figurehead and a few blackened timbers floating on the water remained.[52]

At dawn the fleet below Port Hudson "presented a melancholy spectacle," wrote one observer. Blood, brains, and other parts of human bodies covered the *Richmond*. Men found it difficult to move about the vessel, with the sailors trying to repair the ship, the carpenters making coffins, and most of the survivors of the *Mississippi* resting on board. The *Monongahela*, viewed from the outside, showed that at least eight shots had passed completely through her. A ten-inch solid shot had demolished three staterooms, and another projectile, apparently from an eighty-pounder rifle, had entered the port steerage and engine room. The slight casualties suffered by the *Richmond* (three men killed and twelve wounded), *Genesee* (three wounded), *Monongahela* (six killed and twenty-one wounded), and *Kineo* (none) belie the severity of the fighting. Smith reported only sixty-four men killed or missing from the *Mississippi*'s crew, and Confederate cavalry captured thirty-seven of these.[53]

51. Smith, *Leaves from a Soldier's Diary*, 41; Sprague, *13th Connecticut*, 25, 103–104; Townsend, *Sixteenth New Hampshire*, 85; Memphis *Daily Appeal*, March 20, 1863; Clark, *One Hundred and Sixteenth New York*, 57.

52. Charles McGregor, *History of the Fifteenth Regiment New Hampshire Volunteers, 1862–1863* (N.p., 1900), 249; Jennings, *Plains*, 60; Dixon, Diary, March 14, 1863, Dixon Papers; *ORN*, XIX, 681, ser. II, Vol. I, p. 146; Smith, *Leaves from a Soldier's Diary*, 41–42.

53. Moore (ed.), *Rebellion Record*, VII, 456; *ORN*, XIX, 676, 679, 682, 685, 688–89, 694, 770; Memphis *Daily Appeal*, March 16, 1863.

Upriver, the night passed slowly aboard the flagship. An officer recalled that the fire from the burning *Mississippi* caused extreme "anxiety for the fate of those on board of the absent vessels." When the firing had ended, all expected the other vessels to appear because the *Hartford* and *Albatross* had passed virtually undamaged. Casualties on both vessels amounted to only two killed and two slightly wounded. [54]

All efforts to communicate with the vessels below from the *Hartford*'s masthead failed; the woods on the intervening point blocked the line of sight between the two fleets. Farragut then discharged three guns, the signal agreed on with Banks to indicate a safe passage. The next morning the crew nailed a placard stating their safe arrival on the launch and cast it adrift. At 10:30 A.M. Farragut, undoubtedly anxious and distressed, moved leisurely upstream toward his self-imposed objective—to blockade the Red River. [55]

Confederate casualties totaled three enlisted men killed and three officers and nineteen men wounded. Most of the injuries occurred among the 10th and 30th Tennessee regiments when portions of those units moved from their camp to the breastworks. One shell-burst apparently killed three men and wounded six. While Private O. P. Saltzgiver was carrying a hot shot from the furnace to the battery a shell fragment tore off his heel and forced the amputation of the leg. He was one of only two men admitted to the hospital. Although shells had plowed the ground surrounding the batteries, not one gun sustained damage. An Arkansas infantry officer wrote his wife, "God. is on our Side." [56]

54. Charles B. Boynton, *The History of the Navy During the Rebellion* (2 vols.; New York, 1868), II, 315; *ORN*, XIX, 670, 711.

55. McGregor, *Fifteenth New Hampshire*, 327; *ORN*, XIX, 710, XX, 3; Boynton, *Navy During the Rebellion*, II, 315.

56. W. N. Parish to wife, March 18, 1863, W. N. Parish Civil War Letter, Arkansas History Commission, Little Rock; *OR*, XV, 278; Partin (ed.), "Report of a Corporal," 591; Mobile *Advertiser and Register*, April 2, 1863; Smith, *Company K*, 53; Lindsley (ed.), *Military Annals*, 448; S. R. Simpson, Diary, March 14, 1863, Simpson Papers; William H. H. Farmer to mother, March 27, 1863, Farmer Family Papers; John W. Robison to wife [Josephine], March 18, 1863, Robison Papers; [Tennessee] Centennial Commission, *Tennesseans in the Civil War*, I, 239, II, 354; Hewitt and Bergeron (eds.), *Post Hospital Ledger*, 61–62; Garrett and Lightfoot, *Civil War in Maury County*, 61–62; [Wright], *Port Hudson*, 19; McMorries, *First Alabama*, 102; J. Wes Broom to [Miss G. A. Brigham], March 27, 1863, Brigham Family Papers.

Naturally, the Confederates believed congratulations were in order. Everyone from Gardner on down praised their performance. A lieutenant wrote his beloved, ''This Splended achievement has fully demonstrated that open mud forts can fight gun boats with an advantage, when defended by stout hearts and cool heads.''[57] An editorial in the Franklin (Louisiana) *Junior Register* on March 26 heralded

> the heroic daring and gallant defense . . . the same determination, the same valor and the same cause which urged on the defenders of Vicksburg, now actuate the troops of Port Hudson. They are all aware of the great responsibility resting upon them, and they know that all eyes are turned towards this point. . . . Time and opportunity only wanting to make the name of Port Hudson worthy a place side by side in the annals of history with the ever glorious Hill City. Mississippi will have her Vicksburg and Louisiana her Port Hudson.

Contemporaries and historians have labeled the passage a tactical failure and not because of Confederate gunfire. Yet they also generally described it as an important strategic victory. The failure of five out of seven vessels to pass the batteries confirms the first conclusion, but the Confederate gunners deserve the credit. Even when handicapped by darkness, their six hundred rounds disabled the *Richmond*, *Genesee*, and *Kineo*. One can only speculate about the outcome of a daylight attempt. Nonetheless, Farragut's decision to pass at night undoubtely enabled the *Hartford* and *Albatross* to run the gauntlet almost untouched. Even though his vessel was destroyed, Dewey followed Farragut's example and relied on the cover of darkness thirty-five years later at Manila Bay. Dewey fully appreciated the accuracy of the Confederate fire that night, as he admitted after the war to his friend Chief Justice Edward Douglas White. White, though a mere teenager, served as Gardner's aide during Farragut's passage.[58]

57. J. Wes Broom to [Miss G. A. Brigham], March 27, 1863, Brigham Family Papers; *OR*, XV, 278; Memphis *Daily Appeal*, March 23, 1863; [Tennessee] Centennial Commission, *Tennesseans in the Civil War*, II, 57.

58. *ORN*, XIX, 691; Edwin Cole Bearss, *Vicksburg Is the Key* (Dayton, Ohio: Morningside House, 1985), 684; Stewart, ''Farragut,'' 168; Farragut, ''Passing Port Hudson,'' 321; Irwin, *Nineteenth Corps*, 81; Fletcher Pratt, *Civil War on Western Waters* (New York, 1956), 160; Fletcher Pratt, *The Navy, A History; The Story of a Service in Action* (Garden City, N.Y., 1941), 308; Mahan, *Gulf and Inland Waters*, 138–39; Dewey, *Autobiography*, 88, 208; Smith, *Company K*, 53.

No evidence supports the conclusion that Farragut's passage was an important strategic victory. The admiral could have achieved such a triumph only by forcing the Confederates to evacuate Port Hudson. His two ships above Port Hudson hardly changed the situation. Alone, they could not blockade the Mississippi from Port Hudson to Vicksburg. Only when anchored at the mouth of the Red River did they severely constrict east-west supply lines. Farragut thought his squeeze on foodstuffs reaching troops at Port Hudson from western Louisiana would starve them out. He was wrong. [59]

59. *ORN*, XX, 59, 62, 77–78.

VI

Reorganization and Respite:
March-April, 1863

The object of the expedition is accomplished.
— Major General Nathaniel P. Banks,
Department of the Gulf

The light moving south along the horizon disturbed Major General Banks. His aide, Lieutenant Colonel David Hunter Strother, watched the general pace "to and fro in great perturbation." Fearing the worst, Banks reckoned the naval passage a total failure and blamed the "rash and headstrong" Admiral Farragut. Everyone at headquarters thought the burning ship was only an enemy fire raft, but Banks ordered a retreat anyway. The explosion of the *Mississippi* ended all speculation. Colonel William F. Bartlett led the withdrawal, entering in his journal, "I felt safe from the first, for Banks had made so many good retreats that he must understand it pretty well." [1]

Federals still lounging when the explosion took place quickly deployed for the anticipated Confederate assault. Quiet and determined, the troops stood in line while the morning wore away, the men anxiously awaiting an attack from both front and rear. When the Union soldiers marched toward Baton Rouge, they moved at a fast walk, the rear guard burning bridges and felling trees to slow any pursuers. [2]

---

1. Eby (ed.), *Virginia Yankee*, 157–59; Palfrey, *Memoir of Bartlett*, 75–77; [Banks] to Augur *et al.*, March 15, 1863, 4:45 A.M., Record Group 393; *OR*, XV, 712.

2. Powers, *Thirty Eighth Massachusetts*, 54–55; Townsend, *Sixteenth New Hampshire*, 85–86; [Francis W. Preston], *Port Hudson: A History of the Investment, Siege and Capture* (N.p., 1892), 55.

The soldiers wondered why they were retreating. One private believed "awe and half-panic seized many hearts" and that his comrades were "dispirited, angry, fully believing we had suffered a severe defeat."[3] Rumors of defeat, concluded a regimental adjutant, led officers "who were not accustomed to swear [to do so] and the anxiety and confusion of the men in the ranks, cannot easily be described. We then could see with how little difficulty a panic might be started that would render troops utterly uncontrollable. Had the enemy really made an attack upon us that morning, likely enough there would have been another famous Bull Run disaster."[4] Some men even threw away their guns, though few dropped out to rest for fear of capture. Kind-hearted officers gave up their horses to exhausted soldiers and packed the men's muskets.[5]

The farther the soldiers marched away from the enemy on March 15, the less regard they held for Banks. Cursing him and his tactics, they had no idea that Banks never intended to assault the bastion. A chaplain tried to persuade his comrades they "had not been defeated, that it was a part of the strategy of war. Some were satisfied, others discouraged, and growled."[6] At 8:30 A.M. Banks ordered the division commanders to announce to their troops "that the object of the expedition is accomplished." The message lifted the spirits of some. The 38th Massachusetts cheered Banks when he rode by. Most of the troops, however, took a different view. Members of the 49th Massachusetts thought the announcement "an official lie to cover up a defeat that the unemployed troops might have converted into a victory. . . . *How* we aided [Farragut], we can't see." One officer summed up the feelings of the vast majority of Banks's army: "Our movements resulted like that of the famous king with 40,000 men, who 'marched up hill and then marched down again.' "[7]

---

3. Johns, *Forty-ninth Massachusetts*, 169; Plummer, *Forty-eighth M.V.M.*, 28.

4. Townsend, *Sixteenth New Hampshire*, 90.

5. Hosmer, *Color-Guard*, 99–100; Reports of Companies B, C, E, G, and K, 16th New Hampshire, Box 29, Folder 4, New Hampshire Civil War Records.

6. Moors, *Fifty-second Massachusetts*, 82; Plummer, *Forty-eighth M.V.M.*, 30; *Memorial of Dewey*, 71.

7. [Banks] to Augur *et al.*, March 15, 1863, Record Group 393; Johns, *Forty-ninth Massachusetts*, 169–70; Plummer, *Forty-eighth M.V.M.*, 30; Powers, *Thirty Eighth Massachusetts*, 55; Willis, *Fifty-third Massachusetts*, 71; Moors, *Fifty-*

A shortage of provisions provided an excuse to pillage during the retreat. A corporal described the vandalism in his journal that evening:

> What reckless plunder is carried on, which we would not deem in civilized life capable of being performed by men once living in our enlightened community. Poor defenseless women and children, their houses ransacked by the merciless and demoralized soldiery. It is enough to make a Southerner fight for his home . . . but I being one of the participants, am not obliged to condemn them much, for we *must* live on something; and there is in this world no such merciless dictator, as an empty stomach, craving for food.

Several Yankees entered Mrs. Ramey Delatt's house and proceeded to eat all her food. When she came into the kitchen, threw up her hands, and cried, "Oh, my you have just eaten the poultice from my husband's sore leg," the soldiers quickly exited the building and "unswallowed!" Lieutenant Colonel Strother said, "The soldiers plundered without restraint, keeping up a skirmishing fire all around on pigs, poultry, and cattle. The whole land was covered with blood, guts, horns, hair, and feathers . . . and some houses wantonly robbed."[8]

That afternoon a severe thunderstorm broke over the troops, bringing an end to the unseasonable heat but turning the road into a quagmire that pulled shoes off the feet. A sergeant major cut a hole in the toe of his boots to allow the water to drain out. "We had encountered the worst storm and waded through the deepest mud to be found on the continent and had bivouacked in a field almost as dry as the bottom of Lake Ontario," concluded a man in the 25th Connecticut.[9]

Before the sun rose on March 16 most of the men endured what one called "a night to be remembered a lifetime."[10] The soldiers

---

second Massachusetts, 81; Adjutant General, *Massachusetts Soldiers, Sailors, and Marines*, IV, 621; Palfrey, *Memoir of Bartlett*, 79.

8. Dargan, *Experiences*, Bk. 2, March 15, 1863; Adjutant General, *Massachusetts Soldiers, Sailors, and Marines*, I, 242; Jennings, *Plains*, 62; Eby (ed.), *Virginia Yankee*, 158–59.

9. *Twenty-Fifth Connecticut*, 33; Moors, *Fifty-second Massachusetts*, 81, 88–89; Adjutant General, *Massachusetts Soldiers, Sailors, and Marines*, IV, 585; [Preston], *Port Hudson*, 55.

10. W. A. Croffut and John M. Morris, *The Military and Civil History of Connecticut During the War of 1861–65* (New York, 1868), 403.

cursed at least one general that night, and a colonel commented, "I do not believe our great ancestor, Noah, ever saw a greater" flood.[11] The 116th New York had pitched camp south of Monte Sano Bayou before the torrential rain started. Buffeted by gale-force winds, the men found little protection in their tents. A lieutenant said the rain covered their camp with "a sheet of water, and for two hours we literally swam in the element." Some soldiers built an elevated bed of fence rails, but the men of the 116th New York, lying under wet blankets in the mud and water, found no sleep. The exhausted members of the 16th New Hampshire rested in two to four inches of water; other units had to contend with at least a foot. Alligators and snakes competed with the soldiers for space on fallen trees, earning the encampment the name "Rattlesnake Swamp." The 26th Maine stood all night in line of battle. With mud and water nearly to their knees, one member called it "the bluest night . . . he ever experienced."[12] The men of the 25th Connecticut nicknamed their bivouac "Camp Misery," though they had to share the title. The officers of the 13th Connecticut huddled about a burning stump consuming liquor, and the usually abstemious surgeon distinguised himself by shouting, "If you cant take Port Hudson take Baton Rouge; and if you cant take Baton Rouge, take whiskey!" A sergeant in the 8th New Hampshire agreed, stealing enough whiskey for every enlisted man in his regiment and the 4th Wisconsin.[13]

The men spent the sixteenth moving to higher ground, drying out, vanquishing varmints, and securing food. During the night, one unwelcomed guest crawled into the knapsack of a soldier in the 8th New Hampshire. When aroused, the denizen set his fourteen rattles in motion, and a large crowd formed a circle, at a respectful distance, around the rattlesnake's new home. A captain recalled that when the snake emerged "he was gunned out of

11. Moors, *Fifty-second Massachusetts*, 81, 85.

12. Clark, *One Hundred and Sixteenth New York*, 58; Phisterer, *New York in War of Rebellion*, IV, 3360; Elden B. Maddocks (comp.), *History of the Twenty-Sixth Maine Regiment . . .* (Bangor, 1899), 27, 331; Charles F. Wadsworth to mother, March 23, 1863, Wadsworth Papers, New-York Historical Society, New York; Townsend, *Sixteenth New Hampshire*, 91; [Preston], *Port Hudson*, 55; Stanyan, *Eighth New Hampshire*, 192, 194; Willis, *Fifty-third Massachusetts*, 71.

13. Sprague, *13th Connecticut*, 105–106, 261; *Twenty-Fifth Connecticut*, 7, 22; Dargan, *Experiences*, Bk. 2, March 15, 1863; Stanyan, *Eighth New Hampshire*, 192–93.

existence."[14] Strict orders prohibited foraging, but some soldiers thought survival required otherwise. Sweet potatoes, sugar, hogs, sheep, and fowl came from neighboring plantations; even the officers welcomed without question tasty fowls for breakfast. The officers issued whiskey rations to the men where available.[15]

The Federals deployed along Bayou Monte Sano from west of the Bayou Sara road to east of the Greensburg road. Banks apparently feared an assault, but aside from sporadic skirmishing and the confiscation of cotton, the days passed quietly. A few regiments maneuvered, but most of the men enjoyed the rest, nursed their blistered feet, and continued to loot and pillage. The officers paid extreme courtesy to the women—at least at first—but many residents still chose to leave the vicinity. Rattlesnakes remained a problem, however; an officer in the 49th Massachusetts killed eight by himself. Drinking water posed another problem. One private said he had to drink water that "farmers would hardly wash their hogs in."[16] Although Banks arrested one lieutenant and sixteen enlisted men for "quiting their colors to plunder or pillage" on the fifteenth, the general sanctioned such behavior three days later—so long as proper officers gave receipts for the confiscated property. Officers of the 21st Maine gave receipts only to persons professing loyalty to the Union. The army returned to Baton Rouge March 20–22.[17]

14. Stanyan, *Eighth New Hampshire*, 192, 580; Diary of Aldis, March 16, 1863, Aldis Papers.

15. Jos. T. Woodward, *Historic Record and Complete Biographic Roster 21st Me. Vols. with Reunion Records of the 21st Maine Regimental Association* (Augusta, 1907), 25; Hosmer, *Color-Guard*, 103–104; Dargan, *Experiences*, Bk. 2, March 16, 1863; Journal of Sweetser, March 16, 1863, Hess Collection.

16. Johns, *Forty-ninth Massachusetts*, 173; *OR*, XV, 1114; Townsend, *Sixteenth New Hampshire*, 119, 124; 1st Louisiana (Union) Calvary, Company C, Muster Roll, March and April, 1863, Roll 67, Microcopy 594; [Banks] to Brigadier General William Dwight, March 16, 1863, Record Group 393; Captain Daniel E. Howard, 16th New Hampshire History, Box 33, Folder 10, New Hampshire Civil War Records; Aldis, Diary, March 17, 1863, Aldis Papers; Moors, *Fifty-second Massachusetts*, 88–89, 91; Dargan, *Experiences*, Bk. 3, March 17, 18, 20, 1863; *Twenty-Fifth Connecticut*, 24; Jennings, *Plains*, 60; Palfrey, *Memoir of Bartlett*, 80.

17. [Banks] to Grover, March 18, 1863, [Banks] to 1st Lieutenant Charles A. Bartwell, ADC, March 18, 1863, Record Group 393; Woodward, *21st Maine*, 25; 25th Connecticut, Return, March, 1863, Roll 8, Microcopy 594; 4th Massachusetts Battery, Return, March, 1863, Letters Received by the Office of the Adjutant General (Main Series), 1861–70, Roll 348, Microcopy 619, National Archives; Whitman and True, *Maine in the War*, 503.

Opinion about evenly divided between glorious success and bloody repulse, the Federals debated the likely outcome had they assaulted Port Hudson. A large majority, however, believed the expedition ridiculous and took little solace in the $300,000 worth of cotton and sugar taken during a retreat they found "incomprehensible."[18] A New Hampshire officer concluded that the hardship had made the men "an easy prey to disease and accounts in part for the terrible fatality that came to them a month or more later. There is no doubt that scores of our regiment never after that mud march knew a well day." Lieutenant William L. Haskin, a regular army officer, was one of the few who grasped the only true advantage Banks's campaign secured for his army: "The experience thus gained in field service was undoubtedly of use in the coming campaign, for the improvement in the troops in all respects was wonderful in the short space of time intervening."[19]

Banks also drew criticism from Farragut and General in Chief Halleck, who believed that he should have cut the flow of supplies to Port Hudson and forced Gardner to abandon his defenses and attack. But to provoke a battle, Banks would have had to encircle the fortifications to prevent foodstuffs from reaching the garrison from the east. Such a deployment would have jeopardized his army by stretching the seventeen thousand Federals along a seven-mile front. Gardner could have concentrated nearly fourteen thousand troops for an assault against a portion of Banks's line, or Confederate reinforcements from Mississippi could have attacked his rear or cut him off from Baton Rouge. And the military situation in Mississippi at that time almost ensured that sufficient force would be detached to relieve Port Hudson. Such speculation, however, neglects the fact that Banks had no intention of risking his army until he had received both reinforcements and the cooperation of the forces about Vicksburg.[20]

18. Stanyan, *Eighth New Hampshire*, 190; Hosmer, *Color-Guard*, 236–37; Flinn, *Campaigning with Banks*, 76; Charles F. Wadsworth to mother, March 23, 1863, Wadsworth Papers; Ewer, *Third Massachusetts Cavalry*, 66; *Memorial of Dewey*, 73–74; *OR*, XV, 255–56; Moors, *Fifty-second Massachusetts*, 87, 96; Charles [A. R. Dimon] to parents, March 26, 1863, Dimon Papers.

19. Townsend, *Sixteenth New Hampshire*, 120; Haskin, *History of First Artillery*, 547–48.

20. *ORN*, XX, 55–57; Greene, *Mississippi*, 219n; Harrington, *Fighting Politician*, 119; *OR*, XV, 255, 1032. Fred Harvey Harrington, Banks's recent biographer, agreed with Halleck and Farragut.

Once his army had successfully deployed along Bayou Monte Sano, Banks's primary concern was Farragut. Banks tried several times to communicate with the admiral across the intervening lowland west of the river. On the seventeenth, Colonel Theodore W. Parmele, with the 116th and 174th New York, a squadron of the 2nd Rhode Island Cavalry, and a section of artillery, disembarked at W. D. Winter's plantation, three miles below Port Hudson on the west bank. After leading his command down the wrong road for two and a half miles and making his men march through waist-deep water, Parmele became frightened by reports from slaves of Confederate cavalry ahead and retreated to the landing. That night, Lieutenant David Jones, desiring action, took ten men of the 116th New York out and, without firing a shot, captured the commander of the Confederate signal corps, five of his signalmen, and all their equipment. [21]

Parmele apparently thought his force insufficient to reach Farragut, but Captains Charles F. Wadsworth and David W. Tuttle, believing that Parmele was "stampeded," volunteered to make an attempt. Their two companies of the 116th New York, accompanied by a company of cavalry and section of artillery, reached a point above Port Hudson. After a march of about eighteen miles, the expedition returned with about thirty horses, twenty cattle, plenty of poultry, and a dozen prisoners. "We thus proved that the fears of our stampeded Colonel were groundless," Wadsworth concluded, "and that he could have accomplished his object if he had had the pluck." Of course Wadsworth had no way of knowing that Farragut had steamed northward on the fifteenth, thus making it impossible for Parmele to communicate with the admiral two days later. To foil another such attempt by the Federals, Gardner cut the levee upriver, and the resulting flood prevented any further crossing by infantry. The Yankees burned several buildings that night to vent their frustration. [22]

Disgusted by Parmele's failure to communicate with Farragut,

21. *OR*, XV, 990, 1222; Irwin, *Nineteenth Corps*, 83; Clark, *One Hundred and Sixteenth New York*, 65–66, 68, 307–308; Charles F. Wadsworth to mother, March 23, 1863, Wadsworth Papers.

22. Charles F. Wadsworth to mother, March 23, 1863, Wadsworth Papers; Phisterer, *New York in War of Rebellion*, IV, 3360–61; *OR*, XV, 277; Simpson, Diary, March 18, 1863, Simpson Papers; *ORN*, XX, 785; Memphis *Daily Appeal*, March 31, 1863.

Banks, with an entire brigade, started upriver on the evening of the eighteenth. Steaming through the fog and darkness about ten miles above Baton Rouge, the *Morning Light* and *Empire Parish* passed through a crevasse in the levee and ran aground in a cane field, much to the amusement of the infantrymen and the consternation of Banks. The vessels were freed during the day and proceeded to Winter's plantation.[23]

At 2 P.M. on the nineteenth Colonel Charles J. Paine struck out with the 2nd Louisiana (U.S.), the 174th New York, and about twenty troopers of the 2nd Rhode Island Cavalry. The slaves welcomed the Federals with "God bless you all!" and provided intelligence but were poor judges of numbers and distance. High water forced Paine to leave his infantry behind while he proceeded another four miles with the cavalrymen. Leaving detachments along the route, Paine, almost alone, reached the levee about two miles above Port Hudson, but Farragut's vessels were nowhere in sight. Paine's commander praised "his personal courage, military skill, and indomitable perseverance, [which] has almost individually accomplished the object for which hundreds of troops were deemed necessary."[24] The Federals made two more attempts on March 20 and 24. Both failed to contact Farragut, but the second expedition destroyed considerable property.[25]

Banks finally abandoned the effort and ordered the troops to return to Baton Rouge on the twenty-fifth. The men burned more buildings before leaving the following day. Although the Federals had not contacted the admiral, their efforts did not go unrewarded. Besides the property destroyed, the Federals reportedly shipped to Baton Rouge $10,000 worth of copper, 183 hogsheads of sugar, 200 barrels of molasses, 100 horses plus numerous ponies, 109 beef cattle, 60 wagons and carts, and 375 slaves, of whom 200 were men. This list does not include individual expropriations. Mem-

23. Irwin to Weitzel, March 19, 1863, Banks to Irwin, March 19, 1863, Record Group 393; *OR*, LIII, 552; Stevens, *Fiftieth Massachusetts*, 85, 277; Sweetser, Journal, March 19, 1863, Hess Collection; George H. Hepworth, *The Whip, Hoe and Sword or, The Gulf-Department in '63*, ed. Joe Gray Taylor (1864; rpr. Baton Rouge, 1979), 252–53; Diary of Waters, March 19, 1863, Garb Collection; Howe, *Passages from Howe*, 41–42.

24. *OR*, XV, 266–67; Hepworth, *Whip, Hoe and Sword*, 259–60.

25. Captain Alfred F. Tremaine to Dudley, March 20, 1863, C. C. Augur Papers, Illinois State Archives, Springfield; *OR*, XV, 268.

bers of the 116th New York, for example, confiscated enough tobacco to last several months.[26]

At Port Hudson the day after the battle, soldiers and civilians alike rejoiced over the panic-stricken enemy retreat, although Sarah Morgan felt "positively disappointed! I did want to see them soundly thrashed!" The Port Hudson *Echo* advised General Banks "to get up a balloon expedition, and even then he would not be sure to drop in upon us unawares." The troops' confidence in themselves and their commander knew no bounds. No longer fearing an attack, Gardner allowed two-thirds of the troops to return to camp. The soldiers gathered up spent artillery projectiles, and Colonel I. G. W. Steedman obtained the captain's gig from the *Mississippi*, which furnished recreation for the officers of the 1st Alabama. But a sadness hung over the garrison that day as well, for the bodies of a woman and child were recovered from the creek where they had drowned while attempting to flee the preceding night.[27]

Although the passage of the *Hartford* and *Albatross* worried some in the garrison, Gardner expressed little concern. He believed the vessels would go the way of the *Queen of the West* and *Indianola*, a view shared by others. The threat of siege ended, Gardner changed the daily rations, issuing twice the rice, three times the peas, and an additional quarter pound of meat, but reducing the cornmeal to one pound. The men were pleased because the quality of the beef also improved. Only corn remained scarce. Gardner realized that Farragut would pass above the mouth of the Red River and requested Major General Richard Taylor to send steamboats loaded with corn when the danger had passed. Three transports arrived by the nineteenth and five more the next day; all but one delivered corn. The soldiers worked day and night to unload the vessels.[28]

26. *OR*, XV, 257; *ORN*, XX, 787; Memphis *Daily Appeal*, April 6, 1863; Howe, *Passages from Howe*, 42; Clark, *One Hundred and Sixteenth New York*, 66.

27. Dawson, *Confederate Girl's Diary*, 340; J. S. Gardner to Major D. F. Boyd, March 24, 1863, Boyd Papers; Jennings, *Plains*, 60; Memphis *Daily Appeal*, March 21 (citing Port Hudson *Echo*), 30, 1863; Eakin and Peoples, "In Defense of My Country . . .", 23; Cannon, *Inside Rebeldom*, 86–87; de Gournay, "Siege of Port Hudson"; McMorries, *First Alabama*, 56; Taylor, *Reluctant Rebel*, 195.

28. Wiley (ed.), "Letters of Magee," 209; Partin (ed.), "Report of a Corporal," 591; J. Wes Broom to Beautiful Lady [Miss G. A. Brigham], March 27, 1863, Brigham Family Papers; [Gardner], G.O. No. 28, March 15, 1863, Chap. II, Vol. 198,

Farragut's passage did bring about a few changes to the garrison. It provided an excuse for both Pemberton and Gardner to retain cannon intended for the trans-Mississippi because navigation on the Mississippi "was uncertain and dangerous." With water transportation to Bayou Sara threatened, surplus patients at Port Hudson had to be moved overland to hospitals in Clinton or Jackson instead of to Woodville.[29]

The bombardment of the fourteenth had also kindled fear at Port Hudson. The thought of impending death altered attitudes toward religion by both black and white. To one chaplain, "it was remarkable, the change that the bombardment made in many of the negroes. Before they were a careless, happy-go-lucky set, many of them quite profane. Afterwards they indulged largely in camp meeting songs, and one couldn't twist out an oath with a corkscrew."[30] Negro teamsters, cooks, and others held prayer meetings at night. A private wrote in his diary on March 29, "I believe a revival has already commenced in our midst, and I praise God for it." Some soldiers formed social organizations to promote religion through prayer meetings and other services.[31]

One procedure that did not change was the continued needless loss of foodstuffs. This waste took on added importance because most supplies now moved overland from Osyka. Gardner was repeatedly severely criticized over the handling of stores at Port Hudson during late March and April. By the end of April rations on hand had diminished, and the garrison wondered how much longer provisions would last.[32]

Another brigadier drew assignment to Port Hudson in early March, but he came without troops. A Kentuckian, graduate of West Point, and veteran of the Mexican War, Abraham Buford owned a stock farm in his native state when the war broke out. He maintained the classic neutrality of his state until General Braxton

Record Group 109; Cannon, *Inside Rebeldom*, 88–89; *OR*, XV, 275, 278–79, 1021, XXIV, Pt. I, 291.

29. *OR*, XV, 1024, Vol. XXIV, Pt. 3, p. 668; Hewitt and Bergeron (eds.), *Post Hospital Ledger*, v.

30. M'Neilly, "Under Fire at Port Hudson," 338.

31. Goodloe, *Rebel Relics*, 257–61.

32. *OR*, XV, 1022, 1061, Vol. XXIV, Pt. 1, pp. 297–98, 301, 305, 308–11, 313–15, 772; John W. Robison to My dear Companion [wife, Josephine], April 30, 1863, Robison Papers.

Bragg led a Confederate army into Kentucky during the fall of 1862. Even though Buford had two cousins who were generals in the Union army, he cast his lot with the Confederacy. Appointed a brigadier general to rank from September 2, 1862, he apparently received Port Hudson as his first assignment. Lieutenant General John C. Pemberton had to find a position for him and finally conceived the idea of a mixed brigade of infantry and cavalry in Gardner's district. Gardner found such an arrangement ridiculous. "I respectfully represent that the cavalry are encamped at Olive Branch, 15 miles from here," he replied. "I do not understand how I can make a brigade of infantry and cavalry."[33] On March 15 Buford reported for duty, and Gardner drew units from the other brigades and formed a fifth infantry brigade for him to command, composed of the 10th Arkansas, 3rd and 7th Kentucky, and Jeptha Edwards' and John Snodgrass' consolidated Alabama regiments. The four-gun Watson Louisiana Battery provided the artillery. The men easily identified Buford moving about camp; he weighed at least three hundred pounds.[34]

The 9th Louisiana Battalion Partisan Rangers skirmished with the enemy on March 15 and 16. The troopers spent more time gathering items discarded by the enemy than fighting, which hardly reassured local residents. When Gardner learned on the seventeenth that the enemy had sent out strong detachments to gather cotton, he advanced Beall's and Maxey's brigades to disrupt the Federals and force Banks to develop his army. The Confederates expected a major engagement, but none took place. The infantry gathered so much livestock and equipment—reportedly fifteen wagonloads abandoned by the Yankees in their flight—that a corporal concluded, "I think old Banks is about at his wits' end, and don't know what to do. You recollect Old Stonewall used to make a comissary of Banks, and now General Gardner has commenced making one of him."[35]

33. Warner, *Generals in Gray*, 39; *OR*, XV, 1005; [Gardner] to [Pemberton], March 7, 1863, Chap. II, Vol. 8, Record Group 109. The latter shows significant differences between the original and the version published in *OR*.

34. *OR*, XV, 273; Taylor, *Reluctant Rebel*, 105.

35. Partin (ed.), "Report of a Corporal," 591; Memphis *Daily Appeal*, March 31, 1863; Jennings, *Plains*, 61; *OR*, XV, 275–76; W. N. Parish to wife, March 18, 1863, Parish Civil War Letter; Eugene to Stella, March 18, 1863, Hunter-Taylor Family Papers, Louisiana State University Department of Archives and History, Baton Rouge; M'Neilly, "Under Fire at Port Hudson," 338.

The Federal fleet below Port Hudson repeatedly shelled the garrison following Farragut's passage. On March 19 the *Monongahela* (with Banks aboard), *Genesee*, and *Essex* engaged the enemy batteries for at least an hour at a range of twelve to thirteen hundred yards and drove the Confederate transports from the landing. Shells from the Federal fleet interrupted the unloading of supplies for the next several days, but the Confederates did not return the fire. The naval fire did little damage, but the range of the one hundred- and two hundred-pound Parrotts aboard the *Genesee* and *Monongahela*, apparently six miles, impressed the Confederates. Steamboats docked at the wharves attracted deadly attention. Tiring of this consistent inconvenience from the Federal fleet, Gardner established a landing on Thompson's Creek. He ordered each brigadier to detach his smallest regiment to the new site, where the men worked round the clock to unload the transports.[36]

To add to Gardner's worries, Federal troops advanced up the railroad from New Orleans on March 23. The next day they drove the southerners out of Ponchatoula. The Confederates fell back four miles and telegraphed for assistance. Pemberton rushed forward reinforcements from Mississippi, and Gardner sent troops from Port Hudson under Colonel J. M. Simonton. On the twenty-eighth the Federals fell back to a point eight miles south of Ponchatoula. Simonton arrived the night of the thirtieth, and the following day the southerners advanced to attack the Federals. After observing the enemy's position, Simonton deemed an assault unwise. Garland's Mississippi Battalion Cavalry deployed along the Amite River, and Simonton remained in command at Ponchatoula.[37]

To support the Federal move on Ponchatoula, Colonel Franklin S. Nickerson made a diversion with the 14th Maine and three companies of cavalry. His expedition moved from the Mississippi River at Bonnet Carre toward Springfield and Ponchatoula. Some

36. *ORN*, XX, 784–86, ser. II, Vol. I, pp. 93, 149; Schley, *Forty-Five Years*, 43–44; Smith, *Company K*, 55; Taylor (ed.), *Reluctant Rebel*, 106–107; *OR*, XV, 279; [Gardner], S.O. No. 82, March 21, 1863, Chap. II, Vol. 198, Record Group 109; John A. Morgan to sister, March 24, [1863], John A. Morgan Papers.

37. *OR*, XV, 282–83, 287, 289, 1061, Vol. XXIV, Pt. 3, p. 693; [Gardner], S.O. No. 86, March 25, 1863, Chap. II, Vol. 198, [Gardner] to Simonton, April 9, 1863, Chap. II, Vol. 8, both in Record Group 109.

of the Maine soldiers seized two flatboats on Bayou Manchac to ferry their regiment across the Amite River. Captain B. F. Bryan learned of the movement and led twenty-one Louisiana cavalrymen to a bluff adjacent to the Amite and about one hundred yards below the mouth of the bayou. When the boats floated past about 10 P.M. on the twenty-sixth, the Louisianians opened fire and the Yankees jumped overboard, abruptly ending the diversion. [38]

Following Banks's withdrawal from Port Hudson, the Confederates returned to their routine, improving the fortifications and drilling. March 22 passed quietly, both sides apparently respecting the sabbath. The tranquillity continued except for a violent storm during the night of the twenty-third, and by the following day the opposing pickets had resumed trading various commodities, both sides forgetting the deadly conflict of the preceding week. President Jefferson Davis declared March 27 a day for fasting and prayer, and Gardner suspended all details he could. By the end of the month rumors circulated that the Federals had given up all hope of taking Port Hudson and were vacating Baton Rouge, but the Confederates were in for a surprise. [39]

With Farragut above Port Hudson, Banks turned his attention to western Louisiana. He moved his headquarters to New Orleans on the twenty-fourth. Three days later he began shifting his troops to Donaldsonville for a march on Thibodaux. No shortage of cavalry or water transportation would delay his efforts to destroy or disperse Taylor's forces.

Possibly Banks believed that Farragut's curtailment of food arriving at Port Hudson would force the garrison to evacuate the post and thereby provide him with a bloodless victory. By directing his attention—and troops—west of the Mississippi River, however, he allowed Gardner additional time to strengthen his hold on Port Hudson. Banks's faulty strategy also gave the Confederate high command east of the river the freedom to transfer troops from Port Hudson to more threatened positions.

In a letter on March 13 explaining his situation, Banks requested Grant's cooperation. Grant offered an army corps if Banks could provide water transportation and concluded, ''The best aid

---

38. *OR*, XV, 259, 281, 1062; Memphis *Daily Appeal*, March 30, April 15, 1863.

39. Lindsley (ed.), *Military Annals*, 448; Cannon, *Inside Rebeldom*, 89; Simpson, Diary, March 24, 1863, Simpson Papers; Memphis *Daily Appeal*, April 3, 1863; John [A. Morgan] to sister, March 30, 1863, John A. Morgan Papers.

you can give me, if you cannot pass Port Hudson, will be to hold as many of the enemy there as possible." Grant appeared eager to furnish the necessary manpower to capture Port Hudson so that Banks could move to assist him. Grant expanded on the subject of reinforcements for Banks in a letter to Farragut, stating that he might be able to provide Banks with twenty thousand men on the Red River if the Lake Providence Canal could be completed.[40]

Separated by Confederate forces, the two generals could send messages only by warship, making effective cooperation impossible. Farragut's secretary, Edward C. Gabaudan, committed Grant's letters to memory and slipped past the batteries at Port Hudson in a skiff disguised as a tree. He made it to Banks's headquarters at Brashear City on April 10, the exchange of views taking twenty-eight days. Banks immediately replied that he could cooperate with fifteen thousand men in a movement against Port Hudson by May 10. Gabaudan returned to Baton Rouge, crossed the swamp opposite Port Hudson, and reached the *Hartford* on April 15. Grant received the message on May 2. Both generals also sent other messages that hindered rather than helped any possible cooperation.

The strategic situation had changed drastically since Grant had first written Banks forty days before. Grant now had a foothold east of the Mississippi below Vicksburg, and he saw no reason to delay his advance against that city. Consequently, he decided to retain all his troops for that movement and so notified Banks on May 10. Grant also requested Banks to bring all available troops to operate against Vicksburg. Banks received the message two days later at Alexandria and was able for the first time to evaluate the situation properly. Having dispersed Taylor's forces, he could gain nothing by advancing beyond Alexandria. Limited transportation would require weeks to move his army to Vicksburg, and such a move might leave New Orleans open to attack. Consequently, he chose to move against Port Hudson and immediately set his troops in motion.[41]

Banks's movement west of the Mississippi had indeed prompted

40. *OR*, XV, 258–59, 300–301, 692–94.

41. Greene, *Mississippi*, 221–25; *ORN*, XX, 788; Farragut, "Passing Port Hudson," 320–21; Howard C. Westwood, "The Vicksburg/Port Hudson Gap—The Pincers Never Pinched," *Military Affairs: The Journal of Military History, Including Theory and Technology*, XLVI (1982), 113–18.

Brigadier General William
Nelson Rector Beall
From the author's collection

Confederate Barracks
*Courtesy of the U.S. Army Military History Institute, Carlisle Barracks,
Pennsylvania*

Commander William
David "Dirty Bill" Porter
*Courtesy of the U.S.Army
Military History Institute,
Carlisle Barracks, Pennsylvania*

USS *Essex*
*Courtesy of the Department of Archives and Manuscripts, Hill Memorial Library,
Louisiana State University, Baton Rouge*

Major General Nathaniel Prentiss Banks
From the author's collection

Major General Franklin Gardner

Courtesy of the Department of Archives and Manuscripts, Hill Memorial Library, Louisiana State University, Baton Rouge

Rear Admiral David Glasgow Farragut
Courtesy of William Gladstone, Westport, Connecticut

Lieutenant George Dewey

From Francis T. Miller, The Photographic History of the Civil War
(New York, 1910)

USS *Mississippi*
Courtesy of the Department of Archives and Manuscripts, Hill Memorial Library,
Louisiana State University, Baton Rouge

Colonel Isaiah George
Washington Steedman
Courtesy of the Depart-
ment of Archives and
Manuscripts, Hill Memo-
rial Library, Louisiana
State University, Baton
Rouge

Fort Desperate
Courtesy of the National Archives

Colonel William R. Miles
From the author's collection

Scene of the Negro charge on May 27, 1863
Courtesy of the Illinois State Historical Library, Springfield, Illinois

Recruiting poster sponsored by black abolitionists in
Philadelphia

Courtesy of the Chicago Public Library Special Collections Division

Black infantry at Port Hudson
Courtesy of the National Archives

a Confederate redeployment. Gardner ordered Rust's brigade and most of Buford's to join Pemberton in early April. "Satisfied that the enemy will not make an immediate advance on this point," Gardner unsuccessfully requested an eighteen-day leave on the seventh. By the end of the month Gardner's force, including the garrison at Ponchatoula, numbered fewer than twelve thousand effective troops. And he faced an unusual threat.[42]

Gardner received word on April 24 of a new danger—Union cavalry moving south from Tennessee, possibly headed for Baton Rouge. He immediately ordered the 10th Arkansas and one company of the 9th Tennessee Battalion Cavalry to Tangipahoa. He also sent the 7th Texas, eighty troopers of the 9th Louisiana Battalion Partisan Rangers, and two guns of Bledsoe's Missouri battery to Woodville. Later that day he learned that the enemy was "reportedly" moving on Woodville from Hazlehurst and ordered the cavalry north of Clinton to advance on Woodville. Gardner continued to move units about during the next forty-eight hours in a vain endeavor to capture the Federals. Not until after 10 P.M. on April 30 did he learn that the enemy had doubled back toward Osyka.[43] Gardner correctly surmised that the Federals were attempting to reach Baton Rouge, and he planned to cut them off at Williams' bridge on the Amite River.

While Garland's battalion of weary men and jaded horses and the exhausted Louisianians of Miles's Legion pursued the Federals, Gardner ordered troops from Port Hudson to seize the bridge. Colonel A. J. Brown moved with two regiments and a battery at 3 P.M. on May 1. The men bivouacked for the night at Olive Branch and arrived at the bridge at ten the next morning. But Brown had to notify Gardner, "We were unfortunately about 10 hours too late."[44] Gardner promptly arrested Lieutenant Colonels George Gantt and C. C. Wilbourne, whose disobedience of orders was

42. [Gardner] to Lt. Col. J. R. Waddy, April 7, 1863, Chap. II, Vol. 8, Record Group 109; *OR*, XV, 717, 1035–37, 1059.

43. *OR*, Vol. XXIV, Pt. 1, pp. 545, 553, Pt. 3, pp. 782, 805; [Gardner], S.O. No. 116, April 24, 1863, [Gardner], S.O. No. 120, April 28, 1863, [Gardner], S.O. No. 122, April 30, 1863, Chap. II, Vol. 198, [Gardner] to Gantt, April 28, 1863, [Gardner] to Gantt, April 29, 1863, Chap. II, Vol. 8, all in Record Group 109.

44. Brown to [Gardner], May 2, 1863, Entry 138, Record Group 109; *OR*, XV, 1070, Vol. XXIV, Pt. 1, pp. 543, 545–46; [Tennessee] Centennial Commission, *Tennesseans in the Civil War*, I, 297; Dixon, Diary, May 1, 2, 1863, Dixon Papers. Possibly the 46th Tennessee also formed part of Brown's force.

largely responsible for the enemy's escape. Instead of advancing to meet the Federals, they deployed their men to ambush the approaching enemy west of Hazlehurst; while they waited, the Federals doubled back to Brookhaven. Gardner also renewed his request for "a good cavalry commander." Gardner's embarrassment increased when he learned that the Federals had surprised Captain Bryan's cavalry in camp and captured thirty-eight men before entering Baton Rouge. Bryan managed to escape by climbing a tree and lying flat on a large limb while the Federals passed below.[45]

The monotony at Baton Rouge was broken on the afternoon of May 2, when a lookout atop the Capitol sighted a heavy cloud of dust in the distance. Much to everyone's surprise, it proved to be the 6th and 7th Illinois Cavalry, commanded by Colonel Benjamin H. Grierson. The troopers had successfully passed through six hundred miles of enemy-held territory in fewer than sixteen days. The Federals went wild with enthusiasm and cheered the cavalrymen when they rode into town, the garrison amazed at the daring raid.[46]

With Grant's army having landed east of the Mississippi River below Vicksburg, Pemberton faced a threat much worse than Grierson's cavalry disrupting his communications. He ordered Gardner to gather all supplies possible from the west bank and send him reinforcements. While a portion of the 1st Alabama collected and transported cattle, sheep, and corn across the river with Federal vessels above and below Port Hudson, Gardner began transferring units to Pemberton. Gregg's thirty-three hundred troops marched on May 2. Two days later Pemberton telegraphed Gardner to move with Maxey's brigade. On May 6 Gardner forwarded Maxey's brigade, Colonel Brown's detachment, Miles's Legion, and two cavalry companies and ordered Colonel Simonton to move his command to Port Hudson. Gardner also relinquished command of the Third Military District to Brigadier General Beall. Small compensation for the thousands of departing infantrymen arrived on the sixth in the form of a cannon. Confederates salvaged

45. *OR*, XV, 1075, Vol. XXIV, Pt. 1, pp. 537–38; [Gardner], S.O. 126, May 4, 1863, Chap. II, Vol. 198, Record Group 109; Jennings, *Plains*, 63.

46. Stevens, *Fiftieth Massachusetts*, 98; William Cullen Bryant II (ed.), "A Yankee Soldier Looks at the Negro," *Civil War History*, VII (1961), 143; Clark, *One Hundred and Sixteenth New York*, 70–71; Charles F. Wadsworth to father, May 6, 1863, Wadsworth Papers.

the 4.62-inch rifled bronze gun from the U.S.S. *Barataria*, which the Federals had abandoned at the mouth of the Amite River on April 7. Clumsily mounted on a twenty-four-pounder siege carriage, the cannon was christened "The Baby."[47]

While Grant held Confederate attention, the Federals below Port Hudson also became aggressive. Farragut returned to New Orleans via the Atchafalaya River and ordered the mortar boats to take up a position to shell Port Hudson on May 5. The vessels opened on the eighth, commencing a bombardment that became a ritual during the nights ahead. The first fatality from the mortar fire took place the night of May 9, when a thirteen-inch shell struck a soldier standing in Battery No. 9 about the neck and pushed him head first through the wooden platform, leaving only his feet visible. During the afternoon of the seventeenth, a mortar shell buried itself in the earth below four lounging soldiers. The ensuing explosion killed three and wounded the fourth. Adjusting to the bombardment was impossible, but it did not "cause a good soldier to flinch," concluded one lieutenant. "It has the tendency to make a man either a good Christian or a fatalist, according to his early training or latent religious belief."[48]

On the night of May 9, Lieutenant Colonel Paul F. de Gournay took four rifled cannon three miles downriver. At first light his men opened fire on the *Essex* and *Richmond*. The Confederates peppered the ships for almost two hours, until their guns became disabled or their ammunition was expended. Commander C. H. B. Caldwell on board the *Essex* thought eight cannon had bombarded the vessels. The southerners sustained some half-dozen casualties; the vessels suffered hardly at all. An attempt a few days later to destroy a vessel with a torpedo proved equally unsuccessful.[49]

On May 11 the 3rd Louisiana Native Guards marched from Baton Rouge to Monte Sano Bayou and commenced building

47. *OR*, XV, 1070–71, 1076; Moore (ed.), *Rebellion Record*, VII, 267; D. M. Hughes to Wilson, May 4, 1863, Entry 138, Record Group 109; [Wright], *Port Hudson*, 21; Lindsley (ed.), *Military Annals*, 448; [Gardner], G.O. No. 41, May 6, 1863, Chap II, Vol. 198, Record Group 109; Smith, *Company K*, 56; Edward Bacon, *Among the Cotton Thieves* (Detroit, 1867), 94; Memphis *Daily Appeal*, April 13, 1863.

48. [Wright], *Port Hudson*, 22–23; *ORN*, XX, 178–79, 791–92; Dabney to [Gardner], August 24, 1863, LHA Collection; "Fortification and Siege," 313.

49. Houston *Tri-Weekly Telegraph*, June 1, 1863; *ORN*, XX, 247, 775–76; Smith, *Company K*, 56–58; Kendall, "Recollections," 1110.

bridges. Colonel N. A. M. Dudley led a brigade twelve miles out the Clinton road the next day. After continual skirmishing for the last four miles, he withdrew to the Bayou Sara road, leaving the 50th Massachusetts, two cannon, and a cavalry squadron at the bridge across White's Bayou. Supported by Grierson's Illinois Cavalry, Dudley pushed up the Bayou Sara road on the thirteenth. Severe skirmishing started before the column reached Plains Store, but Company A, 6th Illinois Cavalry, managed to reach the railroad, where the troopers destroyed three hundred yards of track and cut the telegraph line to Clinton. The entire column then withdrew to Mrs. A. D. Alexander's and Ray Turner Merritt's plantations on the Bayou Sara road. Grierson's troops skirmished with the 9th Tennessee Battalion Cavalry at Redwood Creek Bridge on the Plank Road on the fourteenth, but the Federal infantry failed to advance. The Confederates reopened communications with Clinton May 15, and the soldiers rejoiced when they received several weeks' back mail.[50]

On May 2, Pemberton had recommended to Davis that Port Hudson be evacuated unless he received substantial reinforcements. But Davis replied on May 7: "To hold both Vicksburg and Port Hudson is necessary to a connection with Trans-Mississippi. You may expect whatever is in my power to do." Pemberton immediately ordered Gardner to "return with 2,000 troops to Port Hudson and hold it to the last. President says both places must be held."[51]

Gardner resumed command on May 11 and gathered what forces remained. He ordered Colonel William R. Miles to return with his legion and brought in all the infantry from Olive Branch except the 11th and 17th Arkansas. Captain Charles R. Purdy's Lake Providence Cadets (Company C) stayed to guard nearby Jackson when the remainder of the 4th Louisiana left for Mississippi. Receiving no orders, Purdy decided that his men would prove more valuable at Port Hudson, and he marched his company into the garrison.[52]

50. Company G, 3rd Native Guard, Return, May, 1863, Roll 348, Microcopy 619; *OR*, XV, 409–11, 728, Vol. XXVI, Pt. 1, p. 34; Stevens, *Fiftieth Massachusetts*, 286; Howe, *Passages from Howe*, 46; Map Z218; Logan to [Gardner], May 15, 1863, Entry 138, Record Group 109; Smith, *Company K*, 59.

51. *OR*, Vol. XXIV, Pt. 3, pp. 815, 842, XV, 1080.

52. Gardner, G.O. No. 42, May 11, 1863, Chap. II, Vol. 198, Record Group 109; [Wright], *Port Hudson*, 21, 30–31; *OR*, Vol. XXVI, Pt. 2, p. 3; A. Curl, "The Fight

Gardner undoubtedly welcomed this unexpected reinforcement. He would need every one of them if Banks concentrated his troops and moved against Port Hudson.

Twenty-four hours after he despaired over Grant's failure to provide reinforcements and his own inability to join Grant, Banks reversed himself. On May 13 he notified Farragut and Grant that he would move his army via Simmesport to Grand Gulf and unite with Grant. Consequently, he asked the admiral to leave the *Hartford* above Port Hudson while Augur moved to block the supposed Confederate evacuation. But later that day Banks again seemed indecisive. He sent Brigadier General William Dwight with a plea to Grant for reinforcements to enable him to capture Port Hudson quickly. Before contacting Grant, however, Dwight sent word on the evening of the sixteenth that "Port Hudson is evacuated except one Brigade. . . . Move with all disposable force at once, immediately—precipitately against Port Hudson—I will have a Corps on the way to aid you soon—*Very soon*—But you will need only half your force much less aid, to capture Port Hudson." Dwight caught up with Grant the following day, and the latter promised to send troops to Port Hudson—a commitment he quickly forgot. But Banks acted on Dwight's initial correspondence and the advice of his chief of staff and his adjutant. He changed his plans once again. He would move on Port Hudson immediately.[53]

---

at Clinton, La.," *Confederate Veteran*, XIII (1905), 122; Booth, *Louisiana Soldiers*, Vol. III, Bk. 2, p. 218.

53. Dwight to [Banks], May 16, 1863, 8:30 P.M., original in author's collection; *OR*, XV, 731–32, Vol. XXVI, Pt. 1, pp. 488–90; *ORN*, XX, 178; Irwin, *Nineteenth Corps*, 157; Westwood, "Vicksburg/Port Hudson Gap." 117; U. S. Grant, *Personal Memoirs of U. S. Grant* (2 vols.; New York, 1885), I, 524.

VII

Surrounded: May, 1863

*The enemy are coming, but mark you, many a one will get to
hell before he does to Port Hudson.*
— Major General Franklin Gardner,
Third District, Department of
Mississippi and East Louisiana

Once Banks had decisively committed himself, he rapidly deployed his forces to achieve his goals—a swift capture of Port Hudson followed by a junction with Grant. On May 14 three divisions started from Alexandria to Simmesport. The men began crossing the Atchafalaya on the nineteenth and landed at Bayou Sara at 2 A.M. on the twenty-second. If these troops could unite east of Port Hudson with two divisions moving northward from Baton Rouge and New Orleans, the Confederate garrison at Port Hudson would find itself isolated. [1]

To thwart Banks's planned encirclement, Gardner on May 18 sent three companies of the 1st Alabama across the river to prevent enemy communication across the point. When the first company landed at the junction of the Mississippi and False River levees, the twenty-five Alabamians found themselves face to face with the enemy. Five companies of Union cavalry had ridden down the west bank on a reconnaissance to clear out the Confederates who shipped supplies across the river. The troopers attacked immediately and drove the southerners back. When the other two companies arrived, the Confederates advanced, but the enemy had vanished. The initial encounter had convinced the Federals that they faced an overwhelming force. With their commander drunk and five

---

1. *OR*, Vol. XXVI, Pt. 1, p. 492; Irwin, *Nineteenth Corps*, 153–54, 159.

miles in the rear, the troopers fled with all the cattle they had collected and twenty-eight prisoners. The Alabamians returned to the east bank on the twenty-first.[2]

On the night of May 18, Confederates attacked Colonel N. A. M. Dudley's cavalry pickets on the Bayou Sara road. This action convinced Dudley to make a reconnaissance in full force the following day. The northerners drove Stockdale's Mississippians more than seven miles to a point north of Plains Store and then countermarched to Merritt's plantation, where Dudley requested reinforcements from Major General Christopher C. Augur. Colonel Frank P. Powers brought additional cavalry to assist Captain T. R. Stockdale. Some three hundred southerners deployed south of the store and placed two six-pound howitzers in the road.[3]

Both sides sent reinforcements to the Bayou Sara road on the twentieth. Augur joined Dudley with Colonel Edward P. Chapin's brigade and prepared to advance the next morning. Gardner sent Major Erastus L. Black with three hundred infantry from various regiments and Abbay's five-gun battery to assist Powers.[4]

A message from General Joseph E. Johnston reached Gardner on May 21. Written on the nineteenth, it ordered Gardner to "evacuate Port Hudson forthwith." Gardner, recalling the words of President Davis, was determined to fight instead. He shot back: "A large force . . . is moving down to cross at Bayou Sara against this place. His whole force from Baton Rouge is in my front. I am very weak and should be rapidly re-enforced." Johnston telegraphed on the twenty-third to avoid an investment and save the troops, but by then it was too late.[5]

After a meager beefless breakfast, Augur's division moved out at six o'clock on the morning of the twenty-first, with Dudley's brigade in the lead. Three companies of the 30th Massachusetts

2. OR, Vol. XXVI, Pt. 1, pp. 36–37; Wisconsin State Journal, undated clipping, Archives Division, State Historical Society of Wisconsin, Madison; ORN, XX, 793; Townsend, Sixteenth New Hampshire, 175; Record of Events, Company C, 1st Alabama, Compiled Service Records of Confederate Soldiers Who Served in Organizations from the State of Alabama, Roll 83, Microcopy 311, National Archives.

3. OR, Vol. XXVI, Pt. 1, pp. 38–39; New Orleans Daily Picayune, July 30, 1905, Pt. 3, p. 11; Mobile Advertiser and Register, July 17, 1863.

4. [Auger], G.O. No. 1, May 20, 1863, Roll 348, Microcopy 619; Dabney to [Gardner], August 24, 1863, LHA Collection; Estes [comp.], List of Field Officers, 13; Little Rock Arkansas Gazette, October 25, 1936, mag. sect., 3.

5. OR, Vol. XXVI, Pt. 2, p. 9, Vol. LII, Pt. 2, pp. 476, 482.

met stiff resistance when they clashed with Powers' forces three-quarters of a mile south of Plains Store about 10 A.M. The Federals deployed two guns but after thirty minutes failed to silence the enemy's cannon. Eventually eight guns joined the bombardment, but the northerners still could not muffle the opposing battery, which continued to hold them at bay. To end the deadlock, Augur moved two regiments through the woods to the east. Before these units could outflank the southerners, however, the latter had to retreat, their ammunition expended. Augur's men resumed their advance to the store, where they deployed shortly after noon to await the arrival of Banks. One section of Battery G, 5th U.S. Artillery, advanced on the road leading to Port Hudson and the other on the road leading to Bayou Sara. [6]

Powers reformed his command near the railroad. Their ammunition replenished, the Confederates swept southward along the Bayou Sara road that afternoon, most of the troopers fighting on foot. The 174th New York rushed to support the 2nd Vermont Battery, which had deployed two hundred yards north of the store, and the struggle continued. The southerners pushed the Federals back, but the Vermonters, firing canister, finally managed to halt the onslaught and repulse Powers' assault. [7]

At noon, Gardner dispatched Colonel William R. Miles with four hundred infantry and Boone's battery to assist Powers. Two companies of the 15th Arkansas picketed the road to Port Hudson. During the afternoon they skirmished with enemy cavalry moving westward from Plains Store until Miles arrived and quickly dispersed the troopers. Lieutenant Colonel Frederick B. Brand took three companies of Miles's Legion south of the road, while Major James T. Coleman took two companies on a wide detour through the woods on the north. Coleman's Louisianians emerged from an apple orchard on the flank of the enemy's cannon, and the major ordered his men to charge—right into an overwhelming force. Their sheer audacity startled the 48th Massachusetts, which sup-

6. Clark, *One Hundred and Sixteenth New York*, 76; Johns, *Forty-ninth Massachusetts*, 207; [Augur], G.O. No. 1, May 20, 1863, Roll 348, Microcopy 619; *OR*, Vol. XXVI, Pt. 1, p. 121; Martin, "Reminiscences of an Arkansan," 70.

7. Diary of Lt. R. W. Ford (7th Texas Infantry), May 21, 1863 (typescript copy), in possession of Russell Surles, Jr., Dallas, Tex.; Martin, "Reminiscences of an Arkansan," 70; New Orleans *Daily Picayune*, July 30, 1905, Pt. 3, p. 11; *OR*, Vol. XXVI, Pt. 1, p. 121; Captain P. E. Holcomb to [Augur], [n.d.], Augur Papers.

ported the artillery. Lieutenant Colonel James O'Brien mistakenly attempted to wheel his inexperienced regiment to face the rear. Although the 48th had withstood enemy artillery fire earlier, the new threat threw them into confusion and they fled in disgrace to the rear. Their support routed, the U.S. regulars attempted to save their cannon. They managed to remove one gun, but the Confederates shot the horses and drivers of the second piece and seized it. [8]

About 3 P.M., while the 116th New York and 49th Massachusetts were stacking arms in the field southeast of the intersection, the men heard firing in the direction of Port Hudson. One of Dudley's staff officers appeared with an order for Colonel Edward P. Chapin to send the 116th New York to the front. Chapin refused, saying, with some sarcasm, that he had learned neither of Augur's death nor of his relinquishing command of the division to Dudley. Suddenly a member of Augur's staff rode up and ordered Chapin to lead two regiments via a wagon path northwest to support the guns on the Port Hudson road.

The 49th Massachusetts and 116th New York had moved but a short distance when they received a volley of musketry at point-blank range from Brand's Louisianians. Simultaneously, the panic-stricken members of the 48th Massachusetts burst into the ranks of the 49th, throwing the men of both into the 116th New York. Major George M. Love shouted to them to "stand fast," and the New Yorkers held firm while the rabble fled to the rear. The 116th then advanced a short distance, where Augur deployed the men in line of battle.

No sooner had the soldiers executed the order than a volley of musketry swept their rear. The New Yorkers faced about and exchanged some twenty or thirty rounds with the enemy. Augur faced a desperate situation. With few exceptions, none of his troops had combat experience, and only his calm, determined manner helped ease their fear. Finally, Augur asked Major Love if his regiment could manage a charge. Love replied, "The One Hundred and Sixteenth will do anything you order them to." Augur instructed him to advance. Love relayed the message to each captain, and he took position at the center of the regiment. Leading the

---

8. Miles to [Gardner], July 24, 1863, Dabney to [Gardner], August 24, 1863, LHA Collection; Plummer, *Forty-eighth M.V.M.*, 34; *OR*, Vol. XXVI, Pt. 1, pp. 71, 121; [Chapin] to [Augur], May 23, 1863, Augur Papers.

charge twenty paces in advance of the line, Love waved his men on with his hat. The New Yorkers surged forward, shouting demonic yells. The Confederates retreated three hundred yards across an open field and into another patch of woods, just west of a graveyard. There the southerners wheeled about and returned fire. The 116th exchanged a few rounds before Augur ordered a second charge, forcing the Confederates back a second time. Facing encirclement, Miles managed to outflank the enemy's left with two guns of Boone's battery. Lieutenant E. P. Harmanson handled the cannon so effectively that he halted the Federal onslaught and enabled Miles to withdraw in good order. Lacking horses, Coleman had to abandon the captured cannon. The fighting at an end on this portion of the field, the New Yorkers scoured the woods and brought in about seventy prisoners, mostly of French origin, who expressed their loyalty for the Union by crying, "*Vive la Republic.*" The 116th also picked up the abandoned colors of the 49th Massachusetts.[9]

As Powers and Miles were attempting to disengage, Colonel John Logan's Arkansans advanced from the southeast and struck a train of some fifty wagons strung out along the Bayou Sara road in the Federal rear. Eight companies of the 21st Maine advanced to meet them and soon forced the southerners to withdraw to Olive Branch. Black's infantry, dragging some of Abbay's cannon by hand, joined Miles, and together they returned to Port Hudson. Powers' cavalry withdrew to Freeman's plantation, on the road to Clinton.[10]

Both sides congratulated themselves and licked their wounds. Despite the duration and ferocity of the battle, casualties amounted to only about one hundred on either side. A flag of truce the following afternoon allowed the Confederates to remove their dead and gave the northerners a chance to look over the battlefield. The two-story structure that stood at the crossroads attracted the most attention. The first floor contained a drugstore and post office; a

9. Clark, *One Hundred and Sixteenth New York*, 76–80, 82; *OR*, Vol. XXVI, Pt. 1, p. 71; [Chapin] to [Augur], May 23, 1863, Augur Papers; [Wright], *Port Hudson*, 24–25; Booth, *Louisiana Soldiers*, Vol. III, Bk. 1, p. 191; Johns, *Forty-ninth Massachusetts*, 212, 214.

10. Woodward, *21st Me.*, 28–29; Logan to Gardner, May 21, 1863, Entry 138, Record Group 109; Martin, "Reminiscences of an Arkansan," 70; New Orleans *Daily Picayune*, July 30, 1905, Pt. 3, p. 11.

Masonic lodge occupied the upper level. Several artillery rounds struck the building, one bursting open the door of the Masons' hall. [11]

While the Battle of Plains Store raged, Gardner inspected the garrison. As was his custom, he rode unattended. He listened to the distant firing, and his face reddened and his eyes glowed. The cannoneers at the river batteries knew at a glance that he desired combat. After confirming their readiness, he pointed toward the fighting and said, "The enemy are coming, but mark you, many a one will get to hell before he does to Port Hudson." [12]

Banks also heard the firing at Plains Store. Worried that the Confederates might escape, the general hastened to complete the encirclement. On May 22 the curses of southern women and a driving rainstorm accompanied Grover's division southward from Bayou Sara until it linked up with Grierson's cavalry, whereupon Grover's men bivouacked south of Thompson's Creek. Paine's division camped about one mile in Grover's rear. Grierson's troopers occupied the intersection of the Port Hudson and Jackson and Baton Rouge and Bayou Sara roads. Augur's men blocked the road leading from Port Hudson to Clinton via Plains Store. Brigadier General Thomas W. Sherman's division disembarked at Springfield Landing and marched to the Bayou Sara road, where it deployed on Augur's left, blocking any Confederate escape toward Baton Rouge. Thus, by the evening of the twenty-second, the Federals had effectively besieged the garrison of Port Hudson. The following day, the 110th and 162nd New York, two guns of the 6th Massachusetts Battery, and two companies of cavalry occupied the west bank. Together with the naval vessels above and below, Banks believed this force sufficient to block any escape to the west. [13]

Banks continued to tighten his encirclement until the night of

11. Clark, *One Hundred and Sixteenth New York*, 81–82; [Wright], *Port Hudson*, 25; Irwin, *Nineteenth Corps*, 162; Howe, *Passages from Howe*, 47; Johns, *Forty-ninth Massachusetts*, 211, 214; F. N. Deland, *Some Recollections of the Civil War* (Pittsfield, Mass., 1909), 20; Map of Plains Store, Augur Papers. The store was the only structure at the crossroads.

12. McMorries, *First Alabama*, 58.

13. *Twenty-Fifth Connecticut*, 43; Irwin, *Nineteenth Corps*, 160, 165–66; OR, Vol. XXVI, Pt. 1, p. 107; *A Memorial of Brevet Brigadier General Lewis Benedict, Colonel of 162nd Regiment N.Y.V.I., Who Fell in Battle at Pleasant Hill, La., April 9, 1864* (Albany, N.Y., 1866), 54.

the twenty-sixth. Brigadier General Godfrey Weitzel's division moved south on the Telegraph Road with Paine's on its left. Grover's marched southwest on the Jackson road, Augur's west on the Clinton road, and Sherman's northwest on the Baton Rouge road. Banks had to slow his approach the closer he came to his foe, particularly because of the stubborn resistance encountered on his right flank. Gardner had reinforced Confederate pickets in that area until Colonel I. G. W. Steedman had nearly a thousand men deployed from Big Sandy Creek on the west to near the Jackson road on the east, the line generally running one-half mile north of the mill. These troops, drawn from almost every unit in the Port Hudson garrison, bought Gardner the precious time he needed to complete his northern defenses. He placed Steedman in command of the left wing, consisting of the 1st Alabama (six companies), 10th and 15th Arkansas, 39th Mississippi, Herod's, Bradford's (one section), and the Watson (one section) batteries, the 9th Louisiana Battalion Partisan Rangers, and the provost guard battalion. Some twenty-one hundred men covered one-third, or one and one-half miles, of the defenses. [14]

Brigadier General Beall commanded the center, occupied by the 49th Alabama, 8th Battalion, 12th, 14th, 16th, 18th, 23rd, and detachments of the 11th and 17th Arkansas, 1st Mississippi, and Abbay's, the Watson (two sections), and Bradford's (one section) batteries. His twenty-three hundred men also defended one-third of the line. [15]

Gardner placed the right wing under Colonel Miles. Besides his legion, Miles had the 9th Louisiana Battalion, Boone's battery (six guns), Roberts' battery (two sections), and two makeshift battalions, one composed of fragments of Maxey's and Gregg's brigades and one of surplus artillerymen of de Gournay's battalion. With

14. *OR*, Vol. XXVI, Pt. 1, pp. 156, 501, Pt. 2, p. 10; Sprague, *13th Connecticut*, 136–37; Irwin, *Nineteenth Corps*, 166; Steedman to [Gardner], n.d. (two letters), Provision Returns for May, 1863, Entry 138, Record Group 109; Mobile *Advertiser and Register*, August 9, 1863; Miles to [Gardner], May 26, 1863, Shelby to [Gardner], August 5, 1863, LHA Collection; [Wright], *Port Hudson*, 25–26. Confederate troop figures are based on incomplete returns, provision records, and parole lists. Of the 7,450 officers and men in the garrison, roughly 20 percent were too sick at the time of investment to perform their duties. Figures in the text represent those present for duty at the breastworks.

15. [Wright], *Port Hudson*, 26. The 18th Arkansas did not come under Steedman's command until after the fighting had commenced on May 27.

some 950 infantry and 200 cannoneers, Miles had to defend one-third of the breastworks with one-fifth of the available manpower. It was no small task. Three hundred cannoneers manned the heavy artillery, leaving only a single relief crew for each gun. [16]

Gardner also had some twelve hundred troops operating in Banks's rear. This force consisted of all the cavalry, except for most of the 9th Louisiana Battalion Partisan Rangers, under command of Colonel Powers, and Colonel John Griffith's 11th and 17th Consolidated Arkansas mounted infantry. Colonel John Logan had overall command of these forces. Gardner had welcomed Logan's suggestion to mount his infantrymen but vehemently opposed taking horses "from carriages whilst persons were at church or from minors without their consent." Logan also had two guns of Roberts' battery. [17]

Gardner originally had expected a besieging army to advance only from the south and so had no fortifications on the northern sector west of Little Sandy Creek. Thinking the area safe, particularly during periods of high water, the Confederates had built their gristmill and ordnance shops there. While the 9th Louisiana Battalion Partisan Rangers attempted to delay the enemy's advance from Bayou Sara, Gardner hurried to secure his vulnerable left flank. Steedman's troops hastily fortified the high ground immediately south of Little Sandy Creek and choked the ravines with felled timber. Trenches dug behind logs and fence rails, with the excavated dirt thrown in front, provided rifle pits. To safeguard the vital mill, Gardner built a lunette north of the stream, where the creek made a wide detour to the south. On the night of the twenty-fifth Gardner sent all available tools and slaves to his chief engineer, Lieutenant Frederick Y. Dabney. By daylight of the twenty-sixth Dabney had the works laid out. The men worked rapidly. By the next morning rifle pits and lunettes protected the most exposed points of Steedman's line. The southerners also strengthened the existing fortifications, with the men working five hours in the morning and five in the afternoon. [18]

16. Miles to [Gardner], July 24, 1863, LHA Collection; Diary of Ford, May 21, 1863; de Gournay, "Siege of Port Hudson."

17. Logan to Gardner, May 18, 21, 1863, Powers to Gardner, May 23, 1863, Entry 138, [Gardner] to Logan, May 19, 1863, Chap. II, Vol. VIII, all in Record Group 109; Dabney to [Gardner], August 24, 1863, LHA Collection; OR, XV, 1061, Vol. XXVI, Pt. 2, p. 5; Curl, "Fight at Clinton," 122.

18. Diary of Ford, May 23, 1863; Map of Port Hudson, Camp Moore State

Gardner removed several of the heavy cannon from the river bluff to provide more firepower along the land defenses. The southerners positioned one rifled twenty-four-pounder in the center of Steedman's line to sweep a ravine where a road provided a good means of approach for the enemy and a second near Bennett's house; a third went to Slaughter's field. They moved two twenty-four-pounder smoothbores to the intersection of the railroad and breastworks, the thirty-pound Parrott to the extreme right of the land defenses, and "The Baby" to the redan on the Jackson road. The men mounted quaker guns—wood shaped and painted to resemble cannon—in the vacant positions along the river. Faced with the impossibility of forwarding cannon and ammunition to the trans-Mississippi, Gardner acquired a sizable amount of both. This formidable increase in armament included a 4.62-inch Brooke, two 12-pound Blakelys, and two small breechloading guns.[19]

Soon the Federals began showing signs of aggression on Gardner's center and right. On May 24 the navy stepped up its bombardment of Miles's sector for two and one-half hours. The shelling killed three men and wounded three others but did little damage to the fortifications. Along Beall's sector the artillery dueled at long range on the twenty-fifth. Miles's artillery fire dispersed two advances against the Confederate right. Shortly thereafter a white flag appeared, and the northerners immediately began removing their dead and wounded. When Miles sent two officers to receive the flag, the Federals withdrew, violating the rules of war. Colonel Edward Prince moved down the west bank of Thompson's Creek with the 7th Illinois Cavalry and a section of the 1st Illinois Battery. Under orders to block any escape in that direction, Prince seized two steamboats that had anchored in the creek to escape the Union fleet.[20]

Commemorative Area; [Wright], *Port Hudson*, 25–26; Mobile *Advertiser and Register*, August 9, 1863; Lawrence L. Hewitt (ed.), *A Place Named . . . Desperate!* (Baton Rouge, 1982), 1; "Fortification and Siege," 318; [Gardner], Circular, May 23, 1863, LHA Collection.

19. [Wright], *Port Hudson*, 26; "Fortification and Siege," 318, 326; McMorries, *First Alabama*, 62; Smith to Gardner, October 23, 1863, Shelby to [Gardner], August 5, 1863, LHA Collection; Photograph 77-F-133-98-1, showing a 4.62-inch Brooke rifled cannon, National Archives; John W. Robison to wife, April 16, 1863, Robison Papers.

20. Diary of Ford, May 24, 1863; Miles to [Gardner], July 24, 1863, Dabney to

The enemy foiled Confederate expectations of an assault on the twenty-sixth. Scarcely a cannon was fired during the day, and the southerners found everything ominously quiet. They worked on the fortifications well into the night and collapsed behind the trenches, sleeping on their weapons. Only the song of the whippoorwill broke the stillness while some of the men, too nervous to sleep, pondered what the morrow would bring. [21]

Meanwhile, Banks completed his assault preparations. The troops posted on the Plank Road received orders to join the investing force. Signal stations located high in trees enabled a semblance of rapid communication along the investing line. Company K, 42nd Massachusetts, constructed a 280-foot pontoon bridge where the Telegraph Road (running to Bayou Sara) crossed swollen Big Sandy Creek, one-half mile northwest of the Confederate defenses. Cannoneers replenished their ammunition and deployed their guns while officers spent the day reconnoitering. A detachment of the 128th New York drove Confederate pickets from Slaughter's house and burned the plantation buildings, which impeded Union artillery fire. To fill the trenches before the breastworks, the men made fascines of bundles of branches bound with grapevines. Each bundle measured eight feet long and one foot wide and weighed from fifteen to thirty pounds. A call for volunteers for a storming party met overwhelming response from the men. They were eager for the coming fray. [22]

The Federals remained on edge throughout the night of the twenty-sixth. After completing their work that day, many soldiers cried as they penned what might be their last letters to loved ones. Unlike their opponents, the northerners found the evening extremely noisy, especially on the right, where the artillery bombardment kept the pickets awake. Twice that night one regiment

[Gardner], August 24, 1863, LHA Collection; *OR*, Vol. XXVI, Pt. 1, pp. 506, 1013, Pt. 2, pp. 168–69.

21. McMorries, *First Alabama*, 62; Dabney to [Gardner], August 24, 1863, LHA Collection; "Fortification and Siege," 319.

22. [Banks] to Augur, May 26, 1863, Record Group 393; Woodward, *21st Maine*, 110; Bosson, *Forty-second Massachusetts*, 364; *OR*, Vol. XXVI, Pt. 1, p. 506; D. H. Hanaburgh, *History of the One Hundred and Twenty-eighth Regiment, New York Volunteers [U.S. Infantry] in the Late Civil War* (Poughkeepsie, N.Y., 1894), 36; Johns, *Forty-ninth Massachusetts*, 221; Howe, *Passages from Howe*, 48; Map Z218.

mistook stampeding mules for an enemy cavalry attack and fired into its comrades. [23]

A council of war took place at A. M. D. Riley's plantation on the evening of the twenty-sixth. Opinions about an assault varied drastically. Those opposed apparently included Augur and Brigadier Generals Godfrey Weitzel and Thomas W. Sherman. But Banks had made up his mind the previous day and would not be swayed by his subordinates. He surmised that he must attack promptly because of the uncertainty of Grant's situation in Mississippi. [24]

Banks's confidence in making a successful attack was not unfounded. He had an overwhelming advantage in men, his thirty thousand outnumbering the enemy four to one. [25] Excluding the navy, his artillery was superior both in quantity and quality. Although many of his soldiers had not fought a major engagement, his officers were seasoned.

Most of his top subordinates had both military education and combat experience. Weitzel, Cuvier Grover, Augur, and Sherman had graduated from West Point. Graduating second in his class, Weitzel performed engineering duties until 1862, when he commanded an expedition in southwestern Louisiana. Grover had fought in the Seven Days' Battle and at Second Manassas (August, 1862). Augur had seen action in the Mexican War and at the Battle of Cedar Mountain (August, 1862), where he received a severe wound. At the age of eighteen, Sherman walked from Rhode Island to Washington, D.C., to secure his appointment to the military academy from President Andrew Jackson. He served in the Mexican War and successfully commanded the expedition that captured Port Royal, South Carolina, in 1861. William Dwight had attended West Point but "was discharged . . . for deficiency in studies" in his senior year. He proved himself at the Battle of Williamsburg in the spring of 1862, however, where his regiment suffered 50 percent casualties. Dwight was wounded, left for dead, and captured. Halbert E. Paine entered the war as colonel of the 4th

23. Johns, *Forty-ninth Massachusetts*, 222; *History of the Second Battalion Duryee: Zouaves, One Hundred and Sixty-fifth Regt. New York Volunteer Infantry* . . . (rev. ed.; n.p., 1905), 17; Powers, *Thirty Eighth Massachusetts*, 91.

24. Clark, *One Hundred and Sixteenth New York*, 84; Neal Dow, *The Reminiscences of Neal Dow: Recollections of Eighty Years* (Portland, Me., 1898), 690–91; *OR*, Vol. XXVI, Pt. 1, pp. 67–68, 504; Irwin, *Nineteenth Corps*, 166–67.

25. *OR*, Vol. XXVI, Pt. 1, pp. 526–28.

Wisconsin. In July, 1861, while moving his regiment to the front, he declined to transport his soldiers in cattle cars. Instead, he armed his men with pickaxes and seized the next suitable train. He saw minor action in Louisiana and commanded the successful evacuation of Baton Rouge.

Banks's staff and artillery officers had equally impressive credentials. His chief of staff, chief quartermaster, chief commissary, chief engineer, chief of ordnance, and chief of artillery were all alumni of West Point. Several battery officers and a majority of the artillery battalion commanders had attended the academy or experienced combat.

Twelve men commanded brigades in the army advancing on Port Hudson. Apparently only one, Oliver P. Gooding, ever attended West Point. Edward P. Chapin had distinguished himself the preceding year during the Peninsular Campaign, where he received a serious wound. Franklin S. Nickerson fought at the Battle of Baton Rouge. Benjamin H. Grierson had shown his worth by his famous raid just a few weeks earlier, and the others had experienced varying amounts of combat. Regimental commanders included at least one graduate of West Point and several seasoned veterans. William F. Bartlett always commanded the 48th Massachusetts on horseback because he had lost a leg the previous year at the Battle of Yorktown. Possibly even more important, Banks's officers and men felt confident.[26]

But the commander made one mistake he selected the wrong day for the assault. Even taking into account the stiff resistance, Banks's troops should have deployed for an assault no later than the evening of May 25. Had they advanced the following morning, the Federals probably could have crushed Steedman's forces and taken Beall and Miles in reverse. Banks's caution provided Gardner with an additional twenty-four hours to construct fortifications along Little Sandy Creek. After the evening of the twenty-sixth Federal success would hinge on a coordinated assault based on accurate knowledge of the terrain. Banks could have greatly enhanced his chances of victory had he delayed a day or two and

26. Warner, *Generals in Blue*, 10, 12, 24–25, 33, 79, 134–35, 189–90, 193–94, 345–46, 440–41, 503; Cullum, *Biographical Register*, II, 47, 247, 256–57, 278, 346–47, 373, 393–94, 418, 478, 538, 552; *OR*, XV, 158; Boatner, *Civil War Dictionary*, 616; Stanyan, *Eighth New Hampshire*, 321; E.B. Huntington, *Stamford Soldiers' Memorial* (Stamford, Conn., 1869), 103; Irwin, *Nineteenth Corps*, 166–67.

obtained sufficient knowledge of what faced him. Yet, lacking necessary information and undoubtedly worried about Grant, he went ahead and ordered the assault for the next morning.

Sherman held the left, then Augur, Grover, and Weitzel. Weitzel's command included his own brigade, one brigade of Grover's division under Dwight, seven regiments under Paine, and two Negro regiments under Colonel John A. Nelson. The entire line would assault the fortifications simultaneously. The nature of the ground, however, determined that the right wing would advance first. There the Federals would have to drive the foe through wooded hills and ravines, then over precipitous terrain rendered virtually impassable by felled timber, before they could even see the fortifications. In contrast, their comrades on the center and left generally were separated from the enemy only by cleared fields. Consequently, Paine and Dwight had to deploy at 3 A.M. Pioneers would follow the infantry and clear a route for the artillery. Unfortunately for Union forces, Banks failed to specify a time for a simultaneous assault along the entire line. Instead, he instructed his commanders "to take instant advantage of any favorable opportunity . . . afford mutual aid and avoid mistakes . . . [and] commence at the earliest hour practicable." The order concluded: "Port Hudson must be taken to-morrow."[27]

27. *OR*, Vol. XXVI, Pt. 1, pp. 59n, 508–509, 1002; Irwin, *Nineteenth Corps*, 166; Stanyan, *Eighth New Hampshire*, 224.

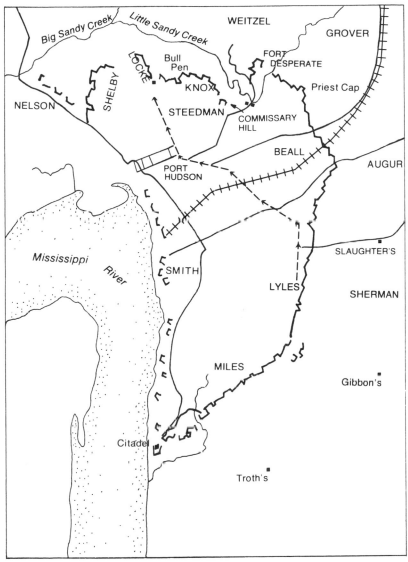

Port Hudson, May 27, 1863

VIII

Holding the Line:
Morning, May 27, 1863

The valley of the shadow of death.

— Captain George W. Carter,
4th Wisconsin Infantry

It was early on May 27 when Colonel I. G. W. Steedman completed preparations for meeting the impending Union onslaught. He sent four companies of the 1st Alabama to strengthen Lieutenant Colonel M. B. Locke's *ad hoc* command occupying the woods almost a mile north of the granary. But this reinforcement failed to match the detachments that returned to construct fortifications, and Locke had only some five hundred infantrymen and no artillery to buy the Confederates additional time to organize their defenses. Steedman's main concern was acquiring additional cannon to sweep the ravines that provided the easiest access to the fortifications. Captain James Madison Sparkman moved two twelve-pound Blakleys to Commissary Hill and deployed at the edge of the ravine, where only some bushes lent protection. His Tennesseans quickly fashioned an abatis of beech and magnolia trees and limbs. [1]

The mortar vessels shelled the garrison throughout the night, but the battle proper opened about 5:30 A.M. Federal land batteries commenced a fierce one-hour bombardment of the Confederate center and right, as an ominous silence prevailed on Steedman's front. The upper and lower fleets approached the fortress and began firing around 7 A.M., but ceased an hour later for fear of

---

1. "Fortification and Siege," 319; *OR*, Vol. XXVI, Pt. 1, p. 163; Garrett and Lightfoot, *Civil War in Maury County*, 51, 62.

injuring their comrades ashore. Their brief participation proved ineffective.[2]

Union Brigadier General Godfrey Weitzel formed his men in a column of brigades. Dwight's division headed the advance, Colonel Jacob Van Zandt's three regiments leading off, supported by Stephen Thomas' four. Paine's division followed, Hawkes Fearing, Jr.'s, four regiments in front and Gooding's three in the rear. Twelve hundred Confederate infantrymen faced an overwhelming force. The fourteen Federal regiments encompassed at least 6,000 soldiers, ranging from the 8th Vermont, about 900 strong, to the 298 members of the 8th New Hampshire. Even so, the column moved forward considerably reduced. Absent from the field were two regiments of Brigadier General William Dwight and four regiments of Brigadier General Halbert E. Paine. The 53rd Massachusetts, 160th New York, and 4th Wisconsin each entered the battle with two companies detached, and the 31st Massachusetts had three absent.[3]

Weitzel began his advance about 6 A.M. During the next hour, the fight raged with great severity while Van Zandt pushed the Confederates back through the forest and ravines. Although heavily outnumbered, Locke held his ground until the enemy threatened both his flanks, at which point he withdrew to the fortifications. Both sides lost frightfully for what amounted to a skirmish. Locke had nearly two hundred men killed, wounded, or missing, including one colonel captured—40 percent of his command.[4]

But the Union column had become disarrayed. The farther south the Federals advanced, the more they drifted to the west, trying to keep their right flank anchored on Big Sandy Creek, which meandered southwesterly. Steep ravines, many over thirty feet in

2. *ORN*, XX, 769, 795; "Fortification and Siege," 319.

3. Irwin, *Nineteenth Corps*, 169; Cunningham, *Port Hudson Campaign*, 122; Stanyan, *Eighth New Hampshire*, 245; George W. Carter, "The Fourth Wisconsin Infantry at Port Hudson," in *War Papers Read Before the Commandery of the State of Wisconsin, Military Order of the Loyal Legion of the United States* (Milwaukee, 1903), III, 227; E. B. Quiner, *The Military History of Wisconsin . . .* (Chicago, 1866), 503; Willis, *Fifty-third Massachusetts*, 121; Edward H. Sentell, Diary, May 27, 1863, Sentell Family Papers, New-York Historical Society, New York; *OR*, Vol. XXVI, Pt. 1, pp. 530–31; Lieutenant Peter Eltinge to father, May 30, 1863, Eltinge-Lord Family Papers, Perkins Library, Duke University, Durham, N.C.

4. *OR*, Vol. XXVI, Pt. 1, p. 530; Irwin, *Nineteenth Corps*, 169–70; "Fortification and Siege," 319–20; Dabney to [Gardner], August 24, 1863, LHA Collection.

depth, and dense woods broke battle lines. To press the attack, Thomas' troops passed through the gaps of Van Zandt's exhausted and widely dispersed men. By the time the Federals gained the crest north of Little Sandy Creek any sense of organization above the regimental level had vanished.[5] And scores of blue-clad infantrymen, confused and separated from their officers, advanced no further.

At the edge of the woods lining the crest the Federals came to a halt, finally beholding their objective. Before them lay the valley of Little Sandy Creek, broken by small hillocks and ravines, in places dense with pines and magnolias, in others interlaced with branches of felled trees—a formidable abatis. Sharpshooters sniped away from the protective cover of the gullies and trees. Beyond the basin lay the opposite crest, crowned with the yellow dirt of unfinished earthworks, behind which the Federals could see the garrison's tents, shanties, and warehouses and the church and dwellings of the village. The only unobstructed route through the bottom was a wagon path leading straight into the blazing guns of the battery atop Commissary Hill.

First to respond to the challenge, Lieutenant Colonel Willoughby Babcock drew his sword and dashed ahead of the 75th New York shouting, "Come On!" A corporal leaped forward, replying, "Here goes the Colonel, boys, we won't leave the Colonel! Charge!" Their crossing over the rugged, obstructed valley soon dispersed the 75th into squads. The regiments that followed met with a similar fate, and an unorganized mob struggled toward the breastworks, their number growing ever smaller as the less steadfast members dropped out to the safety of an inviting crevasse. Fear was not the only factor influencing their actions. The nature of the terrain they had traversed, coupled with the heat and the humidity, undoubtedly exhausted many Yankees.[6]

The Confederates stood in wait, Steedman stationing himself at the battery on Commissary Hill. Through a telescope he watched his men withdraw and the enemy move to positions along the heights north of the creek. Steedman warned the newly arrived gunners of the 15th Arkansas beyond the creek. Lieutenant Jesse

---

5. Irwin, *Nineteenth Corps*, 170.

6. Henry Hall and James Hall, *Cayuga in the Field* . . . (Auburn, N.Y., 1873), [sect. 2], pp. 113–14, 257, 265.

B. Edrington joined in the bombardment with two twelve-pound howitzers stationed in the advanced lunette. The gunners soon obtained the range and exploded shells among the advancing enemy. Their accurate fire caused much confusion, and Steedman watched the Yankees "mowed down in whole ranks, their lines . . . soon broken, yet undismayed they rushed down the hill." Using felled trees and ravines for cover, some of the Federals approached within easy range of the rifle pits.[7]

Pioneers followed the advancing blue-clad infantry to open roads through the woods for the artillery. The cannon soon rolled up, and the artillerists unlimbered their pieces along the crest. The Confederate gunners swiftly directed their fire at the guns of five enemy batteries. The southerners had nailed white crosses to trees on the opposite ridge to mark the range. They zeroed in on a section of the 1st Maine Battery when it wheeled into position, leaving one soldier dead and twelve wounded alongside thirteen dead horses. Premature discharge of another Confederate cannon hurled a rammer toward Battery F, 1st United States Artillery. Just before it reached the battery it struck a tree. Ricocheting off, the whirling staff killed five or six Federals. But it was Battery A of that regiment that suffered the most. The Confederates quickly dismounted two of its guns, killed two men and fifteen horses, and wounded a lieutenant and eleven men.[8]

Yet the deadly precision of the Confederate gunners succeeded only in diverting Federal artillery fire from the retreating gray-clad infantry. Captain Edmund C. Bainbridge's U.S. regulars unlimbered the six guns of Battery A next to the 6th Massachusetts' four cannon at the edge of the woods, four hundred yards from the lunette manned by the 15th Arkansas. Together, the two batteries quickly silenced Edrington's guns. A shell struck the wheel of one cannon; the explosion killed the lieutenant, wounded two of his men, and disabled the piece. The colonel of the 15th, Benjamin W. Johnson, withdrew the remaining gun to a secure place, where the

7. Mobile *Advertiser and Register*, August 9, 1863; Garrett and Lightfoot, *Civil War in Maury County*, 62; "Fortification and Siege," 320; Hewitt (ed.), *Desperate!* 1, 6.

8. Irwin, *Nineteenth Corps*, 171; Stanyan, *Eighth New Hampshire*, 225–26; Whitman and True, *Maine in the War for the Union*, 387; Diary of Elon P. Spink, May 27, 1863 (typescript copy in author's possession); Haskin, *First Regiment Artillery*, 192.

remaining cannoneers double loaded it with canister to cover his vulnerable left flank and rear.

Yankee gunners managed to knock out almost every gun on Commissary Hill. Captain Sparkman jumped atop the breastwork to see if he had correctly cut the fuse to explode the shell directly over the enemy's battery. When he did so, a shell fragment killed him by driving his powder flask into his groin. Another shell cut one soldier in two, tore the leg off another, and stunned several more. Artillery projectiles also riddled the large granary just to the right of the battery.[9]

Three companies of the 12th Connecticut worked their way forward toward Commissary Hill. Dispersed among the fallen trees and firing as sharpshooters, they soon compelled the gunners to lie behind the parapet. The guns silenced, some of the Federals seized a ditch from which they poured an enfilading fire into the battery. Confederate efforts to oust the Yankees proved costly and futile, but they did stop the advance.

The assaulting force hit hardest Major Samuel L. Knox's six companies of the 1st Alabama and two companies of provost guards. The Alabamians stood five feet apart and carried outdated flintlock muskets. With an effective range of forty yards, the men loaded their guns with one ball and three buckshot, a deadly round at close range. They held their fire until the enemy came within forty yards, when the parapet blazed with a volley of musketry. The suddenness of the destruction caused the Federals to hesitate. The more courageous participants rallied quickly, however, and came on with a yell.[10]

Rebel officers now instructed their men to load and fire individually while the Yankees struggled over brush and fired on the run. One Alabamian thought his comrades shot so rapidly that their muskets popped "as fast as canes when the fire is in a canebrake." Fence rails in the breastworks manned by the provost guard battalion caught fire. To prevent a possible breach, the Al-

9. Garrett and Lightfoot, *Civil War in Maury County*, 62–63; Hewitt (ed.), *Desperate!* iv–v, 5–6; Dabney to [Gardner], August 24, 1863, LHA Collection.

10. McMorries, *First Alabama*, 62–64; John William De Forest, *A Volunteer's Adventures: A Union Captain's Record of the Civil War*, ed. James H. Croushore (New Haven, 1946), 111; *OR*, Vol. XXVI, Pt. 1, p. 163.

abamians assisted their comrades in tearing out the burning rails under enemy fire.[11]

A few of the Federals almost reached the parapet before fleeing from the withering fire. The Confederates fired at their backs until the Yankees moved out of range. Two Alabamians especially demoralized the Yankees. John C. Cantey, one of two crack shots in the regiment armed with a long-range rifle, dropped the gallant blue-clad color bearer of the 75th New York at the outset of the advance. And at the height of the assault Captain Richard Williams jumped atop the parapet and emptied his pistol into the charging column. His men had to drag him down from his perilous perch. The Federals who had actually inflicted the most damage were three companies of the 1st Louisiana (U.S.) who lined the ridge in front of the Alabamians before the assault began. Keeping up a deadly fire on the breastworks, these men are credited with killing far more Confederates than their comrades in the advancing column—a clear indication of the limited number of New Yorkers who participated in the final charge. Out of seven hundred, the 75th New York lost only eight-six men the entire day.[12]

Almost in concert with Thomas' attack, the 91st and 131st New York of Van Zandt's brigade struck Major W. K. Bennett's lunette, commanded by Lieutenant Colonel Locke. Bullets and canister spewed forth from the breastworks with telling effect; the 131st New York lost about sixty killed and wounded during the assault. While waving his sword, Union Sergeant Major William H. Aldis, Jr., took a minié ball in his right forearm. With his left hand and teeth he managed to tie a dirty handkerchief about the flesh wound while keeping pace with the advance. Confederate officers acted in a similar vein. A ricocheting bullet struck Locke in the neck, but bandaging it with his handkerchief, he stood his post.[13]

The obliquing of Dwight's brigades and the ensuing extension

11. Moore (ed.), *Rebellion Record*, VII, 268; McMorries, *First Alabama*, 63; A. J. Lewis to [Gardner], July 9, 1863, LHA Collection.

12. Mobile *Advertiser and Register*, August 9, 1863; McMorries, *First Alabama*, 33, 63; "Some incidents connected with the 1st Ala. Regiment which have never been published . . . ," First Alabama Infantry Regiment, Military Records Division; Hall and Hall, *Cayuga in the Field*, [sect. 2], pp. 114, 118–19.

13. Irwin, *Nineteenth Corps*, 170; *OR*, Vol. XXVI, Pt. 1, p. 163; Wm. H. Aldis to wife, June 3, 7, 1863, Aldis Papers; McMorries, *First Alabama*, 63–64.

of the line, coupled with the fragmentation of regiments struggling through the valley, uncovered Paine's front. To fill the gap, Paine ordered Fearing's men forward. At first light, with the paper resting on the pommel of his saddle, Lieutenant Colonel Oliver W. Lull wrote Colonel Sidney A. Bean: "The Eighth New Hampshire greets the Fourth Wisconsin, and will march with you into Port Hudson to-day or die." Lull then dismounted and gave his personal possessions to a friend. He positioned himself twelve paces ahead of the colors, waved his sword, and ordered, "Eighth New Hampshire, forward, smartly and steadily, and follow me." It proved to be his last command. Almost the first to fall, he took a minié ball in his thigh. As he was carried to the rear, he called out, "Don't let the regiment break; we can whip them." He died about six that evening. [14]

Fearing's brigade struck the breastworks at the "Bull Pen," where the Confederates slaughtered their cattle. Steedman had foreseen this possibility and requested reinforcements. Gardner sent Colonel O. P. Lyles with the 14th, 18th, and 23rd Arkansas regiments, who arrived in time to check the enemy's advance. One Union officer aptly labeled the resulting engagement a "huge bushwhack." [15] Under fire from the battery near Major Bennett's quarters, the 4th Wisconsin halted about three hundred yards from the breastworks to dress its line. The shot and shell tore through the trees with devastating effect. One solid shot cleared an entire file from the line. When the men moved forward, they reserved their fire while struggling over and under tree trunks and through branches, all the while under a deadly hail of missiles. By twos and threes they passed through what one officer termed "the valley of the shadow of death," and a few especially determined Federals reached the final summit. One hundred yards away they saw Lyles's Arkansans forming behind an irregular line of entrenchments. Confederate fire soon forced them to withdraw below the crest, where they returned fire. But there they encountered yet another danger. Premature ignition of shells from the 1st Maine Battery caused the projectiles to explode around them, killing one man and wounding several others. Captain John M. Stanyan thought the

14. Stanyan, *Eighth New Hampshire*, 234–37; Irwin, *Nineteenth Corps*, 170; Hall and Hall, *Cayuga in the Field*, [sect. 2], p. 114; *OR*, Vol, XXVI, Pt. 1, p. 71.

15. Irwin, *Nineteenth Corps*, 170; *OR*, XV, 1032; Map of Port Hudson, Camp Moore State Commemorative Area; "Fortification and Siege," 320.

terrain "very peculiar, looking like the skeleton of a hugh fish, the backbone representing the long ridge running from the woods towards the fortifications, and the ribs the short ridges which partially protected us in the gullies." Like too many of his comrades, Stanyan had managed to find a safe refuge. But his regiment, the 8th New Hampshire, lost 124 men killed and wounded. Considering that the men were assaulting fortified defenders, the loss of 42 percent was not exceptional—but it was double the percentage of casualties of any other regiment in that sector.[16]

The Confederates' determination and the timely arrival of reinforcements alone cannot explain their successful defense. Instead, the answer lies with the Federals. Piecemeal attacks contributed to the Union repulse. And the difficult terrain and casualties among officers contributed to the disorganization within Federal ranks. Sheer weight of numbers, however, should have enabled the Federals to breach the fortifications. But not enough Federals reached the Rebel breastworks. Seven regiments—37 percent of the available infantry—did not assault the breastworks. And too many men had dropped out to seek safety. Admittedly, some of these soldiers acted as sharpshooters. But the paucity of casualties reflected the failure of many troops to participate in the final charge against the enemy's parapet. The Federals simply lacked the resolve needed to achieve victory.

Having failed to capture the fortifications along Little Sandy Creek, the Federals looked for any available assistance on either flank. On their right, the 1st and 3rd Louisiana Native Guards anchored that end of the Union line. The 1st, including a majority of its line officers, consisted almost entirely of free blacks from New Orleans. Several of its members were both educated and wealthy. The 3rd consisted of former slaves commanded by white officers. Dwight had stationed both black regiments on the flank because he thought little of the ability of Negroes on a battlefield, even if led by the best white officers. Like many of his colleagues, he believed garrison duty in some rear area the proper place for black soldiers. Dwight never intended to order them forward—and the amount of whiskey given them earlier that morning exceeded the standard ration issued to troops before an assault.[17]

16. Carter, "Fourth Wisconsin," 228–30; Stanyan, *Eighth New Hampshire,* 226, 245.

17. George W. Williams, *A History of the Negro Troops in The War of the*

But Dwight desperately wanted to breach the Confederate defenses. After the assault along Little Sandy Creek ground to a halt, he ordered the black regiments forward. Six companies of the 1st with nine of the 3rd Native Guards crossed the pontoon bridge. Two cannon of the 6th Massachusetts Battery and some dismounted troopers of the 1st Louisiana (U.S.) Cavalry accompanied them. The artillerymen unlimbered the cannon in the road, but enemy fire forced them to withdraw the guns after firing only one round. The infantry, however, filed to the right, where they formed a line of battle among the willow trees that covered the old riverbed. Confederate River Batteries No. 1 and 4 bombarded the area with shell and solid shot, some weighing more than a hundred pounds. [18]

The terrain made the fortifications the Native Guards would assault the strongest at Port Hudson. With the Mississippi near its crest, backwater covered much of the floodplain west of the road. Just south of the creek the road paralleled the inaccessible west slope of an abrupt ridge for a quarter of a mile, at which point both road and ridge intersected the bluff. Stationed along the crest of the ridge, sixty riflemen had a front, rear, and enfilading field of fire on any force assaulting this sector because the attackers would have to move down the road. About three hundred men of Colonel William B. Shelby's 39th Mississippi, supported by four small cannon, manned the rifle pits constructed along the edge of the steep bluff.

At 10 A.M. the Native Guards moved forward. More than a thousand black troops emerged from the woods in fine order, advancing first at quick time and then double-quick toward the bluff, about six hundred yards away. The 1st Native Guards led off, followed closely by the 3rd. Each regiment formed a long line, two ranks deep. [19]

Rebellion, 1861–1865, Preceded by a Review of the Military Services of Negroes in Ancient and Modern Times (1888; rpr. New York, 1969), 216; Stanyan, *Eighth New Hampshire*, 229; Garrett and Lightfoot, *Civil War in Maury County*, 64.

18. Irwin, *Nineteenth Corps*, 172; Joseph T. Wilson, *The Black Phalanx* (New York, 1968), 525; Bosson, *Forty-Second Massachusetts*, 364; Company A, 1st Louisiana Cavalry, Muster Roll, May and June, 1863, and 1st Louisiana Cavalry, Return, May, 1863, Roll 67, Microcopy 594; Shelby to [Gardner], August 5, 1863, LHA Collection; *OR*, XV, 1027.

19. "Fortification and Siege," 321; Shelby to [Gardner], August 5, 1863, LHA Collection; Wilson, *Black Phalanx*, 525–26; New Orleans *Times-Democrat*, April 26, 1906; Williams, *History of Negro Troops*, 216. One source claimes that because

As the black soldiers rushed forward, bullets from the ridge ripped into their flank, causing confusion and disorder. Yet they pressed on toward the bluff, to a point two hundred yards from the Confederate main line. At that moment rebel artillery opened with canister, and Shelby's troops, eager to join in the fight, commenced firing from the bluff without orders. Canister and minié balls mowed down the lead ranks by the dozen. The color sergeant of the 1st fell embracing the flag, a shell having torn off part of his head. Blood and brains stained the riddled banner. A free black and a resident of New Orleans, Captain Andre Cailloux led the advance with his left arm dangling, broken above the elbow by a cannonball. Shouting orders in both English and French, Cailloux pressed on until a second shell struck him dead. After firing one volley, the black soldiers in front fell back in utter confusion. Their uncertainty spread to the men in the second line, and both regiments withdrew to the woods. [20]

While the officers attempted to rally the troops among the willow trees, a few especially brave soldiers attempted to wade through the backwater. Both efforts proved unsuccessful. Another heroic group managed to scale the projecting ridge, but all the men were killed by an enfilading fire or captured. Barely fifteen minutes had passed from the time the black troops exited the woods until they returned to them. Although the Confederates had killed and wounded scores of the enemy, they themselves had not suffered a single casualty. [21]

The black soldiers found little safety in their refuge. Confederate artillery continued to rain shell and solid shot into the woods, and splinters from fragmenting trees proved as dangerous as the projectiles themselves. His Native Guards unable to reach the enemy's breastworks, Colonel John A. Nelson sent an aide with a request to Dwight for permission to withdraw. "'Tell Colonel

---

of their limited number, Shelby's men had three rifles each when the Native Guards attacked on May 27. It is more plausible that Shelby's troops found these surplus weapons on the field after the fighting ended on the twenty-seventh.

20. William Wells Brown, *The Negro in the American Rebellion: His Heroism and His Fidelity* (Boston, 1867), 171; de Gournay, "Siege of Port Hudson"; Williams, *History of Negro Troops*, 217–19; Shelby to [Gardner], August 5, 1863, LHA Collection; [Wright], *Port Hudson*, 36; Wilson, *Black Phalanx*, 525.

21. Wilson, *Black Phalanx*, 525; Frederick (ed.), "Diary of Porter," 313–14; [Wright], *Port Hudson*, 36; Shelby to [Gardner], August 5, 1863, LHA Collection.

Nelson I shall consider he has done nothing unless he carries the enemy's works,'' Dwight responded. Protesting, the aide argued that the black regiments had already suffered 50 percent casualties. But Dwight ended the argument with a pompous, "Charge again, and let the impetuosity of the charge counterbalance the paucity of the numbers."[22]

But troops did not exist who could accomplish the objective Dwight had set for the Negroes. Even if Nelson could induce the men to advance, he undoubtedly realized that another charge would be nothing more than suicide. So he chose not to make the attempt. But neither could he withdraw. To fool Dwight, who remained in the rear, Nelson had his men continue firing. His deception forced the Negroes to remain among the trees and endure the shelling for hours.[23]

To support Weitzel, Brigadier General Cuvier Grover sent the 159th New York and 25th Connecticut on a wide detour to the west to unite with Paine's left flank. Lieutenant Colonel Charles A. Burt moved forward under the mistaken impression that a trifling number of Confederates would oppose him and that his New Yorkers alone could breach the enemy's line. The men double-quicked down the dusty road under a murderous fire from the battery on Commissary Hill and started through the valley choked with felled trees and heavy underbrush—a combination that undoubtedly influenced several of the troops to drop out of the column. Turning west and advancing in single file, they sloshed across Little Sandy, and some of the men finally reached the side of the hill they were to assault. In fearful anticipation they waited a few moments for the order to charge. Then, at 10 A.M., with a terrifying yell, they rose and rushed forward, crashing through brush and bounding over the last tree only to emerge thirty yards from the breastwork, where it seemed to one Federal that "a thousand rifles were cracking our doom." Within seconds, the Federals suffered some fifty

22. Johns, *Forty-ninth Massachusetts*, 254–55; [Wright], *Port Hudson*, 36; Stanyan, *Eighth New Hampshire*, 229.

23. Irwin, *Nineteenth Corps*, 174; Smith, *Company K*, 63; Dabney to [Gardner], August 24, 1863, LHA Collection; Wilson, *Black Phalanx*, 525. Nelson reported that his men made three distinct assaults, and his claim is substantiated by Gardner's report of the siege, as prepared by Dabney. Both Nelson and Dabney must have considered the attempt to wade through the backwater and the scaling of the projecting ridge as independent assaults.

casualties. The survivors dove for cover. The colors of the 159th lay before the parapet, the standard-bearer dead at their side. Sergeant Robert Buckley of the 25th Connecticut worked his way back and brought in the colors, only to be killed when he turned to pick up his gun. [24]

When these two regiments failed to breach the defenses, Grover decided to increase the pressure even more. He extended the fighting eastward to encompass the lunette defended by the 15th Arkansas. Most of the Arkansans had fought in the advance line earlier that morning. Although their lieutenant colonel had fallen badly wounded and the regiment had lost thirty men and several officers during the skirmish, many of them falling prisoner when the Federals blocked their retreat, the majority of the Arkansans managed to escape. Confusion reigned when the survivors entered the lunette, and Colonel Johnson hastened to meet the anticipated attack. Disregarding proper company organization, he assigned the men to new positions. Two hundred Arkansans lined the quarter-mile-long lunette, while the major and thirty men prepared to hold the rear "at all hazards." [25]

Grover dispatched three additional regiments of his division to engage the 15th Arkansas. Marching west, they passed through the woods littered with the dead and wounded of Weitzel's command. About 10:30 A.M. these fresh reinforcements, together with Gooding's brigade, moved toward Johnson's bastion. The 12th Maine led the assault, followed by the 38th Massachusetts; the third wave, composed of the 31st Massachusetts, did not advance. The assaulting column received covering fire from one company of the 12th Connecticut on the right and the 13th and 24th Connecticut on the left. [26]

The Federals advanced in a long, crescent-shaped line that covered Johnson's front and partly overlapped both flanks. Although

24. *Twenty-Fifth Connecticut*, 46–47; Irwin, *Nineteenth Corps*, 171; OR, Vol. XXVI, Pt. 1, p. 530; Thomas McManus, *Twenty-fifth Regiment Battle Fields Revisited* (Hartford, 1896), 22; Tiemann (comp.), *159th New-York*, 40–41; McMorries, *First Alabama*, 63; Croffut and Morris, *Military and Civil History of Connecticut*, 410.

25. Hewitt (ed.), *Desperate!* 1–2, 5, 11–12.

26. Sprague, *13th Connecticut*, 139–40; Irwin, *Nineteenth Corps*, 172; Flinn, *Campaigning with Banks*, 75; *Hampshire Gazette & Northampton Courier*, June 30, 1863; De Forest, *Volunteer's Adventures*, 113.

his situation appeared hopeless, Johnson devised a plan. He forbade his men to look over the parapet until the enemy was within sixty yards, at which point the Federals let out a lusty cheer and quickened their pace. The Arkansans rose with a yell and fired volleys of buck and ball cartridges with such rapidity that the Federal center broke and ran within ten minutes. But the absence of devastating volleys of canister from Confederate artillery enabled the more steadfast of the Federals to close both wings on the center. Onward they came, only to have their center decimated a second time by Johnson's backwoodsmen, who carefully picked off the officers. They rallied a third time and advanced to within fifty yards of the works. Here they dropped behind stumps and logs or sought shelter in ravines.

A steady covering fire of artillery and musketry enabled about three hundred Federals, less than 30 percent of the attacking column, to move up a ravine and into the ditch surrounding the lunette. The Arkansans crouched behind the breastwork, their guns at the "ready," each determined to shoot the foremost of the stormers and then rely on musket butt and bayonet to hold the line. The Federals repeatedly attempted to scale the rampart, each time being bloodily repulsed. Finally, a Federal officer shouted, "Are you ready?" Everyone replied in the affirmative and the officer screamed "Charge!" He scaled the parapet with only four men at his side. When their lifeless bodies rolled down into the ditch, the spectacle sapped whatever courage remained in their comrades. Another officer repeated the attempt, but when he shouted "Charge," not a single man rose above the parapet. The Federals crossed bayonets with the foe and hurled sticks, dirt clods, and verbal abuse, but they quickly discovered they could neither advance nor retreat.[27]

Those infantrymen who had remained in the rear now moved to support their comrades in the advance. The 53rd Massachusetts moved up to relieve the 91st New York, and the reserve companies of the 12th Connecticut rotated with those sharpshooting at the front. The 173rd New York marched to assist the 1st Louisiana, but that unit had the right flank securely anchored on Big Sandy, and the 173rd took position in its rear. Shortly after noon Grover relaxed his efforts because he heard nothing from the left, and

27. Hewitt (ed.), *Desperate!* 6, 11–12; [Wright], *Port Hudson*, 34–35.

Weitzel followed suit. Both men requested fresh orders and awaited their arrival or the sound of battle from the Union left before renewing their assault. Federal victory would have to be achieved elsewhere.[28]

Without question, desperate fighting had occurred along Little Sandy Creek, but such encounters were generally isolated, short-lived, and involved few men on either side. Seven of the nineteen Federal regiments on the field did not actively participate in the assault. With few exceptions, Union losses indicate that the remaining twelve made no serious effort to breach the Confederate defenses. Out of more than eight thousand blue-clad infantrymen, fewer than seven hundred were killed or wounded. One-fourth of these casualties occurred in the 8th New Hampshire and 4th Wisconsin, the units caught in the "huge bushwhack."[29]

The terrain prevented any organized effort by separating most of the enlisted men from their regimental officers. Once this happened, the more faint-hearted soldiers secreted themselves at a safe depth in a ravine. With little chance of embarrassment, these men remained hidden in their sanctuaries until nightfall. Consequently, few participants pressed the attack despite allegations to the contrary. The following account of the 156th New York, coupled with its number of casualties, typifies the "action" of too many Federals on May 27:

> In order to reach the enemy works they had to plunge through a dense forest of magnolias, choked with a thick undergrowth, brambles and wild honeysuckle, before encountering the maze of felled trees. All the time their broken ranks were subjected to a galling fire which pinned them down in ravines, woods or any shelter they could find. The protection thus gained kept their losses down, but they would always remember Port Hudson and May 27, 1863.

The regiment's position indeed protected its members. The 156th

28. Willis, *Fifty-third Massachusetts*, 122; De Forest, *Volunteer's Adventures*, 111; *Memorials of Fowler*, 43; Palfrey, "Port Hudson," 40; Irwin, *Nineteenth Corps*, 175.

29. 12th Connecticut, Return, May, 1863, Roll 7, Microcopy 594; *Twenty-Fifth Connecticut*, 47–48; Willis, *Fifty-third Massachusetts*, 121; Tiemann (comp.), *159th New-York*, 41; Lieutenant Peter Eltinge to father, May 30, 1863, Eltinge-Lord Family Papers; Hall and Hall, *Cayuga in the Field*, [sect. 2], pp. 118–19; Powers, *Thirty Eighth Massachusetts*, 94–95; Stanyan, *Eighth New Hampshire*, 245; Love, *Wisconsin in the War*, 544.

New York did not have a single man killed or wounded that day because all ten of its companies were several miles in the rear; three were detached to Banks's headquarters, and seven guarded a large train of ammunition wagons. This grossly exaggerated account of the performance of the 156th New York does, however, accurately describe the behavior of several Union regiments on the morning of May 27, 1863.[30]

Despite the terrain, and without the aid of covering fire from two regiments and more than twenty cannon, three regiments should have overwhelmed the two hundred Arkansans in the lunette north of the creek. Although Colonel Johnson reported killing ninety and wounding more than three hundred of the enemy in front of the 15th Arkansas, many of these Federals apparently feigned death until nightfall. The combined loss of these three regiments amounted to fewer than eighty men killed or wounded; virtually none of the casualties occurred in the 31st Massachusetts. One can only speculate about the consequences if that regiment had participated in the final advance.[31]

Widespread Yankee shirking should not detract from those Federals who pressed the assault. The 8th New Hampshire, 131st New York, 4th Wisconsin, and the Negro regiments performed gallantly. And the sharpshooters of the 1st (U.S.) Louisiana and 12th Connecticut kept up a withering fire on the enemy. For the outnumbered Confederates, it was a hard-fought engagement. Their view of the fierceness of the battle was best expressed by the men of the 15th Arkansas, who nicknamed their lunette "Fort Desperate."[32]

Although most Civil War commanders favored the tactical offensive, assaults seldom proved decisive, even if successful. And such endeavors proved extremely costly against fortified defenders armed with rifled weapons. In four assaults during his defense of Atlanta, John Bell Hood lost 19 percent of his command. Braxton

30. Will Plank (comp.), *Banners and Bugles: A Record of Ulster County, New York and the Mid-Hudson Region in the Civil War* (Marlborough, N.Y., 1972), 46; Phisterer (comp.), *New York in the War of the Rebellion*, V, 3819; Lieutenant Peter Eltinge to father, May 30, 1863, Eltinge-Lord Family Papers.

31. Hewitt (ed.), *Desperate!* 15; Adjutant General, *Annual Report of the Adjutant General of the State of Maine for the Year Ending December 31, 1863* (Augusta, 1864), 80, 405–32; Adjutant General, *Massachusetts Soldiers, Sailors, and Marines*, III, 397–447, IV, 1.

32. Hewitt (ed.), *Desperate!* 19.

Bragg suffered losses of 27 percent at Murfreesboro and 26 percent at Chickamauga. Robert E. Lee lost 30 percent of his army at Gettysburg, 21 percent during the Seven Days, and 19 percent at Second Manassas and Chancellorsville. And Ulysses S. Grant lost 41 percent during his offensive from the Wilderness to Cold Harbor.[33]

Piecemeal attacks by only 63 percent of the available infantry demonstates incompetence equal to that displayed by George B. McClellan at Antietam. And no force could maintain its organization while advancing over terrain such as that which fronted Steedman's position. Any chance that the Federals had of achieving victory after they descended into the valley of Little Sandy Creek depended upon the individual courage and initiative of the soldiers and junior officers. Their failure to breach the Confederate defenses, coupled with a loss of only 8 percent of the attacking force, strongly indicates that the Federals who entered "the valley of the shadow of death" clearly lacked the determination needed to achieve victory.

33. Grady McWhiney and Perry D. Jamieson, *Attack and Die: Civil War Military Tactics and the Southern Heritage* (University, Ala., 1982), 10–11, 19–21, 69, 72.

IX

Holding the Line:
Afternoon, May 27, 1863

We are poorly led and uselessly slaughtered, and the brains are all within and not "before Port Hudson."
—Private Henry T. Johns,
49th Massachusetts Infantry

By 11 A.M. on May 27 the fighting along the Union right had settled into a stalemate. Despite several fresh regiments available to press the assault, the Union generals there chose to await developments on the Federal left. Banks's division commanders on that flank had allowed the morning to pass without launching an infantry assault. When they advanced that afternoon, however, the blue-clad infantry would press the attack with a determination similar to that shown by the Negroes, instead of performing halfheartedly as their white comrades had along Little Sandy Creek.[1]

While the fighting raged on the left, the bombardment on the center and right continued. The Confederates had the best of it while the Federals deployed their artillery. But soon thirty cannon, lined almost hub-to-hub, were in position at the edge of the woods opposite Beall's center, with the 50th Massachusetts in support. Confederate shells speedily destroyed one gun and caused the adjutant of the 21st Indiana to shout, "For God's sake hurry up, boys, they are shooting us down!" Company E of the 50th quickly stacked their weapons, threw off their accouterments, and helped serve the cannon. Their first time under fire, the men from Massachusetts dodged the artillery projectiles in a lively fashion. Shells flew swift and furious but somewhat careless during the morning.

1. Cunningham, *Port Hudson Campaign*, 56–57.

One did explode in a tree immediately above a sutler, who ran off and abandoned his goods. The men of the 50th appreciated this turn of events because they had not had anything to eat since the previous day.[2]

Two Union field batteries met a similar fate when they deployed on Brigadier General Thomas W. Sherman's front. But the Confederate cannon, inferior in both quantity and quality, could not continue to compete successfully. The tide quickly turned, the Federals dismounted or otherwise disabled several guns, and the Confederate cannoneers suffered heavy casualties. A detachment of Company K, 1st Alabama, manned "The Baby" at the Jackson road redan. Sharpshooters picked off so many of the crew that the lieutenant and sergeant served the gun alone, the former pointing and the latter loading. After several rounds, a minié ball mortally wounded the lieutenant and the sergeant carried him to the rear, both men hoping to secure a fresh crew. Posted near the Slaughter road sally port, Abbay's battery took a different course of action. When Union artillery drove the gunners from their positions, the Mississippians ran the cannon down inclines for protection but kept them loaded for instant use.[3]

Throughout the morning, Banks listened for the sound of musketry on his left but heard only the booming of cannon. About noon Banks rode to Sherman's headquarters, where he found the division commander dining in his tent. Following a heated altercation regarding Sherman's failure to advance, Banks returned to his headquarters and sent his chief of staff, Brigadier General George L. Andrews, to relieve Sherman. When he arrived, Andrews found Sherman leading his men forward and so declined to assume command.[4]

At approximately 2 P.M. the Confederates observed the enemy deploying in line of battle on Slaughter's field and along the Plains

2. Stevens, *Fiftieth Massachusetts*, 135, 137–38; [Preston], *Port Hudson*, 14–15; 1st Lieutenant J. B. Rawles to [Augur], May 30, 1863, Capt. P. E. Holcomb to [Augur], May 30, 1863, Report of 1st Lieutenant Fredr. Wm. Reinhard for May 27, 1863, Augur Papers.

3. *One Hundred and Sixty-fifth New York*, 18; McGregor, *Fifteenth New Hampshire*, 333; Dabney to [Gardner], August 24, 1863, LHA Collection; Smith, *Company K*, 63–64, 139; Kendall, "Recollections," 1113–14.

4. Hanaburgh, *One Hundred and Twenty-eighth New York*, 40–41; *OR*, Vol. XXVI, Pt. 1, pp. 68n, 509–10.

Store road. The transfer of three Arkansas regiments to the "Bull Pen" that morning left 150 pickets at twenty-yard intervals to oppose the Federals. Stretching his remaining troops to the right, Beall called on Colonel William R. Miles for assistance. Miles had already heard of the pressing need and responded swiftly. Without waiting for orders, he extended his line to the left, his men barely arriving in time to meet the threat. Having secured extra rifles from the sick in the hospital and from the arsenal, Miles provided his men with three apiece. He also had them count off by twos. When the order came to fire, every man would discharge his three guns and then the second would confine himself to loading for the first. Having completed his instructions, Miles advised, "Shoot low, boys; it takes two men to take away a man who is wounded, and they never come back."[5]

Standing behind the breastwork opposite the smoldering ruins of the Slaughter residence, Arkansas Lieutenant J. M. Bailey never forgot the anxious moments before the enemy advanced:

> It was a magnificent sight, but the great odds against us looked appalling as our line was weak, averaging about one man to every five feet, and no reserve force. Of one thing we felt sure and that was that our men would do all that it was possible for us to do. Every company officer, as far as I could see, stood in line with his men, musket in hand. To facilitate rapid firing, most if not all of the men, placed their cartridges on the works in their front. Varied were the expressions on the faces of the men. Some were serious and silent. Others joked, danced, or sang short snatches of song, but there was an intense earnestness about it all.
>
> All remembered our defeat at Corinth and many remarked that we would now get even. I don't believe any doubted the result notwithstanding the disparity in numbers.[6]

But the Confederates had little time to ponder the possibilities.

After emerging from the woods, Brigadier General Neal Dow's right flank rested on the road running past the ruins of the Slaughter residence. The brigade advanced shortly after 2 P.M., with 450

---

5. New Orleans *Times-Democrat*, April 26, 1906; Dabney to [Gardner], August 24, 1863, LHA Collection; James M'Murray, "Heroism of Union Officer at Port Hudson," *Confederate Veteran*, XVI (1908), 428; Kendall, "Recollections," 1117; [Wright], *Port Hudson*, 33; *OR*, Vol. XXVI, Pt. 1, p. 169.

6. J. M. Bailey, "The Story of a Confederate Soldier, 1861–5," (typescript copy), Texas State Archives, Austin.

men of the 6th Michigan in the lead. The 15th New Hampshire, 26th Connecticut, and 128th New York followed. Negroes in front of the column carried long poles to place across the moat fronting the breastworks. They were followed by 130 volunteers with heavy planks to lay across the poles.[7]

Within minutes of their appearance, the mounted officers drew enemy fire. Leaving Dow, Sherman and his staff rode across the interval between the brigades to hasten Brigadier General Franklin S. Nickerson's advance. A cannonball struck Sherman's horse, which lurched backward ten yards and fell on the general. Although dazed, he continued on foot until a shot shattered one leg below the knee. "O, my God, my Country!" exclaimed Sherman, who apparently thought the situation hopeless without his leadership.[8]

Four successive parallel fences and the debris of the Slaughter house disrupted Dow's formation. The men threw down the fences dividing the cornfield and pressed on into an abatis immediately in front of the fortifications. The Federals faced a hail of lead when they climbed over trees or shredded their clothes as they forced a passage through entangling limbs. Confederate gunners opened a heavy barrage, which caused considerable confusion in the advancing ranks but failed to arrest the enemy's advance.[9]

While skirmishing in front, a New Hampshire private observed the works in front of Dow's men: "behind the long line of rifle pits there was no sign of life. I looked again to the right and saw the long line of blue advance, with flags waving in the gentle breeze. I turned my eyes to the silent rebel rifle pits. Suddenly above them appeared a dark cloud of slouched hats and bronzed faces; the next moment a sheet of flame. I glanced again to the right; the line of blue had melted away."[10] At that moment the Federals came within two hundred yards of the breastworks, and the cannoneers

7. Irwin, *Nineteenth Corps*, 177, 182; Hanaburgh, *One Hundred and Twenty-eighth New York*, 40–41; John E. Hall to wife, May 29, 1863, John Emory Hall Papers, Regional History Collections, Western Michigan University, Kalamazoo; Dow, *Reminiscences*, 692; McGregor, *Fifteenth New Hampshire*, 378. Union accounts disagree regarding the deployment of Sherman's division, but Confederate sources clearly indicate that Dow formed on Nickerson's right.

8. Dow, *Reminiscences*, 693–94; McGregor, *Fifteenth New Hampshire*, 352.

9. Irwin, *Nineteenth Corps*, 178; McGregor, *Fifteenth New Hampshire*, 353; Dabney to [Gardner], August 24, 1863, LHA Collection.

10. McGregor, *Fifteenth New Hampshire*, 386–87.

switched from shell to double charges of canister. Captain George F. Abbay, wearing a badly crushed kepi and smoking a small, "squatty" pipe, told his men, "Now boys, I want you to stick to the pieces and give the Yankees hell." Running their guns into position, they obeyed by blasting the Yankees with canister at the appropriate moment.[11]

The Federals wavered and broke for the rear. Their officers quickly rallied them, and they moved forward a second time with similar results, the number of casualties constantly increasing as they repeated the process. A spent bullet rendered Dow's arm useless, and, no longer able to control his horse, the brigadier dismounted and proceeded on foot. Before Dow could assume command of the division, a bullet passed through his left thigh, forcing him to leave the field. Colonel David S. Cowles (128th New York) lay dead, a snow-white handkerchief covering his face. The plate of mail he wore on his breast failed to stop the bullet that pierced his side when he turn to cheer his men on. The colonels of the 6th Michigan and 26th Connecticut were wounded, and their regiments suffered nearly 30 percent casualties.[12]

The attack finally dissipated approximately seventy yards from the breastworks, with droves of Dow's men seeking shelter in the ravine to their right. The collapse of the attack, however, brought about something strange. The defeated brigade commenced sharpshooting, and their deadly aim forced the Confederates to take refuge behind the breastworks, unable to reply. The "eastern men" firing over the heads of those from Michigan shot their comrades because their bullets did not carry far enough.[13]

Nickerson's brigade moved forward in column of regiments.

11. Kendall, "Recollections," 1114; Dabney to [Gardner], August 24, 1863, LHA Collection; *OR*, Vol. XXVI, Pt. 1, p. 921.

12. Dabney to [Gardner], August 24, 1863, LHA Collection; Dow, *Reminiscences*, 694–96; *OR*, Vol. XXVI, Pt. 1, p. 68; McGregor, *Fifteenth New Hampshire*, 542; Alan S. Brown (ed.), *A Soldier's Life: The Civil War Experiences of Ben C. Johnson (Originally Entitled, Sketches of the Sixth Regiment Michigan Infantry)*, Faculty Contributions, School of Graduate Studies Western Michigan University, Vol. VI (Kalamazoo, 1962), 83; Harry [Harrison Soule] to father, July 2, 1863, Harrison Soule Collection, Michigan Historical Collections, Bentley Historical Library, University of Michigan, Ann Arbor; Croffut and Morris, *Military and Civil History of Connecticut*, 411.

13. Kendall, "Recollections," 1116; Irwin, *Nineteenth Corps*, 178; M'Murray, "Heroism of Union Officer," 428; John E. Hall to wife, May 29, 1863, Hall Papers.

Out in front, the 14th Maine deployed as skirmishers, followed by the 24th Maine and 177th and 165th New York. With artillery shells tearing gaping holes in their lines, they charged across a field of thick bushes and scrambled through a twenty-foot-deep ravine choked with felled timber. By the time they reformed and emerged upon the open plain, the 165th New York had passed to the front of the column. Dressed in zouave uniforms of red trousers and caps, they made a magnificent spectacle—and a magnificent target. [14]

When the attackers came within two hundred yards, southern infantry poured forth a fusillade of minié balls. "Oh how they fall," commented Texas Quartermaster Sergeant Richard W. Ford, "their red baggy Breeches the prettiest mark in the world." Some of the Confederates concentrated on the color bearers; the flag of the 165th New York went down at least three times. The seven-man color guard had five killed and one fatally and one seriously wounded. Leaping atop a stump, Lieutenant Colonel Abel Smith, Jr., waved his sword in one hand and a small United States flag in the other. He urged his New Yorkers to seize the fallen banner and press on, but marksmen turned their attention to him and he fell mortally wounded. The regiment lost 186 of the 350 men who participated in the assault. [15]

At one time the Confederate commander in this sector ordered his men to cease fire because of the gallant conduct of the New Yorkers. This expression of respect only inspired the New Yorkers to redouble their efforts, however, and the Confederates had to resume firing to prevent a breach in their line. The troops behind the zouaves failed to support them, and the New Yorkers ran or crawled back to the woods or lay on the ground awaiting the coming of darkness to attempt an escape. When he learned of Sherman's disabling injury, Andrews assumed command of the

14. Irwin, *Nineteenth Corps*, 177, 179; Diary of Ford, May 27, 1863; Clarence S. Martin, *Three Quarters of a Century with the Tenth Infantry New York National Guard, 1860-1935* (N.p., n.d.), 20; *One Hundred and Sixty-fifth New York*, 17–18; Dabney to [Gardner], August 24, 1863, LHA Collection.

15. Diary of Ford, May 27, 1863; R. W. Ford, Compiled Service Records of Confederate Soldiers Who Served in Organizations from the State of Texas, Roll 316, Microcopy 323, National Archives; Kendall, "Recollections," 1116; *One Hundred and Sixty-fifth New York*, 70, 99, 142; Irwin, *Nineteenth Corps*, 179, 182; [Wright], *Port Hudson*, 32–33.

division and prepared to implement forthcoming orders. None came, however, and he attempted to reorganize the shattered command.[16]

Cries for water from the wounded often went unheeded because some of Sherman's men had filled their canteens with whiskey before the assault. When the fighting ended, the zouaves' colors lay about seventy yards from the parapet. One youthful Louisianian, Private James Clark, could not resist the temptation to capture the flag. He dashed for the sally port, but Captain Robert L. Pruyn grabbed him, lecturing, "Here, you, boy, you'll be killed out there! and then what will your mother say?" Private Matt Howley managed to seize the coveted trophy, and the indignant Clark howled, "There, now, Matt's got the flag, and he didn't get killed either."[17]

To meet the threat along the Plains Store road, Colonel Benjamin T. Pixlee hurried the 16th Arkansas northward, the movement exposing them to enemy missiles. The six-foot-tall Pixlee unsheathed his sword and shouted, "Sixteenth, follow me, every devil of you!" The remaining Confederates opposite Sherman's division, now having "time to blow," watched their comrades to the left meet the charge against their front.[18]

When Banks heard the rattle of musketry from his left, he instructed Major General Christopher C. Augur to advance. Augur had awaited the order all day and had already deployed his men at the edge of the woods, a quarter-mile from the Confederate lines. Standing near his men while bullets zipped past, the general saw the men jerk their heads. "No use boys to dodge them after you hear them," he told them, something the men learned soon enough.[19] While awaiting the order to advance, Augur's men listened to their officers' words of encouragement and appreciated the whiskey ration, for "it was almost impossible to swallow hard bread and salt beef."[20]

16. McGregor, *Fifteenth New Hampshire*, 517; Diary of Ford, May 27, 1863; Irwin, *Nineteenth Corps*, 179.

17. Kendall, "Recollections," 1117; *One Hundred and Sixty-fifth New York*, 18, 99; Booth, *Louisiana Soldiers*, II, 342, Vol. III, Bk. 1, p. 369, Bk. 2, p. 213.

18. [A. M. Trawick], "Col. Benjamin T. Pixlee, of Arkansas," *Confederate Veteran*, X (1902), 317; Diary of Ford, May 27, 1863.

19. Plummer, *Forty-eighth M.V.M.*, 37; Irwin, *Nineteenth Corps*, 179–80.

20. Johns, *Forty-ninth Massachusetts*, 228; Stevens, *Fiftieth Massachusetts*, 138.

Finally, the order came. Profoundly excited, Lieutenant Colonel James O'Brien shouted, "Come on, boys; we'll wash in the Mississippi to-night."[21] The column advanced down the road until it emerged from the woods, where the men deployed in line of battle. Skirmishers covered the front south of the road, immediately followed by O'Brien's two hundred volunteers of the "forlorn hope." Next came Colonel Edward P. Chapin's five regiments, and four companies of the 50th Massachusetts from Dudley's brigade, and the 2nd Vermont Battery.[22]

The "forlorn hope" believed that half their group was to run from the woods, bridge the ditch fronting the breastworks with cotton bags and fascines, and return to the shelter of the woods, while the remainder crossed the bridge and forced their way inside at bayonet point. None knew the nature of the moat, but they believed it to be fifteen feet wide and twelve feet deep.[23]

They came forward with a whoop and a yell, clawing their way through briars and vines, over logs and around stumps. "Foolishness to talk about cheering or the 'double-quick.' We had no strength for the former, aye, and no heart either. We had gone but a few rods ere our Yankee common sense assured us we must fail," recalled one private. They had hardly moved when everyone found himself inextricably caught in an almost grasping abatis under a withering blaze of artillery and musketry. Fieldpieces shot directly down the road while two twenty-four-pounders raked their flank; the gunners used railroad rails and broken chains for grape and rusty nails and other bits of scrap iron for canister.[24]

The deadly hail of missiles decimated the Federals. A three-inch piece of bayonet struck one captain in the mouth. Almost on exiting the woods, Chapin, conspicuous in his dress coat and white Panama hat, took a slight wound in the knee. The brigade commander continued but a few steps when a ball struck his face and passed completely through his brain. Blood stained the flag of 48th Massachusetts, the color bearer having embraced the banner when he fell dead. After a bullet passed through his wrist, Color Sergeant

21. Johns, *Forty-ninth Massachusetts*, 228; *OR*, Vol. XXVI, Pt. 1, p. 71.
22. Dabney to [Gardner], August 24, 1863, LHA Collection; Irwin, *Nineteenth Corps*, 179–80; Stevens, *Fiftieth Massachusetts*, 139.
23. Johns, *Forty-ninth Massachusetts*, 219.
24. *Ibid.*, 229, 384; Dabney to [Gardner], August 24, 1863, LHA Collection; Irwin, *Nineteenth Corps*, 180.

Hadley P. Dyer seized the banner of the 21st Maine with his good hand and cradled it with his injured arm. He hastened forward until falling with a lethal wound. One member of the 50th Massachusetts described the deluge of lead and iron as "perfect hell."[25]

With a driving determination the Federals pressed onward. The color sergeant of the 116th New York, riddled with bullets, fell near the breastworks. Captain Francis M. Smith of the 48th Massachusetts seized the fallen banner and rallied the men until he fell wounded; miraculously he survived, even though thirty-eight bullets had pierced his uniform. Colonel William F. Bartlett seized a regimental flag and rode ahead of the column. Severely wounded, he fell from his horse only sixty yards from the parapet. He lifted the flag to signal his men to come on. Confederate officers thought this "the bravest and most daring thing we have yet seen done in the war" and shouted "Don't shoot him!"—and so he lay unmolested.[26]

None of the Federals managed to struggle through the abatis. When they neared the fortifications, their line lost all sense of regularity, and it became evident that the assault was doomed. Word passed through the line to halt, and the men sought safety behind stumps, logs, and uprooted trees, where they lay listening to missiles of death strip the bark from their shelters. The battery kept abreast of the advancing infantry and maintained a steady barrage, but the garrison's reply seemed hardly diminished. The underbrush burst into flames on the left of Augur's line, and the smoke and flames posed additional danger and discomfort to the men. Pinned down for nearly an hour, O'Brien suddenly sprang forward over the logs. Waving his sword, he screamed, "Charge! boys, charge!" Fewer than a dozen men followed him in the foolhardy effort that ended his life. The seven assaulting companies of the 49th Massachusetts suffered 35 percent casualties, the 116th New York 29 percent. Comrades assisted some of the injured to the rear, and friends managed to spread blankets over a few of the dead, but most had to lie where they fell till nightfall. Even so, Banks prepared to order the remainder of Dudley's brigade forward until

25. Stevens, *Fiftieth Massachusetts*, 279–80; Plummer, *Forty-eighth Regiment*, 64–65; Woodward, *21st Me.*, 33; Clark, *One Hundred and Sixteenth New York*, 90; Bryant (ed.), "Yankee Soldier," 146.

26. Palfrey, "Port Hudson," 83–84; [Preston], *Port Hudson*, 17–18; Plummer, *Forty-eighth Regiment*, 123; M'Murray, "Heroism of Union Officer," 428.

word arrived of Sherman's repulse, and it became immeasurably clear that he had lost the battle.[27]

The Federals on the left had lacked neither determination nor courage. Although the Confederates lost fewer than thirty men, the enemy suffered more than a thousand casualties. At least one man out of five was killed or wounded. Filled with admiration for their bravery, the Confederates sought out the Federals on the field and gave them water. They brought nine zouaves inside and took them to the hospital.[28]

The intense heat of the afternoon sun beat down on the men still engaged in deadly conflict. About five o'clock word passed through the ranks on the Confederate left that someone had raised a white flag. Hopelessly pinned down for almost six hours, the commander of the 159th New York hoisted a white handkerchief on a stick. Major Samuel L. Knox of the 1st Alabama met the flag, and Lieutenant Colonel Charles A. Burt erroneously informed him that Banks desired a cessation of hostilities to bury the dead. Knox detained Burt while he notified Gardner, who "at once rejected it as informal, and an unwarranted use of the white flag, and ordered that hostilities be resumed in half an hour."[29]

Knox informed the enemy, and both sides sought cover, for the Confederates had taken advantage of the cease-fire to stretch out atop the breastwork. They "swarmed out on the parapet like ants on an ant hill," commented one Federal lieutenant, who believed the enemy sufficient in number to sweep away any force assaulting across the plateau "like chaff from the summer threshing floor" before it reached the breastwork.[30]

But during the interval, hundreds of Federals who had worked their way close to the Confederate works took advantage of the short truce to retire to safer positions. Burt's men had got themselves into a perilous position, and Colonel I. G. W. Steedman

27. Johns, *Forty-ninth Massachusetts*, 231, 241; Irwin, *Nineteenth Corps*, 180–81; Stevens, *Fiftieth Massachusetts*, 140; Woodward, *21st Me.*, 33–34; Bosson, *Forty-Second Massachusetts*, 365; Charles F. Wadsworth to mother, May 30, 1863, Wadsworth Papers.

28. Dabney to [Gardner], August 24, 1863, LHA Collection; McGregor, *Fifteenth New Hampshire*, 517–18; Hewitt and Bergeron (eds.), *Post Hospital Ledger*, 95.

29. "Fortification and Siege," 323; Hall and Hall, *Cayuga in the Field*, [sect. 2], 116; De Forest, *Volunteer's Adventures*, 113.

30. Smith, *Leaves from a Soldier's Diary*, 65–66; "Fortification and Siege," 323.

concluded: "I have now no doubt but that the flag was presented for the unlawful and cowardly purpose of withdrawing the troops from the dangerous position in which they found themselves. Had not this been done many must have been killed, as there was no possibility of escape until night came on." When Colonel Benjamin W. Johnson received orders to respect the white flag, the Yankees marched from the moat with supreme impudence to a safe refuge in the woods. But the 15th Arkansas had held "Fort Desperate" with the loss of about forty men.[31]

When Federal buglers sounded "cease firing" that evening, stretcher parties moved over the battlefield, The Confederates lounged atop the parapet and watched the enemy remove the dead and wounded. Both sides refrained from firing a shot or even shouting an unfriendly remark. The Federals buried twenty of their comrades without coffin or shroud in a long trench beside the Plains Store road. While the injured sought medical assistance, the able-bodied searched for missing friends, deployed to meet a counterattack, or began to entrench. Two fallen trees lying parallel to the enemy's breastworks enabled the 75th New York to build a crude fortification which they dubbed "Fort Babcock," in honor of their gallant commander.[32]

After nightfall, the division commanders reported to Banks's headquarters. It then became known that the repulse was worse than anticipated. Banks called up reinforcements and ordered arms for the Negro engineers. The utmost confidence of the morning was now gloomy, surprised regret. "It was long indeed before the men felt the same faith in themselves, and it is but the plain truth to say that their reliance on the department commander never quite returned," concluded Banks's adjutant.[33]

When the firing ceased that evening, the 1st Alabama had lost thirty-two killed and forty-four wounded. Blood saturated parts of the ramparts and flowed through the trenches to form puddles. The

31. "Fortification and Siege," 323–24; Hewitt, *Desperate!* 12.

32. Stevens, *Fiftieth Massachusetts*, 140–41, 150; Plummer, *Forty-eighth Regiment*, 38; Woodward, *21st Me.*, 35; Hall and Hall, *Cayuga in the Field*, [sect. 2], 117.

33. Irwin, *Nineteenth Corps*, 181; [Banks] to Emory, May 27, 1863, 10 P.M., Record Group 393; Woodward, *21st Me.*, 35; Lawrence L. Hewitt, Introduction to Richard B. Irwin, *History of the Nineteenth Army Corps* (1893; rpr. Baton Rouge, 1985), [insert], ii.

groans of the dying and pitiful cries for water from injured Federals lying before the breastworks brought the deepest sympathy from the Alabamians. Several risked their lives to carry canteens of water to those they had just engaged in deadly strife. While on their mission of mercy, the southerners discovered the ground littered with Enfield rifles. After they reported this information, their comrades quickly secured some, so that in the future each member of the regiment had two loaded guns, the Enfield for the "long taw" and the flintlock for close quarters. Members of the 12th Arkansas managed to secure a fresh supply of percussion caps, ammunition, and Enfield rifles, which were far superior weapons to their indifferent shotguns.[34]

Like his subordinates, Gardner prepared to meet the next assault. Almost every able-bodied southerner, even though he had fought all day, had to perform fatigue duty during the night. They strengthened the hastily constructed rifle pits on the left wing and throughout the garrison repaired any damage inflicted by artillery projectiles. Units redeployed along the line, and Gardner issued an order that if a white flag appeared his men should open fire if the enemy refused to halt "some distance" from the breastworks. He added, "A battle does not necessarily cease on the presentation of a white flag."[35]

The Confederates felt great satisfaction that evening. They believed that only their cool determination had saved them. Had they wavered but a moment or slackened their murderous fusillade at a critical time to seek shelter, the enemy would have breached their works and forced them to surrender. The southerners also learned a valuable lesson that day—determined men could hold a fortified position against considerable odds.[36] Yet the outcome of the battle on May 27 still amazed them. And this unexpected turn of events had far-reaching consequences.

The Confederate triumph that day resembled Robert E. Lee's stand against George B. McClellan at Sharpsburg the previous fall. And it was just as surprising. The only significant difference be-

34. McMorries, *First Alabama*, 63–64; Mobile *Advertiser and Register*, December 29, 1863; *OR*, Vol. XXVI, Pt. 1, p. 929.

35. [Gardner], G.O. No. 49, May 27, 1863, Chap. II, Vol. 198, Record Group 109; Dabney to [Gardner], August 24, 1863, A. J. Lewis to [Gardner], July 9, 1863, LHA Collection.

36. [Wright], *Port Hudson*, 37; McMorries, *First Alabama*, 65.

tween the two engagements was that McClellan ordered his troops to attack piecemeal. Had Banks's subordinates implemented his plan for a simultaneous assault, his troops would surely have breached the Confederate defenses. Brigadier General Thomas W. Sherman's delay allowed Confederates on the right to reinforce Colonel Steedman on the left. Had these troops not arrived at the "Bull Pen" when they did, even the halfhearted Federal attack against Steedman would have overwhelmed his line.

Having moved against Port Hudson, Banks had committed himself to capturing the garrison. His initial failure brought an irreversible stalemate, one that would drag on until the fall of Vicksburg ended the need for a Confederate bastion on the Mississippi below the mouth of the Red River. By the time the struggle for Port Hudson ended on July 9, 1863, the longest true siege in American military history (forty-eight days) would occur, and the men in gray would undergo the greatest deprivation ever experienced in the Confederacy.

In spite of their isolated position, southerners felt confident after their initial success and seemed more determined than ever to hold out. And despite shortages of everything except gunpowder, Gardner apparently never despaired. He divided his perimeter defenses into zones, with an engineer in charge of each. The soldiers strengthened the fortifications and constructed loopholes in the top of the parapet for sharpshooters. The Confederates had fewer than sixty cannon, and most of them were obsolete, of small caliber, or lacked projectiles. Officers and men quickly realized that they must improvise if they were to defend the post successfully. Gardner ordered the cannon positioned where their fire would have greatest effect. He also had his men dig pits in which to place the guns when not in use to protect them against incoming shells. At least three of the guns along the river lay on center-pivot carriages, which enabled their crews to swing them around and fire at the Federal army. The ten-inch columbiad in Battery No. 4 proved so menacing that the Yankees christened the gun "The Demoralizer" and incorrectly believed, because of its wide range of fire, that the Confederates had it mounted on a railroad car. The men tore off their shirt sleeves and filled them with spent bullets and pieces of iron to provide rounds of canister for the cannon.

Gardner desperately needed and could not replace four items: men, cannon, medicine, and food. Rifles dropped by the enemy or a fallen comrade and hand grenades made from unexploded enemy projectiles increased firepower and compensated for the loss of manpower. Land mines or "torpedoes" made from unexploded thirteen-inch mortar shells also increased the killing power in front of the breastworks. [37]

Such measures could not make up for desertions, however, which steadily increased as the siege progressed. Colonel Steedman noted, "Our most serious and annoying difficulty is the unreliable character of a portion of our Louisiana troops. Many have deserted to the enemy, giving him information of our real condition; yet in the same regiments we have some of our ablest officers and best men." Confederates, especially members of Miles's Louisiana Legion, eventually entered the Federal lines in droves. [38]

Outgunned three to one, Confederate cannon became choice targets for enemy gunners. Captain L. J. Girard was responsible for maintaining Gardner's cannon, and if any individual deserved special recognition for his performance, it was he. Almost single-handedly and without proper tools or materials, Girard kept the cannon firing. The enemy's cannonade disabled, dismounted, or destroyed virtually every gun at least once, but Girard worked day and night making the necessary repairs. Another especially attractive target was the gristmill. Its destruction left the Confederates in dire straits until someone came up with an ingenious idea. The southerners blocked up the locomotive, passed a belt from the drivewheel to a grindingstone, and in this way the engineer "furnished meal at the rate of several miles an hour." [39]

Endless labor and improper diet sapped the soldiers' health. The number of sick increased daily. "Six ounces of quinine would save the army," commented Steedman, "as the mass of our diseases are intermittent and bilious fevers, with their many complications."

37. Cunningham, *Port Hudson Campaign*, 68, 70–72, 106; de Gournay to [Gardner], September 12, 1863, LHA Collection.

38. Mobile *Advertiser and Register*, August 9, 1863; Eli [A. Griffin] to wife, June 30, 1863, Eli A. Griffin Letters, Michigan Historical Collections, Bentley Historical Library, University of Michigan, Ann Arbor; Bergeron and Hewitt, *Miles' Legion*, 40–44, 68, 72–74, 79, 82–83, 85–91.

39. George N. Carpenter, *History of the Eighth Regiment Vermont Volunteers, 1861–1865* (Boston, 1886), 131; [Wright], *Port Hudson*, 30, 52, 62; Smith to Gardner, October 23, 1863, de Gournay to [Gardner], September 12, 1863, Dabney to [Gardner], August 24, 1863, LHA Collection.

The lack of stimulants and nourishment augmented the fatality rate from wounds and debility. By the end of June, daily rations consisted of three small ears of corn, nicknamed "pinewoods nubbins" by the soldiers. Yet the men retained their humor. When he distributed the rations, the commissary sergeant of Boone's Louisiana battery would call out, "Pig-gee, pig-gee, pig-goo-ah!" The artillerymen promptly fell in on all fours and began squealing and grunting, keeping up the jollity of the camp.[40]

But men could not long subsist on such a diet. Gardner had a mule butchered and set the example for his troops; fifteen pounds of the beast were prepared for his mess. On July 3 Steedman described the desperate situation in a letter to his uncle: "For two days a number of horses have been slain and eaten by men and officers. *Rats*, which are very numerous in our camps, are considered a dainty dish, and are being considerably sought after . . . I have eaten a piece of horse this morning. I do not fancy it, but will eat it as long as I can sustain life upon it, before I will give any consent to surrender. The whole army exhibit the same spirit."[41] One private "believed that good fat mule (not sore back) is a better and juicier as well as a finer grained meat than beef, and would have or make no objection to eating it if it is properly dressed and cooked." His comrades often imitated a mule by uttering "ye-haw," kicking, or trotting.[42] The shortage of food, however, nearly proved the undoing of the garrison. The men preferred mule meat to surrender, but even that delicacy would have been exhausted by mid-July.

Banks was as determined as the Confederates. And unlike Gardner, Banks could draw on the resources of his entire department, which stretched from Texas to Florida. Shocked by the initial repulse, he strengthened his command and thereby increased the lopsidedness of the contest. By June 1 nine additional regiments had joined the besieging army, more than enough fresh troops to offset the Federal losses of May 27. And reinforcements continued to arrive throughout the siege. Banks also brought up

40. Mobile *Advertiser and Register*, August 9, 1863; Linn Tanner, "The Meat Diet at Port Hudson," *Confederate Veteran*, XXVI (1918), 484.

41. Mobile *Advertiser and Register*, August 9, 1863; West Baton Rouge *Sugar Planter*, February 24, 1866.

42. Linn Tanner, "Port Hudson Calamities—Mule Meat," *Confederate Veteran*, XVII (1909), 512; Booth, *Louisiana Soldiers*, Vol. III, Bk. 2, p. 766.

additional cannon. Soon, eighty-nine fieldpieces, forty siege cannon and mortars, four nine-inch Dahlgrens brought ashore from the *Richmond*, and the long-range rifled cannon and six thirteen-inch mortars of the fleet pounded the Confederates.

His preparations complete for a second assault, Banks began an hour-long bombardment at 11:15 A.M. on June 13. The Confederates hugged their trenches while the projectiles fell at the rate of more than one a second. When the shelling ended, Banks demanded that Gardner immediately surrender to avoid unnecessary bloodshed. "My duty requires me to defend this position, and therefore I decline to surrender," responded Gardner.[43]

Banks resumed the bombardment, and the firing continued throughout the night. Gardner's refusal apparently caught Banks by surprise because he did not issue the final orders for the second assault until 1 A.M. on June 14—only two and a half hours before the assault was to begin. These last-minute preparations and a heavy fog almost assured the disorganization of the simultaneously scheduled three-pronged assault. And a piecemeal attack against a fortified enemy alerted by an artillery barrage made failure a foregone conclusion.

The middle column struck the center of Beall's line about 4 A.M. Initial Federal success ended quickly, and the struggle there had almost ceased by the time the right wing of the assault struck "Fort Deperate" some three hours later. The left wing failed to make any serious effort. As unsuccessful as the May 27 attack, the one of June 14 only lengthened the casualty list and lowered Union morale to an all-time low. One regiment even mutinied. Banks and his staff had made plans for a third assault led by a "forlorn hope" of more than a thousand volunteers,[44] but the garrison surrendered before the attack took place.

The outcome of May 27 had convinced many men on both sides that the garrison could withstand anything the besiegers threw at it. The second assault only intensified this belief. Undoubtedly the morale of both sides significantly influenced the ability of the Confederates to maintain such a one-sided contest. The south-

43. *OR*, Vol. XXVI, Pt. 1, pp. 141, 553; Cunningham, *Port Hudson Campaign*, 70, 72, 79.

44. Cunningham, *Port Hudson Campaign*, 79, 83–93, 111–13; *Forlorn Hope Storming Column, Port Hudson, Louisiana*, Box 38, Folder 38, Historic New Orleans Collection, New Orleans.

erners also realized the absolute necessity of holding Banks's troops at Port Hudson until General Joseph E. Johnston could drive Major General Ulysses S. Grant from the rear of Vicksburg. One Alabama private recalled, "All through the siege we cherished hope of relief . . . we had no fears of the enemy, who was thoroughly whipped and demoralized already, yet having nothing to eat and being nearly out of ammunition, all foresaw our inevitable doom." A Federal lamented, "We are poorly led and uselessly slaughtered, and that the brains are all *within* and not *'before* Port Hudson.'"[45] This mental outlook, together with the unwillingness of Banks to admit defeat by withdrawing and of Gardner to surrender or attempt an evacuation, made a lengthy siege inevitable.

Contemporaries and historians have criticized Gardner for his passivity during the siege. Edward G. Cunningham contended, "At any time after 10 A.M. on June 14, a major Confederate counterattack at the 'Priest Cap' would have almost certainly broken the siege. . . . By using the ravines and gullies running along Confederate Battery No. XI, the Confederates could have broken the backbone of the Federal works and lifted the siege by destroying Banks's heavy guns." Such remarks ignore Gardner's objective of holding Port Hudson to the last. He had no desire to evacuate the garrison. Nor did he wish to expend lives and ammunition in sorties at the cost of hastening his capitulation.[46]

The deadlock could have ended differently only if a Confederate relief force had raised the siege. Colonel John Logan's troops did an excellent job harassing Banks's rear, but they lacked the strength to compel him to withdraw. Confederate authorities had forces for such an expedition but committed these soldiers to relieve Vicksburg. When troops finally moved to aid Port Hudson, they succeeded in disrupting Banks's supply line to New Orleans. By then, however, the fall of Vicksburg had determined the outcome at Port Hudson, and it is impossible to determine what effect a shortage of supplies would have had on Banks's army. But one does not have to speculate about the consequences of the unsuccessful assault by the Federals on May 27.[47]

45. McMorries, *First Alabama*, 68; Mobile *Advertiser and Register*, August 9 1863; Johns, *Forty-ninth Massachusetts*, 302.

46. Elias P. Pellet, *History of the 114th Regiment, New York State Volunteers* . . . (Norwich, N.Y., 1866), 130; Cunningham, *Port Hudson Campaign*, xii.

47. Cunningham, *Port Hudson Campaign*, xii–xiii, 113–16.

X

Besieged, Surrendered— The True Significance

They fought splendidly!

—Major General Nathaniel P. Banks,
Department of the Gulf

Although Port Hudson became the last Confederate stronghold on the Mississippi River, its capitulation following the loss of Vicksburg had little strategic effect on the war. But despite having to surrender the entire garrison, Gardner could claim a significant tactical victory. Fewer than three thousand men could stand in line during the surrender ceremony on July 9; yet Gardner's army had held nearly forty thousand Federals at bay for almost two months. His men had inflicted more than five thousand casualties on the enemy while sustaining only five hundred. Sunstroke or disease hospitalized an additional four thousand Federals; only two hundred Confederates died from these causes. [1] Port Hudson had proven a field of slaughter for the Federals.

One historian had suggested that the Confederates, "by their dogged resistance, stalled the Union victory schedule and thereby prolonged the conflict." [2] And this statement has considerable merit. Union operations against Mobile and Texas were delayed, troops desperately needed at Vicksburg had to be drawn from other departments, and the Confederates regained southwestern Louisiana. But a closer examination of the consequences of the failure

1. *OR*, Vol. XXVI, Pt. 1, p. 144; Cunningham, *Port Hudson Campaign*, 123.
2. T. Harry Williams, Foreword to Cunningham, *Port Hudson Campaign*, vi.

of the Federal assault on May 27 tells a different story, one that had a far-reaching and devastating effect on the Confederacy.

One of these consequences centers on the Union commander. When the fighting ended on May 27, the opponents were deadlocked. To avoid the stigma of defeat, Banks had to remain until he forced Gardner to capitulate—thus delaying his juncture with Grant. In fact, the garrison at Port Hudson held out until Banks and his troops were no longer needed at Vicksburg. Thus Banks never joined Grant.

If Port Hudson had fallen on May 27, Banks would have arrived at Vicksburg the conquering hero who had dispersed Confederate forces in western Louisiana and won at Port Hudson. As ranking officer, Banks would have assumed overall command of the combined armies, his and Grant's, and received the credit for capturing the doomed city. Considering his political connections, it is not improbable that Banks would have become supreme commander in the West and even general in chief.

Political considerations instead of military experience had initially influenced Lincoln to commission Banks a major general. Politics had sustained Banks through military reverses in 1862, and politics would have sustained him through all but the most disastrous campaign. Lincoln also favored him because he appeared to share the president's views, particularly on slavery. This position made Banks popular with the moderate faction of the Republican party and especially its leader, Secretary of State William H. Seward. And the politically astute Banks could change his views as circumstances dictated.[3] Once Grant became his subordinate, Banks would have indefinitely, if not forever, blocked Grant's rise to supreme command. This change in command would have extended the war far longer than the delay brought about by the Confederates' "dogged resistance" at Port Hudson.

The initial success by Colonel I. G. W. Steedman's men on the morning of the twenty-seventh ironically dealt the Confederacy a deadly blow. And it had a more direct impact on the war than simply the possibility of Banks superseding Grant, for it drew black troops into the attack. Their assault proved the last undertaken by the Federals on their extreme right and the last in which the 1st and 3rd Louisiana Native Guards participated at Port

3. Harrington, *Fighting Politician*, 61, 288.

Hudson. Withering fire made their sector a death trap for any attacker. Casualties among the black soldiers probably totaled nearly 600; proof of their losses lay in the arms and legs piled behind their hospital the night of the twenty-seventh. Confederate officers counted 250 Federals lying on the field where the Native Guards had charged. These casualties included only the dead or those too badly wounded to crawl off.[4]

The performance of the black troops impressed Banks. "They fought splendidly!" he wrote his wife. He gave Brigadier General William Dwight command of a division and, needing every man possible, ordered additional black soldiers at Baton Rouge to hasten to the front.[5]

All major engagements during the Civil War made headlines in the newspapers, but an assault by black troops drew special attention from northern reporters. One correspondent wrote: "One negro was observed with a rebel soldier in his grasp, tearing the flesh from his face with his teeth, other weapons having failed him. After firing one volley they did not deign to load again, but went in with bayonets, and wherever they had a chance it was all up with the rebels." An illustration in *Harper's Weekly* depicted the black soldiers in hand-to-hand combat atop a parapet that bristled both with cannon and an abundance of Confederates.[6]

Many Yankees who fought at Port Hudson agreed with the press's view. These men believed that the black troops had fought valiantly and looked forward to the day when thousands of former slaves would swell the ranks of the Union army. On May 28 Colonel Benjamin H. Grierson wrote his wife: "There can be no

4. Garrett and Lightfoot, *Civil War in Maury County*, 64; Wilson, *Black Phalanx*, 525; Stanyan, *Eighth New Hampshire*, 230; [Wright], *Port Hudson*, 36; de Gournay, "Siege of Port Hudson," in "Annals of the War"; *OR*, Vol. XXVI, Pt. 1, 68. Casualty figures for the black regiments vary widely and cannot be precisely determined. Considering the number of attackers, the terrain, the lengthy shelling they had to endure, and the number and firepower of their opponents, a loss of 50 percent is not unusual. The official casualty return for both regiments for the entire siege lists 44 killed, 133 wounded, and 3 captured or missing for a total loss of 180 men—a figure so low as to make one wonder if there was a deliberate attempt to cover up what was little short of a massacre.

5. Banks to wife, May 30, 1863, Banks Papers; *OR*, LIII, 559; [Banks] to commanding officer at Baton Rouge, May 27, 1863, 10 P.M., Record Group 393.

6. Jno. Robertson (comp.), *Michigan in the War* (rev. ed.; Lansing, 1882), 267; *Harper's Weekly*, July 18, 1863.

question about the good fighting quality of negroes, hereafter, that question was settled beyond a doubt yesterday.'' Captain Robert F. Wilkinson wrote his father on June 3: ''One thing I am glad to say, that is that the black troops at P. Hudson fought & acted superbly. The theory of negro inefficiency is, I am very thankful at last thoroughly Exploded by facts. We shall shortly have a splendid army of thousands of them.''[7]

Banks, too, praised the black soldiers in his official report. He took pleasure in writing

> that they answered every expectation. In many respects their conduct was heroic. No troops could be more determined or more daring. . . . Whatever doubt may have existed heretofore as to the efficiency of organizations of this character, the history of this day proves conclusively . . . that the Government will find in this class of troops effective supporters and defenders. The severe test to which they were subjected, and the determined manner in which they encountered the enemy, leaves upon my mind no doubt of their ultimate success.[8]

Not everyone accepted the newspaper accounts. Confederate Lieutenant Howard C. Wright gave a different evaluation of the media coverage in a letter to his mother: ''The N.Y. Herald correspondence & all the Illustrations I have seen of the fighting, in Leslie & Harper, are preposterous, particularly the story about the negro troops fighting well. . . . The story must have been gotten up for political effect.'' Other readers, including numerous Yankees, agreed with Wright. Colonel Halbert S. Greenleaf of the 52nd Massachusetts described the charge by the Native Guards as ''an exhibition of cowardice on the part of the entire gang instead of that courageous and valiant spirit of which so much has been written.'' When the Confederates read that the black units had suffered six hundred casualties, many of them concluded that the white soldiers supporting the Negroes must have shot them. One Alabama private even reported hearing volleys of musketry from the direction the black troops fled, but apparently the Negroes fired

---

7. Dudley Taylor Cornish, *The Sable Arm: Negro Troops in the Union Army, 1861–1865* (New York, 1956), 142–43; Grierson to Alice, May 28, 1863, 6 P.M., B. H. Grierson Papers, Illinois State Historical Library, Springfield; Capt. Robert F. Wilkinson to father, June 3, 1863, Wilkinson Papers.

8. *OR*, Vol. XXVI, Pt. I, p. 45.

these discharges to convince Dwight they were pressing the assault.[9]

The truth lay between the extremes. Despite their failure to penetrate or even reach the principal fortifications, the black soldiers deserve no criticism for their performance on May 27. Their baptism of fire came from an order to accomplish the impossible. Who can blame them for withdrawing after scores of their comrades lay dead and dying? Many white regiments failed to advance any closer than two hundred yards to the Confederate works during the attack; some hardly moved forward at all. And only the 165th New York suffered a higher percentage of casualties. Banks even ordered one of his division commanders relieved for not attacking promptly.[10] The black troops deserved the praise they received—even if it was somewhat exaggerated.

Abolitionist reporters and military officers made the Negroes' assault one of the turning points of the war—a turning point long overlooked by both contemporaries and historians. On June 11, 1863, the New York *Times*, noted for its accurate reporting and sober editorial policy, published extracts from Banks's report with the comment:

> This official testimony settles the question that the negro race can fight with great prowess. Those black soldiers had never before been in any severe engagement. They were comparatively raw troops, and were yet subjected to the most awful ordeal that even veterans ever have to experience—the charging upon fortifications through the crash of belching batteries. The men, white or black, who will not flinch from that, will flinch from nothing. It is no longer possible to doubt the bravery and steadiness of the colored race, when rightly led.

The excitement generated by the newspaper coverage of the black soldiers' charge at Port Hudson almost singularly convinced northern whites to accept the enlistment of Negroes in the U.S. Army.

9. [Howard C. Wright] to mother, July 16, 1863, Lieut. H. C. Wright Letters, New-York Historical Society, New York; New Orleans *Daily Picayune*, August 19, 1863, quoting correspondent of Chicago *Times*; *OR*, Vol. XXVI, Pt. 1, p. 530; Charley [Moulton] to brother and sister, June 19, 1863, Charles Moulton Letters, Michigan Historical Collections, Bentley Historical Library, University of Michigan, Ann Arbor; Smith, *Company K*, 63, 83.

10. Cunningham, *Port Hudson Campaign*, 55, 60–62; *OR*, Vol. XXVI, Pt. 1, pp. 509–10.

It also stimulated free blacks in the North to volunteer. By sponsoring a recruitment poster heralding the "VALOR AND HEROISM" displayed by the Negro soldiers at Port Hudson, black abolitionists in Philadelphia alone induced more than eight thousand Negroes to enlist. The bravery exhibited by black troops in the July 18 assault on Battery Wagner, outside Charleston, South Carolina, dashed any serious doubts that remained after the Negroes' performance at Port Hudson on May 27. The black man had earned the right to fight for his freedom.[11]

Nearly 180,000 black soldiers served in the Federal army before the war ended. Although the Negroes generally found themselves stationed in rear areas doing guard duty, this service freed white troops for combat. By the spring of 1865 black soldiers nearly equaled in number Confederate infantrymen present for duty throughout the South. In addition, this fresh source of manpower appeared when the war-weary North had grown tired of the seemingly endless list of casualties.[12] And the positive impact the presence of these additional soldiers had on the Union war effort should not be underestimated.

Ramifications of a Confederate defeat on May 27 could have extended beyond the war. Imagine how different Reconstruction would have been if white troops had formed the bulk of the occupation forces and Banks, instead of Grant, had become the eighteenth president of the United States.

One does not have to speculate about events that actually occurred, however. Grant went on to defeat Lee and become president. Banks remained in command of the Army of the Gulf until his disastrous defeat in the Red River Campaign in the spring of 1864 brought about his removal from field duty. And black soldiers distinguished themselves in several major battles and numerous

11. Cornish, *Sable Arm*, ix, 143, 145, 155–56; Charles L. Blockson, "Escape from Slavery: The Underground Railroad," *National Geographic*, CLXVI (July, 1984), 33; Long and Long, *Civil War Day by Day*, 363, 387; Benjamin Quarles, *The Negro in the Civil War* (Boston, 1953), 224; Bell Irvin Wiley, *Southern Negroes, 1861–1865* (1938; rpr. Baton Rouge, 1974), 336–37. Some historians emphasize the Negroes' performance at Milliken's Bend, Louisiana, on June 7, 1863, as having a major impact on public opinion. But the black troops in that engagement merely fought on the defensive—and behind earthworks and supported by gunboats— hardly as impressive as Negroes equaling the performance of white soldiers in a full-scale assault.

12. "Notes on the Union and Confederate Armies," 767–68.

smaller engagements following their performance at Port Hudson. At the Battle of Olustee, Florida, the 8th U.S. Colored Infantry lost 303 officers and men, one of the most severe regimental losses of the entire war. On June 15, 1864, a division of black troops succeeded in capturing the works in its front, along with seven cannon, at Petersburg, Virginia. Another division composed entirely of Negroes formed the final wave of the assault column at the Battle of the Crater. Despite the failure of the attack before they moved forward, the black soldiers fought bravely; their casualties exceeded 1,300. About 10,000 Negroes engaged the Confederates at the Battle of Chaffin's Farm, where the 6th U.S. Colored Infantry sustained losses in excess of 57 percent. The 29th Connecticut (Negro) held a skirmish line for several hours under heavy pressure along the Darbytown Road in Virginia on October 27. The 54th Massachusetts (Negro) endured the heaviest loss of any regiment at the Battle of Honey Hill, South Carolina. Two brigades of black troops participated in the victorious charge at Nashville, Tennessee, where the 13th U.S. Colored Infantry lost 221 officers and men killed and wounded—the largest loss of any regiment in the assault. And in the last battle of the war, the successful Federal attack on Fort Blakely, Alabama, on April 9, 1865, yet another black division distinguished itself. More than 32,000 Negroes died while in the army. Undoubtedly, the performance of black soldiers on the battlefield had some impact on the Confederate government's decision to enlist slaves in its army, although too late to turn the tide of the war. [13] The Confederates' "dogged resistance" on May 27, 1863, brought about this participation by Negroes in the war and prevented Banks from superseding Grant— thereby hastening the downfall of the Confederacy and making Port Hudson a turning point of the Civil War.

13. William F. Fox, *Regimental Losses in the American Civil War 1861–1865* . . . (1889; rpr. Dayton, 1985), 54–56; Long and Long, *Civil War Day by Day*, 641, 708.

Appendix I

Confederate Troop Strength at Port Hudson

	Present for Duty	Aggregate Present
August 31, 1862	946	1,175
October 22, 1862[1]	NA	2,594
January 31, 1863	12,372	15,802
February 28, 1863	11,977	15,572
March 31, 1863[2]	16,287	20,388
April 29, 1863[3]	11,700	NA
May 19, 1863	4,652	5,715
June 30, 1863	2,803	4,098
July 9, 1863[4]	NA	6,404
June 25, 1863 (Logan's command)	1,296	1,571

NA = not available.

SOURCE: *OR*, XV, 804, 841, 965, 1000, 1032, 1059, 1062, Vol. XXVI, Pt. 2, pp. 10, 82, 99.

1. Includes 182 men at Baton Rouge.

2. Includes Herren's and Lester's companies at Ponchatoula.

3. Includes McLaurin's Battalion, Cochran's command, and Herren's and Lester's companies at Ponchatoula.

4. Confederate Paroles, Record Group 393. Includes 5,953 noncommissioned officers and privates paroled and 451 officers retained as prisoners of war. Available evidence indicates that approximately 100 additional officers and enlisted men escaped.

Appendix II

Port Hudson Garrison, March 14, 1863

MAXEY'S BRIGADE
4th Louisiana
30th Louisiana
42nd Tennessee
46th Tennessee
48th Tennessee
49th Tennessee
53rd Tennessee
55th Tennessee
1st Texas Battalion
  Sharpshooters
Fenner's Louisiana
  Battery
Roberts' (Seven Stars)
  Mississippi Battery

BEALL'S BRIGADE
8th (Jones) Arkansas Battalion
11th Arkansas
12th Arkansas
14th Arkansas
15th Arkansas
16th Arkansas
17th Arkansas
18th Arkansas
23rd Arkansas
1st Mississippi
39th Mississippi
Battery B (Herod's), 1st
  Mississippi Light Artillery
Battery F (Bradford's), 1st
  Mississippi Light Artillery
Battery K (Abbay's), 1st
  Mississippi Light Artillery

SOURCE: The troop organization tables in Appendixes II-V are based on the *Official Records*, unpublished records in the National Archives and the Louisiana Historical Collection, state and county histories and compilations, individuals' memoirs, and regimental histories.

GREGG'S BRIGADE
9th Louisiana Battalion
3rd Tennessee
10th Tennessee
30th Tennessee
41st Tennessee
50th Tennessee
51st Tennessee
1st Tennessee Battalion
7th Texas
Hoskins' (Brookhaven)
    Mississippi Battery
Bledsoe's (1st) Missouri
    Battery

BUFORD'S BRIGADE
27th Alabama
49th Alabama
6th Alabama Battalion
16th Alabama Battalion
10th Arkansas
3rd Kentucky
7th Kentucky
Watson Louisiana Battery

RUST'S BRIGADE
35th Alabama
9th Arkansas
1st Confederate Battalion
12th Louisiana
6th Mississippi
15th Mississippi
Hudson's Mississippi Battery
Battery A, Pointe Coupee
    Louisiana Artillery
Battery C, Pointe Coupee
    Louisiana Artillery

MILES'S COMMAND
Miles's Louisiana Legion
Boone's Louisiana Battery

PROVOST GUARD
English's Mississippi Battery
    (without guns)
Claiborne Mississippi
    Infantry Company

HEAVY ARTILLERY BATTERIES

No. 1 Captain J. F. Whitfield, Company K, 1st Alabama: 30-
       pound Parrott
No. 2 Lieutenant A. W. Harmon, Company A, 1st Alabama: one
       42-pounder smoothbore and two rifled 24-pounders
No. 3 Captain R. H. Riley, Company G, 1st Alabama: one rifled
       32-pounder and one 42-pounder smoothbore
No. 4 Captain W. B. Seawell, Company E, 12th Louisiana Bat-
       talion Heavy Artillery (Mohawk Alabama Artillery): one
       8-inch and one 10-inch columbiad
No. 5 Captain D. Wardlaw Ramsay, Company B, 1st Alabama:
       one 10-inch columbiad, one 42-pounder, and one
       32-pounder, both smoothbores
No. 6 Captain John M. Kean, Company A, 12th Louisiana Bat-
       talion Heavy Artillery: two rifled 24-pounders

No. 7   Captain James Madison Sparkman, 1st Tennessee Battalion Heavy Artillery (hot shot battery): two 24-pounder smoothbores

No. 8   Captain W. Norris Coffin, Company D, 12th Louisiana Battalion Heavy Artillery (Bethel Virginia Artillery): two rifled 24-pounders

No. 9   Captain Felix Le Bisque, Company B, 12th Louisiana Battalion Heavy Artillery: one 8-inch shell gun (Lieutenant O. Rodrigues) and one 32-pounder smoothbore (Lieutenant E. C. McDowell)

CAVALRY

9th Louisiana Battalion Partisan Rangers
Bryan's Louisiana Company
Cage's Louisiana Company
Daigre's Louisiana Company
Stuart's Louisiana Company
Garland's Mississippi Battalion
Norman's Mississippi Company
Rhode's Mississippi Company
Stockdale's Mississippi Company
Terrell's Mississippi Company
Wilbourn's Mississippi Battalion
9th Tennessee Battalion

Appendix III

Port Hudson Garrison, May 27, 1863

Left Wing: Colonel I. G. W. Steedman
1st Alabama (six companies)
10th Arkansas
15th Arkansas
9th Louisiana Battalion Partisan Rangers (dismounted)
1st Mississippi (five companies)
39th Mississippi
Provost Guard Battalion: Claiborne Mississippi Infantry Company
     and English's Mississippi Battery (without guns)
Watson Louisiana Battery (two guns)
Battery B (Herod's), 1st Mississippi Light Artillery (six guns)
Battery F (Bradford's), 1st Mississippi Light Artillery (two guns)
Detachment, 1st Tennessee Battalion Heavy Artillery (two guns)
Company A, 1st Alabama Infantry (two guns)

Center: Brigadier General William N. R. Beall
49th Alabama
8th (Jones) Arkansas Battalion
11th and 17th Arkansas (detachment)
12th Arkansas
14th Arkansas
16th Arkansas

18th Arkansas

23rd Arkansas

1st Mississippi (five companies)

Watson Louisiana Battery (four guns)

Battery F (Bradford's), 1st Mississippi Light Artillery (two guns)

Battery K (Abbay's), 1st Mississippi Light Artillery (five or six guns)

Detachment, Company K, 1st Alabama Infantry (one gun)

Detachment, Company D, 12th Louisiana Battalion Heavy Artillery (one gun)

Detachment, 1st Tennessee Battalion Heavy Artillery (two guns)

Right Wing: Colonel William R. Miles

9th Louisiana Battalion

Miles's Louisiana Legion

Battalion composed of members of the 12th Louisiana Battalion Heavy Artillery serving as infantry: Major Anderson Merchant

Battalion composed of fragments of Maxey's and Gregg's Brigades: Lieutenant Colonel W. N. Parish

Boone's Louisiana Battery (six guns)

Roberts' (Seven Stars) Mississippi Battery (four guns)

Heavy Batteries

No. 2   Company A, 1st Alabama: one 42-pounder smoothbore

No. 3   Company G, 1st Alabama: one rifled 32-pounder and one 42-pounder smoothbore

No. 4   Company E, 12th Louisiana Battalion Heavy Artillery: one 8-inch and one 10-inch columbiad

No. 5   Company B, 1st Alabama: one 10-inch columbiad, one 42-pounder, and one 32-pounder, both smoothbores

No. 6   Company A, 12th Louisiana Battalion Heavy Artillery: two rifled 24-pounders

No. 8   Detachment, Company D, 12th Louisiana Battalion Heavy Artillery: one rifled 24-pounder

No. 9   Company B, 12th Louisiana Battalion Heavy Artillery: one 8-inch shell gun and one 32-pounder smoothbore

No. 11   Lieutenant L. A. Schirmer, one 30-pound Parrott

Colonel John Logan's Command
11th and 17th Arkansas (consolidated; mounted infantry)
Cochran's Arkansas Battalion
Garland's Mississippi Battalion
Hughes's Mississippi Battalion
Stockdale's Mississippi Battalion
9th Tennessee Battalion
Robert's Mississippi Battery (two guns)

Appendix IV

Union Army, March 14, 1863

GROVER'S DIVISION

DWIGHT'S BRIGADE
1st Louisiana
22nd Maine
6th New York
91st New York
131st New York

BIRGE'S BRIGADE
13th Connecticut
25th Connecticut
26th Maine
159th New York

VAN ZANDT'S BRIGADE
24th Connecticut
12th Maine
52nd Massachusetts

ARTILLERY
2nd Massachusetts
Battery L, 1st United States
Battery C, 2nd United States

CAVALRY
Companies C, D, and E, 1st
Louisiana

EMORY'S DIVISION

INGRAHAM'S BRIGADE
4th Massachusetts
16th New Hampshire
110th New York
162nd New York

PAINE'S BRIGADE
8th New Hampshire
133rd New York (nine
companies)
4th Wisconsin

GOODING'S BRIGADE
31st Massachusetts
38th Massachusetts
53rd Massachusetts
156th New York

ARTILLERY
4th Massachusetts
Battery F, 1st United States
2nd Vermont

CAVALRY
Companies B, C, D, and E, 2nd
   Rhode Island

AUGUR'S DIVISION

CHAPIN'S BRIGADE
21st Maine
49th Massachusetts
116th New York
174th New York

DUDLEY'S BRIGADE
2nd Louisiana
30th Massachusetts
50th Massachusetts
   (seven companies)
161st New York

THOMAS' BRIGADE
12th Connecticut
75th New York
8th Vermont

UNATTACHED
1st Louisiana Native Guards

ARTILLERY
Battery A, 1st United States
Battery G, 5th United States
   (two sections)

CAVALRY
Company B, 2nd Massachusetts
   Battalion

MISCELLANEOUS

WAGON GUARD
48th Massachusetts
Battery G, 5th United States Artillery (one section)
Company A, 2nd Rhode Island Cavalry

PONTOON BRIDGE, MONTE SANO BAYOU
Company K, 42nd Massachusetts

BATON ROUGE GARRISON
3rd Louisiana Native Guards

41st Massachusetts
173rd New York
175th New York
21st Indiana (serving as heavy artillery)
12th Massachusetts Battery
18th New York Battery
Company F, 2nd Rhode Island Cavalry

Appendix V

Union Army, May 27, 1863

Right Wing: Brigadier General Godfrey Weitzel

DWIGHT'S DIVISION

VAN ZANDT'S BRIGADE
1st Louisiana
91st New York
131st New York

THOMAS' BRIGADE
12th Connecticut
75th New York
160th New York
8th Vermont

NELSON'S BRIGADE
1st Louisiana Native Guards
    (at least six companies)
3rd Louisiana Native Guards
6th Massachusetts Battery
    (two guns)
1st Louisiana Cavalry
    (detachment)

PAINE'S DIVISION

FEARING'S BRIGADE
8th New Hampshire
133rd New York
173rd New York
4th Wisconsin (nine companies)

GOODING'S BRIGADE
31st Massachusetts (seven
    companies)
38th Massachusetts
53rd Massachusetts
    (eight companies)
156th New York

DETACHMENT ON WEST BANK
110th New York
162nd New York
6th Massachusetts Battery
    (two guns)
1st Louisiana [?] Cavalry,
    (two companies)

WEITZEL'S ARTILLERY
1st Maine Battery
2nd Massachusetts
4th Massachusetts
6th Massachusetts (two guns)
Battery A, 1st United States
Battery F, 1st United States

Right Center: Brigadier General Cuvier Grover

KIMBALL'S BRIGADE
24th Connecticut
12th Maine
  (nine companies)

BIRGE'S BRIGADE
13th Connecticut
25th Connecticut
159th New York

ARTILLERY
Battery L, 1st United States
Battery C, 2nd United States

CAVALRY
2nd Massachusetts Battalion
14th New York (one company)

Left Center: Major General Christopher C. Augur

CHAPIN'S BRIGADE
2d Louisiana
21st Maine
48th Massachusetts
49th Massachusetts
116th New York

DUDLEY'S BRIGADE
30th Massachusetts
50th Massachusetts
161st New York
174th New York

MISCELLANEOUS
1st Louisiana Native Guards
  Engineers
1st Louisiana Cavalry
  (detachment)
2nd Rhode Island Cavalry

ARTILLERY
21st Indiana Infantry
  (seven companies)
18th New York
Battery G, 5th United States
2nd Vermont

Left Wing: Brigadier General Thomas Sherman

DOW'S BRIGADE
26th Connecticut
6th Michigan
15th New Hampshire
128th New York

NICKERSON'S BRIGADE
14th Maine
24th Maine
165th New York
177th New York

ARTILLERY
21st Indiana Infantry (one company)
21st New York
1st Vermont

Cavalry

GRIERSON'S BRIGADE
6th Illinois
7th Illinois
14th New York (five or eight companies)

Bibliography

Primary Sources

MANUSCRIPT COLLECTIONS

Alabama Department of Archives and History, Montgomery
  First Alabama Infantry Regiment. Military Records Division.
  Thirty-Fifth Alabama Infantry Regiment. Military Records
    Division.
  Forty-Ninth Alabama Infantry Regiment. Military Records
    Division.
Arkansas History Commission, Little Rock
  Parish, W. N. Civil War Letter.
Duke University, Perkins Library, Durham, North Carolina
  Confederate States of America Papers.
  Eltinge-Lord Family Papers.
  Ruggles, Daniel. Papers.
Essex Institute, Salem, Massachusetts
  Banks, N. P. Papers.
Historic New Orleans Collection, New Orleans
  Forlorn Hope Storming Column, Port Hudson, Louisiana.
Illinois State Archives, Springfield
  Augur, C. C. Papers.
  Grierson, B. H. Papers.

Library of Congress, Division of Manuscripts, Washington, D.C.
  Stanton, Edwin M. Papers.
Louisiana State University, Department of Archives and Manu-
  scripts, Baton Rouge
  Allen, William M. Correspondence. Merritt M. Shilg Memorial
    Collection.
  Boyd, David F. Papers.
  Dixon, William Y. Papers.
  Hunter-Taylor Family Papers.
  Lea, Lemanda E. Papers. Merritt M. Shilg Memorial
    Collection.
  McKinney, Jeptha. Papers. Merritt M. Shilg Memorial
    Collection.
  Morgan, Henry Gibbes. Letter.
  Morgan, John A. Papers.
  Terry, William, and Family. Papers.
University of Michigan, Michigan Historical Collections,
  Bentley Historical Library, Ann Arbor
  Griffin, Eli A. Letters.
  Moulton, Charles. Letters.
  Soule, Harrison. Collection.
Mississippi Department of Archives and History, Jackson
  "Order Book, Withers Artillery."
  Ruggles, Daniel. Papers.
  Withers Artillery Papers.
National Archives, Washington, D.C.
  Compiled Service Records of Confederate Soldiers Who Served
    in Organizations from the State of Alabama. Microcopy 311.
  Compiled Service Records of Confederate Soldiers Who Served
    in Organizations from the State of Texas. Microcopy 323.
  Compiled Service Records of Confederate Soldiers Who Served
    in Organizations Raised Directly by the Confederate Govern-
    ment. Microcopy 258.
  Compiled Records Showing Service of Military Units in Volun-
    teer Union Organizations. Microcopy 594.
  General and Special Orders, Port Hudson, La., 1862–63, Third
    Military District, Department of Mississippi and East Louisi-
    ana. Chap. II, Vol. 198, Record Group 109.
  Letters and Reports, Port Hudson, La., 1862–63, Third Military

District, Department of Mississippi and East Louisiana. Entry 138, Record Group 109.

Letters and Telegrams Received, Department of Mississippi and East Louisiana, 1862–65. Record Group 109.

Letters Received by the Office of the Adjutant General (Main Series), 1861–70. Microcopy 619.

Letters Sent, December, 1862–August, 1863, Department of the Gulf. Record Group 393.

Letters Sent, December, 1862–August, 1863, Department of the Gulf. Entry 2134, Record Group 393.

Letters Sent, Port Hudson, La., 1862–63, Third Military District, Department of Mississippi and East Louisiana. Chap. II, Vol. VIII, Record Group 109.

Photograph 77-F-133-98-1, showing a 4.62-inch Brooke rifled cannon. Signal Corps Collection, Still Picture Branch.

Roster, Third Military District, Department of Mississippi and East Louisiana. Chap. I, Vol. 166, Record Group 109.

New Hampshire Division of Records Management and Archives, Department of State, Concord
New Hampshire Civil War Records.

New-York Historical Society, New York
Aldis, Wm. H. Jr. Papers.
Rider Collection.
Sentell Family Papers.
Wadsworth Papers.
Wilkinson Papers.
Wright, Lieut. H. C. Letters.

University of North Carolina Library, Southern Historical Collection, Chapel Hill
Dimon, Charles A. R. Papers.

Northwestern Louisiana University, Department of Archives, Natchitoches
[J. M.] Jones Collection.
Melrose Collection.

Port Hudson Battlefield Museum, Port Hudson, Louisiana
Steedman, I. G. W. Letter.

Tennessee State Library and Archives, Nashville
Brigham Family Papers.
Butts, Melmon Marion. Questionnaire.

Campbell, Andrew Jackson. Civil War Diary.

Farmer Family Papers, 1838–89.

Farrar, Lee H. Letters. Copies. Confederate Collection.

Harmon, J. W. Memoir, 1861–65. Civil War Collection.

Robison, John Wesley. Papers.

Simpson, Capt. S. R. Papers.

Tyler, C. W. "Fiftieth Tennessee Infantry." Roster—50th Tennessee Infantry.

Texas State Archives, Austin

Bailey, J. M. "The Story of a Confederate Soldier, 1861-5." Typescript copy.

Tulane University Library, Manuscript Department, Special Collections Division, New Orleans, Louisiana

Louisiana Historical Association Collection.

U.S. Army Military History Institute, Carlisle Barracks, Pennsylvania

Hughes, R. H. Collection.

Sweetser, Private Elbridge, Company E, 50th Massachusetts Infantry. Journal. Earl Hess Collection.

Western Michigan University, Regional History Collections, Kalamazoo

Hall, John Emory. Papers.

State Historical Society of Wisconsin, Archives Division, Madison

Fyfe Family Papers.

PRIVATE COLLECTIONS

Ford, Lt. R. W. Diary. Typescript copy. In possession of Russell Surles, Jr., Dallas, Texas.

Medearis, R. A. Letter. Xerox copy. In possession of David R. Perdue, Pine Bluff, Arkansas.

Muster and Pay Roll of Captain B. D. Martin's Company A of the [1st Texas] Battalion of Sharp Shooters. February 28 to April 30, 1863. In possession of Philip B. Eckert, Baton Rouge, Louisiana.

Owens Papers. Xerox copies. In possession of E. Russ Williams, Monroe, Louisiana.

Stankiewicz, Captain Peter K. Letter. In possession of Gary Hendershott, Little Rock, Arkansas.

Waters, Private James Very, Company A, 50th Massachusetts Infantry. Diary. In possession of Maurice Garb, Baton Rouge, Louisiana.

AUTHOR'S COLLECTION

Dwight, William. Letter.
Myers, Thomas R. Memoirs. Typescript copy.
Spink Elon P. Diary. Typescript copy.
Trask, Lieutenant William. Notebook. Xerox copy.

GOVERNMENT PUBLICATIONS

FEDERAL

Bourne, Edward G., *et al.*, comps. *Sixth Report of Historical Manuscripts Commission: With Diary and Correspondence of Salmon P. Chase*. Vol. II of *Annual Report of the American Historical Association for the Year 1902*. Washington, D.C., 1903.
Cowles, Calvin D., comp. *Atlas to Accompany the Official Records of the Union and Confederate Armies*. 1891–95; rpr. New York, 1958.
U.S. Naval Records Office. *Register of Officers of the Confederate States Navy, 1861-1865*. Washington, D.C., 1931.
U.S. Navy Department. *Dictionary of American Naval Fighting Ships*. 8 vols. Washington, D.C., 1959–81.
————. *The War of the Rebellion: Official Records of the Union and Confederate Navies*. 30 vols. Washington, D.C., 1894–1922.
U.S. Senate. *Medal of Honor Recipients, 1863-1963*. Washington, D.C., 1964.
U.S. War Department. *The War of the Rebellion: A Compilation of the Official Records of the Union and Confederate Armies*. 128 vols. Washington, D.C., 1880–1901.

STATE

Adjutant General. *Annual Report of the Adjutant General of the State of Maine for the Year Ending December 31, 1863*. Augusta, 1864.

Adjutant General. *Massachusetts Soldiers, Sailors, and Marines in the Civil War.* 9 vols. Norwood, Mass., 1931–37.

Booth, Andrew B. *Records of Louisiana Confederate Soldiers and Louisiana Confederate Commands.* 4 books in 3 vols. New Orleans, 1920.

Brewer, W. *Alabama: Her History, Resources, War Record, and Public Men, from 1540 to 1872.* Montgomery, 1872.

Phisterer, Frederick, comp. *New York in the War of the Rebellion, 1861 to 1865.* 3d ed. 5 vols. and index. Albany, 1912.

[Tennessee] Civil War Centennial Commission. *Tennesseans in the Civil War: A Military History of Confederate and Union Units with Available Rosters of Personnel.* 2 pts. Nashville, 1964–65.

Wallace, Lee A., Jr., comp. *A Guide to Virginia Military Organizations, 1861–1865.* Richmond, 1964.

NEWSPAPERS

Baton Rouge *Weekly Gazette and Comet*, November 19, 1862–March 4, 1863.

Franklin (La.) *Junior Register*, March 26, 1863.

Hampshire Gazette & Northampton Courier, June 30, 1863.

Harper's Weekly, July 18, 1863.

Houston *Tri-Weekly Telegraph*, September 10, 1862, June 1, 1863.

Little Rock *Arkansas Gazette*, October 25, 1936.

Little Rock *True Democrat*, March 25, 1863.

Memphis *Daily Appeal*, August 15, 1862–April 15, 1863.

Mobile *Advertiser and Register*, March 18, 1863–December 29, 1863.

Natchez *Weekly Courier*, March 25, 1863.

New Orleans *Daily Picayune*, August 19, 1863, July 30, 1905.

New Orleans *Times-Democrat*, April 26, 1906.

Opelousas *Courier*, February 21, 1863.

Port Hudson *Evening Courier*, January 3, 1863.

Vicksburg *Daily Whig*, February 13, March 19, 1863.

West Baton Rouge *Sugar Planter*, February 24, 1866.

Wisconsin State Journal, undated clipping, Archives Division, State Historical Society of Wisconsin, Madison.

MAPS

Camp Moore State Commemorative Area, State of Louisiana
Office of State Parks, Department of Culture, Recreation and
Tourism, Tangipahoa, Louisiana
Map of Port Hudson and Its Defences. Drawn by Major J. de
Baun.
National Archives, Washington, D.C.
"Baton Rouge to Port Hudson; Showing, Position of 19th Army
Corps, Maj. Gen. N. P. Banks Com'd'g. On the 14th of March
1863." Map Z218, Record Group 77.
Champion Map of Baton Rouge, Louisiana. Charlotte, N.C., n.d.

MEMOIRS AND DIARIES

Bacon, Edward. Among the Cotton Thieves. Detroit, 1867.
Bacon, Thomas Scott. "The Fight at Port Hudson: Recollections
of an Eyewitness." Independent, LIII (1901), 589–98.
Beers, Fannie A. Memories: A Record of Personal Experience and
Adventure During Four Years of War. Philadelphia, 1889.
Brown, Alan S., ed. A Soldier's Life: The Civil War Experiences
of Ben C. Johnson (Originally Entitled, Sketches of the Sixth
Regiment Michigan Infantry). Faculty Contributions, School of
Graduate Studies, Western Michigan University, Vol. VI.
Kalamazoo, 1962.
Bryant, William Cullen II, ed. "A Yankee Soldier Looks at the
Negro." Civil War History, VII (1961), 133–48.
Butler, Benjamin F. Butler's Book. Boston, 1892.
———. Private and Official Correspondence of Gen. Benjamin F.
Butler During the Period of the Civil War. 5 vols. Norwood,
Mass., 1917.
Cannon, M. D. Inside of Rebeldom: The Daily Life of a Private in
the Confederate Army. Washington, D.C., 1899.
Curl, A. "The Fight at Clinton, La." Confederate Veteran, XIII
(1905), 122.
[Dabney, Frederick Y.] "The Sinking of the Mississippi." Con-
federate Veteran, XXXII (1924), 181.
Dargan, James F. My Experiences in Service, or a Nine Months
Man. 4 vols. Los Angeles, 1974.

Dawson, Sarah Morgan. *A Confederate Girl's Diary*. Edited by James I. Robertson, Jr. 1913; rpr. Bloomington, 1960.

De Forest, John William. *A Volunteer's Adventures: A Union Captain's Record of the Civil War*. Edited by James H. Croushore. New Haven, 1946.

[De Gournay, Paul F.] "D'Gournay's Battalion of Artillery." *Confederate Veteran*, XIII (1905), 30–33.

De Gournay, P. F. "The Siege of Port Hudson." In "Annals of the War," scrapbook of miscellaneous newspaper clippings. Tulane University, New Orleans, Louisiana.

Deland, F. N. *Some Recollections of the Civil War*. Pittsfield, Mass., 1909.

Dewey, George. *Autobiography of George Dewey: Admiral of the Navy*. New York, 1913.

Dow, Neal. *The Reminiscences of Neal Dow: Recollections of Eighty Years*. Portland, Me., 1898.

Eakin, Sue Lyles, and Morgan Peoples. *"In Defense of My Country . . .": The Letters of a Shiloh Confederate Soldier, Sergeant George Washington Bolton, and His Union Parish Neighbors of the Twelfth Regiment of Louisiana Volunteers (1861–1864)*. Bernice, La., 1983.

Eby, Cecil D., Jr., ed. *A Virginia Yankee in the Civil War: The Diaries of David Hunter Strother*. Chapel Hill, 1961.

Farragut, Loyall. "Farragut at Port Hudson." *Putnam's Monthly and the Reader*, V (October, 1908), 44–53.

———. "Passing the Port Hudson Batteries." In James Grant Wilson and Titus Munson Coan, eds., *Personal Recollections of the War of the Rebellion: Addresses Delivered Before the New York Commandery of the Loyal Legion of the United States, 1883–1891*. 1st ser. New York, 1891.

Flinn, Frank M. *Campaigning with Banks in Louisiana, '63 and '64, and with Sheridan in the Shenandoah Valley in '64 and '65*. Lynn, Mass., 1887.

"Fortification and Siege of Port Hudson—Compiled by the Association of Defenders of Port Hudson; M. J. Smith, President; James Freret, Secretary." *Southern Historical Society Papers*, XIV (1886), 305–48.

Frederick, J. V., ed. "War Diary of W. C. Porter." *Arkansas Historical Quarterly*, XI (1952), 286–314.

Freeman, Douglas Southall, comp. *A Calendar of Confederate Papers with a Bibliography of Some Confederate Publications.* Richmond, Va., 1908.

Goodloe, Albert Theodore. *Confederate Echoes: A Voice from the South in the Days of Secession and of the Southern Confederacy.* Nashville, 1907.

——. *Some Rebel Relics from the Seat of War.* Nashville, 1893.

Goodrich, John T. "Humorous Features as Well as Tragedies." *Confederate Veteran,* XVI (1908), 126.

Gower, Herschel, and Jack Allen. *Pen and Sword: The Life and Journals of Randal W. McGavock, Colonel, C.S.A.* Nashville, 1959.

Grant, U. S. *Personal Memoirs of U. S. Grant.* 2 vols. New York, 1885.

[Harding, George Canaday]. *The Miscellaneous Writings of George C. Harding.* Indianapolis, 1882.

Hepworth, George H. *The Whip, Hoe and Sword or, The Gulf-Department in '63.* Edited by Joe Gray Taylor. 1864; rpr. Baton Rouge, 1979.

Hewitt, Lawrence L., ed. *A Place Named . . . Desperate!* Baton Rouge, 1982.

——, and Arthur W. Bergeron, Jr., eds. *Post Hospital Ledger, Port Hudson, Louisiana, 1862–1863.* Baton Rouge, 1981.

Hoffman, Wickham. *Camp, Court and Siege: A Narrative of Personal Adventure and Observation During Two Wars, 1861–1865, 1870–1871.* New York, 1877.

Hosmer, James K. *The Color-Guard: Being a Corporal's Notes of Military Service in the Nineteenth Army Corps.* Boston, 1864.

Howe, Henry Warren. *Passages from the Life of Henry Warren Howe, Consisting of Diary and Letters Written During the Civil War, 1861–1865. . . .* Lowell, Mass., 1899.

Kendall, John S. "The Diary of Surgeon Craig, Fourth Louisiana Regiment, C.S.A., 1864–65." *Louisiana Historical Quarterly,* VIII (1925), 53–70.

——. "Recollections of a Confederate Officer." *Louisiana Historical Quarterly,* XXIX (October, 1946), 1041–1228.

Martin, R. T. "Reminiscences of an Arkansan." *Confederate Veteran,* XVII (1909), 69–70.

M'Murray, James. "Heroism of Union Officer at Port Hudson." *Confederate Veteran,* XVI (1908), 428.

M'Neilly, James H. "A Good Place to Die." *Confederate Veteran*, XXVI (1918), 45.

———. "Under Fire at Port Hudson." *Confederate Veteran*, XXVII (1919), 336–39.

Meredith, William T. "Admiral Farragut's Passage of Port Hudson." In A. Noel Blakeman, ed., *Personal Recollections of the War of the Rebellion: Addresses Delivered Before the Commandery of the State of New York, Military Order of the Loyal Legion of the United States*. 2d ser. New York, 1897.

Miller, Mrs. S. G. *Sixty Years in the Nueces Valley, 1870 to 1930*. San Antonio, 1930.

Moore, Frank, ed. *The Rebellion Record: A Diary of American Events with Documents, Narratives, Illustrative Incidents, Poetry, etc.* 12 vols. New York, 1861–71.

Overcash, John S. Letter to editor. *Confederate Veteran*, XV (1907), 141.

Palfrey, Francis Winthrop. *Memoir of William Francis Bartlett*. Boston, 1878.

Palfrey, John C. "Port Hudson." In *The Mississippi Valley, Tennessee, Georgia, Alabama, 1861–1864*, pp. 21–63. Vol. VIII of *Papers of the Military Historical Society of Massachusetts*. Boston, 1910.

Parker, John C. "With Farragut at Port Hudson: A First Person Account by Lt. John C. Parker, USN." *Civil War Times Illustrated*, VII (November, 1968), 42–49.

Partin, Robert, ed. "Report of a Corporal of the Alabama First Infantry on Talk and Fighting Along Mississippi, 1862–63." *Alabama Historical Quarterly*, XX (1950), 583–94.

Poe, J. C., ed. *The Raving Foe: The Civil War Diary of Major James T. Poe, C.S.A., and the 11th Arkansas Volunteers and a Complete List of Prisoners*. Eastland, Tex., 1967.

[Preston, Francis W.] *Port Hudson: A History of the Investment, Siege and Capture*. N.p., 1892.

Read, C. W. "Reminiscences of the Confederate States Navy." *Southern Historical Society Papers*, I (1876), 331–62.

"Reminiscences of R. J. Tabor." *Southern Bivouac*, III (1885), 420.

Schley, Winfield Scott. *Forty-Five Years Under the Flag*. New York, 1904.

Skipwith, Thomas W. "A Letter from Port Hudson." *Louisiana Genealogical Register*, XVIII (1971), 68.

Smith, George G. *Leaves from a Soldier's Diary. . . .* Putnam, Conn., 1906.

Smith, H. D. "With Farragut on the Hartford." in George Morley Vickers, ed., *Under Both Flags: A Panorama of the Great Civil War as Represented in Story, Anecdote, Adventure, and the Romance of Reality,* pp. 1–68. Chicago, 1896.

Stewart, Edwin. "Address on Admiral Farragut." In A. Noel Blakeman, ed., *Personal Recollections of the War of the Rebellion: Addresses Delivered Before the Commandery of the State of New York, Military Order of the Loyal Legion of the United States,* 4th ser., pp. 162–70. New York, 1912.

Tanner, Linn. "The Meat Diet at Port Hudson." *Confederate Veteran,* XXVI (1918), 484.

———. "Port Hudson Calamities—Mule Meat." *Confederate Veteran,* XVII (1909), 512.

Taylor, F. Jay, ed. *Reluctant Rebel: The Secret Diary of Robert Patrick, 1861–1865.* Baton Rouge, 1959.

Taylor, Richard. *Destruction and Reconstruction: Personal Experiences of the Late War.* Edited by Richard B. Harwell. 1879; rpr. New York, 1955.

Thompson, Robert Means, and Richard Wainwright, eds. *Confidential Correspondence of Gustavus Vasa Fox, Assistant Secretary of the Navy, 1861–1865.* 2 vols. New York, 1920.

Tricc, C. W. "The Battleship Mississippi." *Confederate Veteran,* XXV (1917), 112.

Waterman, George S. "Afield—Afloat." *Confederate Veteran,* VI (1898), 390–94.

Webster, Harrie. *Some Personal Recollections and Reminiscences of the Battle of Port Hudson.* N.p., n.d.

Wiley, Bell Irvin, ed. "The Confederate Letters of Warren G. Magee." *Journal of Mississippi History,* V (1943), 204–13.

[Wright, Howard C.] *Port Hudson: Its History from an Interior Point of View as Sketched from the Diary of an Officer.* St. Francisville, La., 1937.

Secondary Sources

UNIT HISTORIES

Bergeron, Arthur W., Jr., and Lawrence L. Hewitt. *Miles' Legion: A History and Roster.* Baton Rouge, 1983.

Bosson, Charles P. *History of the Forty-Second Regiment Infantry, Massachusetts Volunteers, 1862, 1863, 1864.* Boston, 1886.

Carpenter, George N. *History of the Eighth Regiment Vermont Volunteers, 1861–1865.* Boston, 1886.

Carter, George W. "The Fourth Wisconsin Infantry at Port Hudson." In *War Papers Read Before the Commandery of the State of Wisconsin, Military Order of the Loyal Legion of the United States.* Vol. III, pp. 226–40. Milwaukee, 1903.

Clark, Orton S. *The One Hundred and Sixteenth Regiment of New York State Volunteers.* . . . Buffalo, 1868.

Ewer, James K. *The Third Massachusetts Cavalry in the War for the Union.* Maplewood, Mass., 1903.

Gallup, L. A., *et al. Roster, Muster Roll—and—Chronological Record of The Twenty-Sixth Regiment, Connecticut Volunteers.* . . . Norwich, Conn., 1888.

Hall, Henry, and James Hall. *Cayuga in the Field.* . . . Auburn, N.Y., 1873.

Hanaburgh, D. H. *History of the One Hundred and Twenty-eighth Regiment, New York Volunteers [U.S. Infantry] in the Late Civil War.* Poughkeepsie, N.Y., 1894.

Haskin, William L., comp. *The History of the First Regiment of Artillery from Its Organization in 1821, to January 1st, 1876.* Portland, Me., 1879.

History of the Second Battalion Duryee: Zouaves, One Hundred and Sixty-fifth Regt. New York Volunteer Infantry. . . . Rev. ed. N.p., 1905.

Howell, H. Grady, Jr. *Going to Meet the Yankees: A History of the "Bloody Sixth" Mississippi Infantry, C.S.A.* Jackson, Miss., 1981.

Irwin, Richard. *History of the Nineteenth Army Corps.* 1893; rpr. Baton Rouge, 1985.

Johns, Henry T. *Life with the Forty-ninth Massachusetts Volunteers.* Pittsfield, Mass., 1864.

Maddocks, Elden B., comp. *History of the Twenty-Sixth Maine Regiment.* . . . Bangor, 1899.

Maglathlin, Henry B. *Company I, Fourth Massachusetts Regiment, Nine Months Volunteers, in Service, 1862–3.* Boston, 1863.

Martin, Clarence S. *Three Quarters of a Century with the Tenth Infantry New York National Guard, 1860–1935.* N.p., n.d.

McGregor, Charles. *History of the Fifteenth Regiment New Hampshire Volunteers, 1862–1863.* N.p., 1900.

McManus, Thomas. *Twenty-fifth Regiment Battle Fields Revisited.* Hartford, 1896.

McMorries, Edward Young. *History of the First Regiment Alabama Volunteer Infantry C.S.A.* 1904; rpr. Freeport, N.Y., 1970.

A Memorial of Brevet Brigadier General Lewis Benedict, Colonel of 162d Regiment N.Y.V.I., Who Fell in Battle at Pleasant Hill, La., April 9, 1864. Albany, N.Y., 1866.

A Memorial of Lt. Daniel Perkins Dewey, of the Twenty-fifth Regiment Connecticut Volunteers. Hartford, 1864.

Memorials of William Fowler. New York, 1875.

Moors, J. F. *History of the Fifty-second Regiment Massachusetts Volunteers.* Boston, 1893.

Pellet, Elias P. *History of the 114th Regiment, New York State Volunteers. . . .* Norwich, N.Y., 1866.

Plummer, Albert. *History of the Forty-eighth Regiment M.V.M. During the Civil War.* Boston, 1907.

Powers, George W. *The Story of the Thirty Eighth Regiment of Massachusetts Volunteers.* Cambridge, Mass., 1866.

Richards, A. P. *The Saint Helena Rifles.* Edited by Randall Shoemaker, N.p., 1968.

Smith, Daniel P. *Company K, First Alabama Regiment, or Three Years in the Confederate Sevice.* Prattville, Ala., 1885.

Sprague, Homer B. *History of the 13th Infantry Regiment of Connecticut Volunteers, During the Great Rebellion.* Hartford, 1867.

Stanyan, John M. *A History of the Eighth Regiment of New Hampshire Volunteers. . . .* Concord, N.H., 1892.

Stevens, William B. *History of the Fiftieth Regiment of Infantry Massachusetts Volunteer Militia in the Late War of the Rebellion.* Boston, 1907.

Tiemann, William F., comp. *The 159th Regiment Infantry, New-York State Volunteers, in the War of the Rebellion, 1862–1865.* Brooklyn, 1891.

Townsend, Luther Tracy. *History of the Sixteenth Regiment, New Hampshire Volunteers.* Washington, D.C., 1897.

The Twenty-Fifth Regiment Connecticut Volunteers in the War of the Rebellion. . . . Rockville, Conn., 1913.

Whitcomb, Caroline E. *History of the Second Massachusetts Bat-*

tery (Nims' Battery) of Light Artillery, 1861–1865. . . . Concord, N.H., 1912.

Willis, Henry A. *The Fifty-third Regiment Massachusetts Volunteers: Comprising Also a History of the Siege of Port Hudson.* Fitchburg, 1889.

Woodward, Jos. T. *Historic Record and Complete Biographic Roster 21st Me. Vols. with Reunion Records of the 21st Maine Regimental Association.* Augusta, 1907.

STATE AND LOCAL HISTORIES

Croffut, W. A., and John M. Morris. *The Military and Civil History of Connecticut During the War of 1861–65.* New York, 1868.

Dimitry, John. *Louisiana.* Vol. X of Clement A. Evans, ed., *Confederate Military History.* Atlanta, 1899.

Garrett, Jill K., and Marise P. Lightfoot. *The Civil War in Maury County, Tennessee.* N.p., 1966.

Harrell, John M. *Arkansas.* Vol. X of Clement A. Evans, ed., *Confederate Military History.* 12 vols. Atlanta, 1899.

Harrington, Fred Harvey. "Arkansas Defends the Mississippi." *Arkansas Historical Quarterly*, IV (1945), 109–17.

Huntington, E. B. *Stamford Soldiers' Memorial.* Stamford, Conn., 1869.

Jennings, Virginia Lobdell. *The Plains and the People: A History of Upper East Baton Rouge Parish.* New Orleans, 1962.

Lindsley, J. B., ed. *The Military Annals of Tennessee.* Nashville, 1886.

Love, William DeLoss. *Wisconsin in the War of the Rebellion* . . . . Chicago, 1866.

Plank, Will, comp. *Banners and Bugles: A Record of Ulster County, New York and the Mid-Hudson Region in the Civil War.* Marlborough, N.Y., 1972.

Quiner, E. B. *The Military History of Wisconsin.* . . . Chicago, 1866.

Roberts, O. M. *Texas.* Vol. XI of Clement A. Evans, ed., *Confederate Military History.* Atlanta, 1899.

Robertson, Jno., comp. *Michigan in the War.* Rev. ed. Lansing, 1882.

Rowland, Dunbar, comp. *The Official and Statistical Register of the State of Mississippi.* Nashville, 1908.

Whitman, William E. S., and Charles H. True. *Maine in the War for the Union: A History of the Part Borne by Maine Troops in the Suppression of the American Rebellion*. Lewiston, 1865.

Willis, Henry A. *Fitchburg in the War of the Rebellion*. Fitchburg, 1866.

Winters, John D. *The Civil War in Louisiana*. 1963; rpr. Baton Rouge, 1979.

GENERAL WORKS

Abbott, John S. C. "Heroic Deeds of Heroic Men," IV. "Siege and Capture of Port Hudson." *Harper's New Monthly Magazine*, XXX (1865), 425–39.

Bearss, Edwin Cole. *Vicksburg Is the Key*. Dayton, 1985.

Blockson, Charles L. "Escape from Slavery: The Underground Railroad." *National Geographic*, CLXVI (July, 1984), 3–39.

Boatner, Mark M. III. *The Civil War Dictionary*. New York, 1959.

Bonham, Milledge L., Jr. *Man and Nature at Port Hudson: 1863, 1917*. Baton Rouge, 1965.

Boynton, Charles B. *The History of the Navy During the Rebellion*. 2 vols. New York, 1868.

Brockett, L. P. *Battle-Field and Hospital: or, Lights and Shadows of the Great Rebellion*. . . . N.p., n.d.

Brown, William Wells. *The Negro in the American Rebellion: His Heroism and His Fidelity*. Boston, 1867.

Cornish, Dudley Taylor. *The Sable Arm: Negro Troops in the Union Army, 1861–1865*. New York, 1956.

Cullum, George W. *Biographical Register of the Officers and Graduates of the U.S. Military Academy, from 1802 to 1867. Revised Edition, with a Supplement Continuing the Register of Graduates to January 1, 1879*. 3 vols. New York, 1879.

Cunningham, Edward. *The Port Hudson Campaign, 1862–1863*. Baton Rouge, 1963.

Davis, William C. *Breckinridge: Statesman, Soldier, Symbol*. Baton Rouge, 1974.

"Dr. F. M. Mumford." *Confederate Veteran*, XIX (1911), 444–45.

Edmonds, David C. *The Guns of Port Hudson*. 2 vols. Lafayette, La., 1983–84.

Estes, Claud, comp. *List of Field Officers, Regiments and Battalions in the Confederate States Army, 1861–1865*. Macon, Ga., 1912.

Foltz, Charles S. *Surgeon of the Seas.* . . . Indianapolis, 1931.

Fox, William F. *Regimental Losses in the American Civil War, 1861–1865.* . . . 1889; rpr. Dayton, 1985.

Greene, Francis Vinton. *The Mississippi.* New York, 1882.

Harrington, Fred Harvey. *Fighting Politician: Major General N. P. Banks.* 1948; rpr. Westport, Conn., 1970.

Hartje, Robert G. *Van Dorn: The Life and Times of a Confederate General.* Nashville, 1967.

Hattaway, Herman, and Archer Jones. *How the North Won: A Military History of the Civil War.* Urbana, 1983.

"Heroic Deed of Lieutenant Mumford." *Confederate Veteran,* X (1902), 365.

Hewitt, Lawrence L. Introduction to Richard B. Irwin, *History of the Nineteenth Army Corps.* 1893; rpr. Baton Rouge, 1985.

Irwin, Richard B. "The Capture of Port Hudson." In Robert Underwood Johnson and Clarence Clough Buel, eds., *Battles and Leaders of The Civil War,* III, 586–98, 4 vols. 1887–88; rpr. New York, 1956.

Johnson, Ludwell H. *Red River Campaign: Politics and Cotton in the Civil War.* Baltimore, 1958.

Jones, Archer. *Confederate Strategy from Shiloh to Vicksburg.* Baton Rouge, 1961.

Kerby, Robert L. *Kirby Smith's Confederacy: The Trans-Mississippi South, 1863–1865.* New York, 1972.

Kesler, James W. "Loss of the U.S.S. *Mississippi.*" *United Service,* XII (1885), 650–56.

Kettell, Thomas P. *History of The Great Rebellion.* . . . 3 vols. New York, 1865.

Lewis, Charles Lee. *David Glasgow Farragut: Our First Admiral.* Annapolis, 1943.

———. *Famous American Naval Officers.* Rev. ed. Boston, 1948.

Long, E. B., and Barbara Long. *The Civil War Day by Day: An Almanac, 1861–1865.* Garden City, N.Y., 1971.

Mahan, A. T. *Admiral Farragut.* 1892; rpr. New York, 1916.

———. *The Gulf and Inland Waters.* New York, 1883.

McElroy, Robert. *Jefferson Davis: The Unreal and the Real.* 2 vols. New York, 1937.

McWhiney, Grady, and Perry D. Jamieson. *Attack and Die: Civil War Military Tactics and the Southern Heritage.* University, Ala., 1982.

"Notes on the Union and Confederate Armies." In Robert

Underwood Johnson and Clarence Clough Buel, eds., *Battles and Leaders of the Civil War*, IV, 767–68. 4 vols. 1887–88; rpr. New York, 1956.

Potter, E. B., *et al.*, eds. *Sea Power: A Naval History*. Englewood Cliffs, N.J., 1960.

Pratt, Fletcher. *Civil War on Western Waters*. New York, 1956.

——. *The Navy, A History: The Story of a Service in Action*. Garden City, N.Y., 1941.

Quarles, Benjamin. *The Negro in the Civil War*. Boston, 1953.

Ripley, Warren. *Artillery and Ammunition of the Civil War*. New York, 1970.

Roland, Charles P. *Louisiana Sugar Plantations During the American Civil War*. Leiden, 1957.

Soley, James Russell. "Naval Operations in the Vicksburg Campaign." In Robert Underwood Johnson and Clarence Clough Buel, eds., *Battles and Leaders of the Civil War*, III, 551–70. 4 vols. 1887–88; rpr. New York, 1956.

Sword, Wiley. *Shiloh: Bloody April*. New York, 1974.

[Trawick, A. M.] "Col. Benjamin T. Pixlee, of Arkansas." *Confederate Veteran*, X (1902), 317–18.

Truesdale, John. *The Blue Coats, and How They Lived, Fought and Died for the Union*. Philadelphia, 1867.

Warner, Ezra J. *Generals in Blue: Lives of the Union Commanders*. Baton Rouge, 1964.

——. *Generals in Gray: Lives of the Confederate Commanders*. Baton Rouge, 1959.

Westwood, Howard C. "The Vicksburg/Port Hudson Gap—The Pincers Never Pinched." *Military Affairs: The Journal of Military History, Including Theory and Technology*, XLVI (1982), 113–19.

Wiley, Bell Irvin. *Southern Negroes, 1861–1865*. 1938; rpr. Baton Rouge, 1974.

Williams, George W. *A History of the Negro Troops in the War of the Rebellion, 1861–1865, Preceded by a Review of the Military Services of Negroes in Ancient and Modern Times*. 1888; rpr. New York, 1969.

Williams, T. Harry. *Lincoln and His Generals*. New York, 1952.

——. Foreword to Edward Cunningham, *The Port Hudson Campaign: 1862–1863*. Baton Rouge, 1963.

Wilson, Joseph T. *The Black Phalanx*. New York, 1968.

Index